New Financial Horizons

New Financial Horizons
The Emergence of an Economy of Communion

Lorna Gold

Foreword by
Michael Naughton

New City Press
Hyde Park, New York

Published in the United States by New City Press
202 Comforter Blvd., Hyde Park, NY 12538
www.newcitypress.com
©2010 Lorna Gold

Cover design by Durva Correia

Library of Congress Cataloging-in-Publication Data:

Gold, Lorna.
   New financial horizons : the emergence of an economy of communion / Lorna
Gold ; foreword by Michael Naughton.
      p. cm.
   Includes bibliographical references.
   ISBN 978-1-56548-354-5 (pbk. : alk. paper) 1. Economics—Religious aspects—
Christianity. 2. Economy of Communion (Movement) 3. Focolare Movement.
I. Title.
   BR115.E3G645 2010
   261.8'5—dc22   2010016229

Printed in the United States of America

Contents

Foreword

In a New York skyscraper overlooking Central Park, I was giving a talk to business and religious leaders about the emerging financial crisis. During the question/answer session, one CEO of a large publicly-traded company spoke of his sense of being betrayed by so many of his fellow corporate leaders who maximized their own particular self-interests at the expense of the common good. He was shocked and dismayed by such behavior and highly critical of those executives whose lack of moral leadership had shaken society's confidence in business as an institution.

While one is sympathetic to such critiques, and one admires corporate leaders who can call their fellow colleagues to higher moral standards, this CEO's criticism concealed an even deeper problem: that our financial crisis is not just about failures of individual business leaders, but is part of a much larger cultural crisis. The lack of moral responsibility demonstrated at every level of the financial system suggests that a broader cultural failure is at work. This is not to underestimate the complexity of the structural causes which brought down Bear Stearns, Fannie Mae, Freddie Mac, AIG, Washington Mutual, and others. It does suggest, however, that our political and economic institutions were not solely to blame, and that the prevention of similar failures in the future will require more than just improved regulations and financial incentives.

For the most part, the perpetrators of the 2008 calamity were neither vicious nor cutthroat; rather, they are people who lacked moral character, who demonstrated moral thoughtlessness, who blindly followed the money. Consumers, loan officers, investment bankers, and speculators all attempted to capitalize within a particular part of the financial system; in so doing, each myopically passed on problems to other parts of that system. They were technically competent, hard working, and for the most part law abiding, but their moral and spiritual center failed to help them see their role in a broader, destructive whole.

Without stable and nurturing families, without dynamic religious institutions and movements, without a moral and spiritual

9

educational system, businesspeople will not be able to resist the corrupting influence of our current global economic system. It is precisely such a dynamic culture that has the capacity to prevent us from reducing the purpose of business to either the financial theory of the firm (maximizing shareholder wealth — market as the principal source of understanding business), or to social contract theory (stakeholder — law is the principle source of understanding business), both of which fail to build up authentic communities of persons within the corporation. By reconnecting economic life to a culture informed by a unity of faith and reason, we have richer starting points on the first principles of the fundamental realities that inform economic life, realities such as work, property, capital, community, contracts, technology, and most importantly the human person.

We have to come to the realization that business does not create culture, but culture plays an important and embedded function that creates the conditions of business. This is precisely what this book does and it is precisely why it is of critical importance for academics, businesspeople, nonprofit leaders, religious leaders, and politicians. It is an extraordinarily timely book. What Lorna Gold does in this book is to contextualize the practicality of the Economy of Communion (EoC) movement, which has close to 800 businesses in its association, within a broader theoretical rethinking of the relationship between culture, in particular religious culture, and the economy.

Gold illuminates the complex relation between the culture and the economy, and she provides a massive case study of sorts which shows that when religious culture is at its best, it can generate an economic order that humanizes the business realm and still be competitive. This relationship that Gold maps out for the reader is important since all sorts of companies are and have been influenced by their religious culture: Quaker and Cadbury, Dutch Reformed and Herman Miller, Catholic and Ouimet Industries, Protestantism and Reell, Buddhism and the Kikkoman Corporation, Parsi and Forbes Marshall, etc. Rarely does a Harvard case study or Forbes article examine the deep relations between the cultural roots of a company and its economic policies and practices, which makes Gold's book a rarity among books today.

It has been said that the one who tells the story defines the culture. Gold tells a story about a culture of giving within commercial enterprises. It is a story that responds to Benedict XVI's encyclical *Caritas in Veritate* and its principal concern for today's economic situation. He states that the "great challenge before us … is to demonstrate, in thinking and behavior, not only that traditional principles of social ethics like transparency, honesty and responsibility cannot be ignored or attenuated, but also that in *commercial relationships* the *principle of gratuitousness* and the logic of gift as an expression of fraternity can and must *find their place within normal economic activity.*" This is the story of the EoC. It is how this "logic of gift" animates and informs a commercial enterprise. Gold's book is a gift to us who rarely see in print a sophisticated examination of the cultural resources brought to bear in creating conditions in the workplace to humanize the relationships among people in a competitive economic environment.

Michael Naughton
Moss Chair in Catholic Social Thought
Director, John A. Ryan Institute for Catholic Social Thought
University of St. Thomas, MN

1

In Search of a New Economic Vision

INTRODUCTION

The end of the twentieth century was marked by the so-called "triumph of capitalism" and the failure of the socialism regimes in Eastern Europe. It was accompanied by a wave of optimism that the "evils" of communism could be overcome by the forces of the free market. Its closing decade saw an unprecedented expansion of the global economy, based on the ideals of free market liberalization. Globalization became the buzzword of the 1990s and the rate of international financial transactions burgeoned. A new age of international co-operation and solidarity seemed to be dawning. In the autumn of 2000, the UN *Millennium Summit* epitomized the sense of "unique occasion" offered to the "world's peoples" to "reflect on their common destiny."[1] Amid great ceremony, over 100 heads of state gathered at UN headquarters to sign a declaration that set ambitious goals, including the promise to cut poverty in half by 2015.

Just two decades on from the "triumph of capitalism," the world appeared a very different place. A world of prosperity delivered by free market globalization seemed like a distant dream. All over the world, governments were forced to step in to shore up banks, the stalwarts of market capitalism. Massive inequalities in opportunity remain the norm. Environmental destruction threatens. A series of truly global crises challenges us to think carefully about the assumptions on which economy and society is based.

A MULTI-FACETED GLOBAL CRISIS

So what is the nature of the crisis the world faced at the dawn of a new millennium? It is highly complex and multifaceted, but had four principal intersecting and interconnected crises: economic recession, social inequality, environmental threat, and political instability.

13

Economic Recession

The first crisis was an economic recession of such magnitude that it could truly be called "global." It is the first during the era of globalization — indeed since the Second World War. For the first time since 1946, across the world international trade began to fall. Hundreds of countries faced declining consumer demand, shrinking economic growth, and rising unemployment.

Many factors contributed to this situation. What was experienced as a recession in the "real economy" started out as a financial crisis on Wall Street. For several years, the financial sector had been expanding rapidly. At the root of this expansion was phenomenal growth in home ownership. Unlike in previous decades, where there were tight regulations on eligibility for mortgages and other loans, throughout the late 1990s and early 2000s a new kind of market emerged — the sub-prime. "Sub-prime" referred to a type of mortgage designed for people who presented a risk higher than normal. These individuals and families were often in low-paid and insecure work, or were even supported by public assistance. By 2006, such mortgages amounted to $600 billion, 20 per cent of the United States housing market.[2] Purchasers were often offered mortgages with little or no down payment. The expansion of mortgage finance, in turn, fuelled a massive property speculation bubble based on the illusion that this was a win-win situation. So long as you were on the property ladder, there was nothing to lose. Nothing was as safe as bricks and mortar.

Within the financial sector, money flowed in on an unprecedented scale and speed. Individual packets of sub-prime debt borrowed from banks and thrift institutions were "bundled up" and sold as "securities" to other institutions, which then used the capital from such sales to speculate on the stock market. At each stage of these transactions, however, the original risk of the sub-prime market began to disappear. The whole scheme was riding on two basic assumptions: that people would continue to make their mortgage payments and that house prices would continue to rise. So long as the whole system worked, everyone made money and was happy.

Then in 2007 omens began to appear in the mortgage markets. Sub-prime lenders began to report losses, leading to the suspension of sub-prime products. By September, the property speculation bubble clearly had begun to burst. People began to find it harder to get mortgage approval and many were unable to keep up with their payments. The Federal Reserve lowered its interest rates and pumped billions of dollars into the economy in an attempt to shore it up, but the scale of the crash was still only at the beginning. The institutions concerned all held their breath and waited for others to make the first move.

As the situation unfolded throughout 2008, it became apparent that the problem in the financial sector had reached astronomical proportions. It affected many of the best known institutions, and the scale of the losses risked pulling down the entire economy. A number of factors compounded the situation. First, mounting evidence suggested that lax rules within the financial sector had given rise to widespread fraudulent practices. Not only were institutions lending to people who could not afford mortgages, but they were covering up the precarious state of their fiscal integrity. Second, the nature of the securitized products linked to the sub-prime market had become so complicated, nobody knew really what they were or who they belonged to. This may seem ridiculous, but the products had been resold so many times that it became unclear where the original risk lay.

The impact of financial crises always comes in waves. At the start of this crisis, some people could have been forgiven for wondering what the fuss was about. It seemed remote. As time passed, however, the impact on the real economy — both in the US and globally — became apparent. Money is the life blood of the economy and the financial breakdown was like a massive blockage in an artery. Money stopped moving; people stopped buying and selling. As a result, what had started as a bank problem spilled over into the lives of real people with real businesses, jobs, homes, and families to feed. Businesses could no longer access credit. Bank managers froze overdrafts or hiked up interest rates on them. People could no longer get credit for major purchases like cars. Unable to buy and sell, consumer demand, which had driven the American economy for years, plummeted.

The effect of this crisis, however, was not restricted to the United States. In a globalized world with global financial institutions, whatever happens in one jurisdiction has an impact on another. The same securities, in fact, had become entangled in a web of transactions that stretched from London to Singapore, from Reykjavik to Sydney. Such was the scale of the crisis in the US, the banking system across the globe soon became paralyzed and similar scenarios began to unfold in other countries. Although there had not been anywhere near the same scale of sub-prime lending in these other countries, they too found themselves caught in a stalemate where no banking institution trusted another. Rumors spread like wildfire and governments were finally forced to step in to prevent a global financial collapse. But this was too little too late to stave off a global downturn. What started as a crisis in one sector in one country became the tipping point for the global economy from stability into recession.

The depth of this recession took many by surprise. The speed and depth of the financial crisis has led some to dub those years the "Goldilocks Economy."[3] People were living in a fairytale world, believing that the machine could create money forever so long as they made sure the porridge was "not too hot or not too cold." Like in the fairytale, however, Goldilocks got a rude awakening when the bears came home to find her asleep. A similar tale could be told in relation to the collapse of the financial sector.

Social Inequality

The second facet of this global crisis was social inequality. Rapid growth in technology during the twentieth century made the world truly a village. Whether living in the slums of Nairobi or the skyscrapers of Chicago, people acquired the ability to connect with one another. Satellites and mobile technology revolutionized communications, enabling cheap and easy ways for people from around the world to keep in touch. Moreover, despite enduring visa restrictions, people can travel more freely than ever before. Global media groups have created a truly global culture, where people in every part of the world share moments together in real time, whether the Soccer World Cup final or a global rock concert.

Access to information and communications enables people to see what life is like in other parts of the global village. The village, however, contains stark inequality. The human development statistics between Ireland and Sub-Saharan Africa, for example, reveal startling differences. In Ireland, average life expectancy is 77 years and rising; in Zambia, it is 37 years and falling. In Ireland, six in a thousand children die before their fifth birthday; in Zambia it is nearer 2 in every 10 children.

Table 1: Economic and Social Inequalities

	Ireland	Zambia	High Income (OECD)	Sub-Saharan Africa
Income (GNI per capita $)	34,280	450	32,040	660
Education (Adult literacy) (%)	99	67.9	99	60.5
Access to health (Infant mortality per 1000 children)	6	102	5	104
Average life expectancy (years)	77	37	78	46

Sources: World Development Indicators (World Bank) 2004/
UNDP Human Development Report 2005

The 2005 Human Development Report reveals another striking statistic. In certain African countries average life expectancy has been declining since the mid-1990s, meaning that a child born there today may well be outlived by his or her parents, and possibly grandparents. Moreover, while the number of people trying to survive on less than $1 a day has fallen globally,[6] the gap between those in absolute poverty and those who live in relative luxury has widened substantially.[7] In 2004, the wealth of the richest twenty people in the world was greater than the income of the entire population of Sub-Saharan Africa.[8] The World Food and Agriculture Organization, moreover, announced in 2009 that as a result of the food crisis and economic recession, for the first time in history the number of hungry people in the world had risen to over one billion — one person in six.[9]

Inequalities between the rich and the poor endure within countries and between countries. The differences of lifestyle, however, become tangible if one compares items that may be regarded as luxuries with the bare necessities. Table 2 below illustrates the income and spending gap between those living in developing countries and northern countries. Such inequalities call to question the values underpinning the global economy. These figures also suggest the lack of efficiency — indeed the possible lack of morality — in a system that is so inequitable.

Table 2: The Scale of Global Inequality

- In 2005, the wealth of the richest 20 people in the world was $432.2 billion. This is more than the income of 719 million people living in Sub-Saharan Africa.[10]

- The cost of meeting the Millennium Development Goals, an estimated $50 billion, is roughly equal to 0.2% of the global income.[11]

- Europeans and Americans spend over $1 billion a month on pet food while 852 million people experience chronic hunger.[12]

- Europeans spend $1 billion a week on cosmetics and toiletries, while nearly 3 billion people in the world lack access to basic sanitation.[13]

These statistics point to a growing gap between those able to grasp the benefits of globalization and those left behind. Yet the numbers do not disclose fully the human cost of such inequality. Behind each statistic lies a real person with real cares and dreams as mothers and fathers, friends, children, grandparents, and cousins. They strive for a safe home and clean environment, a secure income to provide for their family, a healthy and long life, and a better life for their children. However, they often face dire circumstances that make these most basic human needs impossible to attain: they have meager incomes, but no state safety net to keep them going in times of need; they often face chronic or terminal illnesses, but lack hospitals or medicines; they may manage to build a small home, but have to flee due to armed conflict or natural disasters. The daily experience of poverty is often felt in a lack of control, a sense of powerlessness, injustice, exclusion, and a denial of rights.

Such poverty has become part and parcel of the process of globalization. On the one hand some, through geographical location, privilege, or hard work, grasp the opportunities of a market-based global economy. On the other hand the majority, as a result of unjust social and economic structures, cannot avail of the benefits. In many instances such exclusion is created by lack of access to basic resources such as land or water. In others, it is the result of instability and conflict, often begun through mismanaged development and fuelled by a culture of impunity and corruption. In other countries, the denial of access to basic health and education effectively traps people, making their participation in the market economy practically impossible.

In situations such as these, the market failure is compounded by the inability of governments to intervene effectively.[14]

The scale of the poverty trap on the African continent merits particular concern. African countries consistently rank in the bottom 37 places of the 177-country UN Human Development Index, which tracks access to the basics of human survival such as water, health, education and housing.[15] The current crisis has compounded this poverty trap. While to a greater or lesser extent countries on other continents have benefited from globalization, on balance Africa has not. Indeed, the current form of globalization may have exacerbated its problems. Large flows of unethical investment and illegal trade in minerals, other natural resources, and arms have gone unrecorded and unregulated.[16] This trade in arms has deepened the level of insecurity across many regions of the continent. Its abundant natural resource base is sometimes more of a curse than a blessing.[17] Private investment and trade in extractive industries in the Democratic Republic of Congo, Sierra Leone, Angola and Sudan have contributed not to inclusive development but to the creation of war economies. Such economies serve the needs of armed political elites within these countries while undermining governance, stability and economic growth.[18]

Environmental Threat

The social and economic impacts of the crisis are linked to a third facet of the global crisis — environmental threat. Since the 1980s, various international bodies have been warning about the environmental consequences of an economic model based on limitless consumption and growth. Just before the financial collapse in 2008, there was the strange global phenomenon of a huge spike in resource prices. That massive and sudden increase in the cost of basic commodities like food, minerals, and oil raised the question of whether the planet was nearing its limits of growth. Unprecedented demand for basic resources compounded by speculation sent prices through the roof. The food crisis and the financial crisis are joined like two sides of the one coin. The shift of land away from agricultural production to other commodities pushed up the price of food and left many countries poorly equipped to deal with the global recession.[19]

Demand for basic resources is one dimension of the environmental threat facing the planet. As the global economy accelerated in the years before the crisis, the demand for resources outstripped the ability to produce them. The result was that while economic figures might have looked good, from an environmental perspective many countries were facing ecological breakdown in order to make hasty profits. Across the world, the widespread destruction of rainforests for timber and the accessing of remote wilderness for oil degraded sensitive biodiversity and caused pollution. The global recession offered a small breathing space from the frenetic pace of using up natural resources, but it will likely prove only temporary.

Linked to the cavalier use of natural resources is the impact of climate change, which has begun affecting the everyday lives of millions of people throughout the world. Climate change, compounded by economic and social inequality, is ratcheting up the vulnerability of the poorest countries. Evidence of human interference with the climate, particularly through the burning of fossil fuels, is now stronger than ever.[20] As warmer temperatures lead to greater evaporation and the warmer atmosphere holds more moisture, the possibility of torrential rain in already wet regions increases. In a similar dynamic, hotter weather causes dry regions to lose still more moisture, exacerbating droughts and desertification. The total available water in Africa's largest catchment basins, Niger, Lake Chad, and Senegal, has decreased by 40 to 60 per cent, and desertification has worsened because of lower average annual rainfall, runoff, and soil moisture.

The minimum predicted shifts in climate for the 21st century are likely to be "significant and disruptive." Estimates of changes vary: global temperature may climb from 1.4 °C to 5.8 °C; the sea level may rise from 9 cm to 88 cm. This range of predicted effects reflects the complexity, interrelatedness and sensitivity of the natural systems that make up the climate. But while predictions of future climate impacts may be inexact, they are not meaningless. They do suggest consequences that could vary from disruptive to catastrophic. The *minimum* warming forecast for the next century is more than twice the 0.6 °C increase that has occurred since 1900, and that earlier increase is already having marked consequences. Sea levels have already risen by 10 to 20 cm over pre-industrial averages and are likely to climb higher.

Although regional and local effects may differ widely, a general reduction is expected in potential crop yields in most tropical and sub-tropical regions. Mid-continental areas, such as the United States' grain belt and vast areas of Asia, are likely to dry. Where dry land agriculture relies solely on rain, as in Sub-Saharan Africa, even minimal increases in temperature would decrease yields dramatically. Such changes are already disrupting the food supply in regions already afflicted by shortages and famines, such as Malawi and Niger. In the future, this effect may well become more acute.

Salt-water intrusion from rising sea levels may also reduce the quality and quantity of freshwater supplies.[21] This is a major concern, since billions of people already lack access to fresh water. Higher ocean levels are already contaminating underground water sources in Israel and Thailand, in various small island states in the Pacific and Indian Oceans and the Caribbean Sea, and in some of the world's most productive alluvial plains, such as China's Yangtze Delta and Vietnam's Mekong Delta. Higher temperatures can also expand the range of vector-borne diseases such as malaria.

The rich world does not always see how climate change increases the pressure upon a world already under stress from poverty, injustice and environmental mismanagement. A critical challenge in Africa, in particular, is the "way in which multiple stressors — such as the spread of HIV/AIDS, the effects of economic globalization, the privatization of resources and conflict — converge with climate change."[22]

Overgrazed land, deforested mountainsides, and depleted agricultural soils leave nature vulnerable. Those most at risk are those who lack the resources and, increasingly, the mobility to adapt through migration. Millions live in dangerous places such as floodplains or shantytowns on exposed hillsides around the enormous cities of the developing world. Often they are literally trapped in poverty — they can go nowhere else. Climate change would "accelerate social stratification" in Africa, meaning that "those who don't have sufficient wealth to buffer the effects of climate vulnerability will plunge deeper into poverty."[23] In reality, for many vulnerable people climatic changes may mean the difference between life and death.

Corporations and countries in the industrialized global north are responsible for most of past and current greenhouse gas emissions. Arguably, these emissions are a debt unwittingly incurred for the high standards of living enjoyed by a minority of the world's population. By and large, the wealthy have abundant resources and opportunities to adapt that shield them from the largest impacts. Those already suffering most from climate change are in the developing world, where there are fewer resources for coping with storms, floods, droughts, outbreaks of disease and disruptions to food and water supplies. They are often eager for economic development themselves, but find that this already difficult process is becoming even more difficult. For example, the mounting costs of dealing with the health problems associated with changing disease patterns could eat up any additional aid, thus preventing essential investments in economic development.

Political Instability

The final facet of the global crisis is the growing political instability affecting many parts of the world, particularly in the rapidly urbanizing areas of Africa, Asia, and Latin America. The rapid spike in prices in 2008 provoked an upsurge in political violence in over forty cities around the world in the form of food riots.

Political scientists predict that growing pressure over basic resources such as food and water may spark new wars in many parts of the world. If freshwater sources such as those in the high Andes dry up, new conflicts may emerge. In many respects, some of the conflicts in the eastern Horn of Africa are wars over access to water. The mass migration of refugees, moreover, may increase social tension within and between countries as different ethnic groups seek to resettle in smaller tracts of land.

Elsewhere, the economic downturn fostered nationalist politics. Rising unemployment rates lead people to seek scapegoats for their problems. In pluralistic societies with relatively open labor markets, such scapegoats are readily available. Increasing racial tensions, particularly within Western Europe, led to a revival in the far right and the return of the specters of economic protectionism.

On a global scale, the crisis exposed an institutional vacuum of leadership. Despite its Charter, which outlines its role in governing economic affairs, the UN has proved ineffective in providing coordinated economic action. Other coalitions such as the G7 group of industrialized nations have begun stepping in to lead the way, and expanded groups such as the G20 have brought rising economic powers like China, India, Russia, Brazil and South Africa into the conversation. Nevertheless, other smaller countries feel excluded from decision-making that will have a considerable impact on their affairs. This lack of cohesion at a global level and the breakdown of the existing processes pose a serious risk as the world attempts to address crises. In *Caritas in Veritate,* Pope Benedict XVI has echoed the calls of his predecessors for a true global authority which has the capacity to show real leadership on worldwide issues.

A CRISIS WITH DEEP ROOTS

The section above delineates the main dimensions of the crisis the world faced as it entered the third millennium. It points to some of the proximate causes of some facets of this crisis, and exposes some of the contradictions that must be faced. This crisis has exposed the fragility of globalization as we know it and the real possibility that twentieth-century gains could reverse as a result of environmental and social decline. Returning to business as usual through increased debt and wastage of resources would only deepen the crisis. Although such a complex crisis has many proximate causes, at its heart it is based on a small number of flawed basic principles. To address these, however, means looking at the very foundation of modern economics.

In 1808, one of the most controversial scientists in modern history was born — Charles Darwin. The celebration of his bi-centenary in 2008 called attention to the controversy between those who see opposition between his theory of natural selection and biblical accounts of creation. Very little attention, however, was directed to the link between the misappropriation of Darwin's theory of natural selection and the economic crisis. Although he himself would have pointed out how such arguments are based on only a partial understanding of his theory, repercussions of what has been popularly deemed "Darwinist" thinking have extended beyond the natural sciences into social and economic theories. The fascist regime in Germany, for example, invoked Social Darwinism to justify extermination of the Jews.

It could be argued that Economic Darwinism has become a prevailing doctrine within free market economies. Economic Darwinism refers to a simplistic economic belief that found some currency during the latter part of the twentieth century and the first decade of the next: the economy, like the natural environment, is essentially about the survival of the fittest. Within the economy, individuals and businesses battle for survival by pursuing their own self-interest, dominating others to the point of elimination. In the natural order of things, according to this theory, the strong prevail and the economically weak are eliminated. One of the most influential economists, Milton Friedman, has referred explicitly to the "economic elimination of the unfit."

This notion that has held such sway, however, is a fallacy. It is based largely on a misunderstanding of the nature of human persons and how they act in economic situations. Economic Darwinism sits side by side with another pillar of modern economic theory — the notion that self interest alone can guide the market. This theory was first proposed by the 18th century Scottish philosopher and economist Adam Smith, who said: "It is not from the benevolence of the butcher, the brewer, or the baker that we expect our dinner, but from their regard to their own interest. We address ourselves, not to their humanity but to their self-love, and never talk to them of our own necessities but of their advantages."[24] In other words, within economic transactions the over-riding principle is self-interest.

The notion that economic transactions are founded in self-interest gave rise to the 19th century notion of *homo oeconomicus*, a term coined by another Scottish philosopher, John Stuart Mill. In his view, the science of political economy, which preceded modern economics, should not be concerned with "the whole of man's nature as modified by the social state, nor of the whole conduct of man in society. It is concerned with him solely as a being who desires to possess wealth, and who is capable of judging the comparative efficacy of means for obtaining that end."[25] He later describes this notion as "an arbitrary definition of man, as a being who inevitably does that by which he may obtain the greatest amount of necessaries, conveniences, and luxuries, with the smallest quantity of labor and physical self-denial with which they can be obtained." This arbitrary notion of the "economic man" caught on. Throughout the 19th century influential economists like Wilfredo Pareto used it as the basic assumption of their economic models. By the 20th century, it had become mainstream, with rational choice theory dominating modern economics.[26]

Despite the complexity of the theories built around it, the basic notion of human beings who base rational economic decisions purely on self-interest remains shaky. Although it may have served a useful purpose for some theoretical approaches to economics, in practice it has been less useful. In reality, it is difficult, if not impossible to differentiate the motivations of human behavior, some of which may seem irrational. Many counter-theories have emerged that highlight its complexities. These theories call attention to the psychological factors as well as the impact of partial information on choices. Nonetheless, no convincing proposition has emerged to counter the simple notion of "rational economic man."

The crisis at the beginning of the third millennium is bound up in this notion. One could argue that this is only a theory, but unlike theories in natural sciences that study immutable laws, in some ways social theories have the power to create the reality they seek to explain. Supposedly objective theories soon become normative by influencing the discourse of public policy and by influencing popular culture. This is especially true with the notion of "rational economic man." It is widely acknowledged that under-regulation was a central cause of the post-millennial collapse. Another way of looking at it, however, is to say that there was a misplaced belief that a market founded on rational economic human beings seeking their own self-interest would look after itself. Deep down, markets are thought to be founded on a notion of the natural order of things, combined with a belief in rational self-interest. Any interference with that order is thought to do more harm than good. Yet what has that apparent natural order led to?

Its fundamental fallacy has been exposed in spectacular fashion. The massive bailout of banks has demonstrated that markets fail if based solely on the profit motive, and that the consequences extend well beyond the reach of those who perpetrated the acts. According to the Social Darwinist/Adam Smith model, a Gordon Gekko (the infamous financier from the film "Wall Street" whose watchword was "Greed is good") would represent the peak of human selection, the perfect *homo oeconomicus*, the top of the human food chain so to speak!

Key Considerations

Nature reveals that the complex web of life exists due to collaboration and symbiosis, not because of a survival of the fittest who prevail because of their cunning or strength. Survival is as much about learning to co-exist in harmony and observing limits as it is about competition to the death.

Likewise, Adam Smith is often misinterpreted. His writings make it clear that he was quite aware of the difference between self-interest in the broad sense of the word and narrow selfishness. His notion of self-interest is rooted in a theory of moral sentiments based upon "sympathy" for the other. It is now widely accepted that in fact, the economy hangs together through an intangible force, trust. Trust can only be formed by honest, ethical relationships or "relational capital."[27] The formation of such relationships requires an understanding of human beings deeper than the caricature of *homo oeconomicus*. The economic literature on this is widespread.[28]

The critiques of "rational economic man" are manifold. Some have argued that the impossibility of perfect knowledge makes the idea of a rational actor implausible. Others have criticized the over-emphasis on "self-interest" implicit within "utility maximization," stressing that different forms of utility can be conflicting (Etzioni, 1989: 31) and that the interests of the individual may not necessarily contribute to the common good (Daly & Cobb, 1990). Others have pointed out the limitations of the assumption that human activity is always motivated by a single-minded desire to maximize.

One key finding that has begun to undermine the notion comes from research into the social nature of markets — something antithetical to *homo oeconomicus*. The revival of the work of economist Karl Polanyi (1957) has led to renewed interest in the ways that particular markets are "embedded"[29] within social and cultural relations. According to Polanyi, once societies accept the market as the main form of social organization, human relationships within these societies are transformed into the "epiphenomenon of the market." The market may appear as the central organizing factor, but it is supported by social relationships based on "reciprocity," in addition to other modes of interaction such as "market exchange" and "redistribution."[30]

According to this analysis, mainstream economics has grossly underestimated the degree to which markets are "embedded" within social and cultural norms. The market, a social creation, exists only as a result of prevailing cultural and social values. One such value is self-interest, but the assumption of a rational actor who constantly seeks to maximize personal or corporate utility and in so doing contributes to the wider economy and therefore benefits society as a whole, has been severely criticized (Daly & Cobb 25–43).

Despite the complexity of economic life in the early twenty-first century, a single concept of the market has been applied to the most astonishing range of social relationships on a variety of scales. Financial markets deal in moneys or derivatives of money of various kinds. Stock markets, which span the globe through the various institutions of the international financial system and increasingly through cyberspace, engage in evaluating and distributing the ownership of companies. Markets for various products and services function according to supply and demand. There are housing and labor markets, and finally some "market markets" still operate — occasions where people still physically come together to sell and buy things. The word "market" is also still used to name the physical location where such events are

CHAPTER 1

held. The same word is also used as a verb to indicate the process of making something sellable because of its real or imagined attributes. There is growing agreement that the concept of "the market" cannot take in such a range of relationships, suggesting that other concepts are needed to represent the changes in the economic system.

Although "market" clearly has multiple meanings, it has come to be linked with the term "economic" to indicate a space in which one can assume the outworking of an underlying instrumental logic in social relations. By its nature, such logic cannot include ethical judgments on the part of its participants; indeed, it is antithetical to anything forming an alternative basis for decision-making. In this way, ethical considerations such as social justice are circumscribed within the interplay of "market forces" through which the system rather than the individual decides on the most efficient allocation of resources.

The Problem of Trust

Although such considerations undermine the notion of "rational economic man," it is completely negated by a force which is apparent only when it is absent: trust. The problem with assuming rational human behavior in economic markets is thrown into sharp relief against the basic issue of trust, which is widely recognized as the foundation stone of the economy. Nobel Prize winning economist Amartya Sen, among others, has written extensively on this issue. Trust presents a conundrum: it is indispensable to the economy, yet an economy founded on rational economic people pursuing only their self-interest is unable to generate it.

So where does trust come from? Like all simple ideas, the more it is examined, the more complex it appears. The formation of trust within the economy relies on a myriad of social relationships such as family ties, friends, neighbors and community to provide the behaviors on which the economy thrives. Such values and behaviors, often taken for granted but indispensable to the functioning of the money economy, have been termed "social capital" (Coleman, 1988).[31] Social capital has come to signify a whole range of cultural and social values such as trustworthiness, honesty, reliability, and neighborliness on which the capitalist system arguably rests. This "non-market" space uses a different vocabulary for exchange: rather than buying, selling or bidding, exchange is often expressed as sharing, caring, gift-giving, or even "doing one's duty" (Putnam, 1993). A different set of assumptions underpins such forms of exchange, since giving and receiving is often based on the subjective relationship between individuals and those with whom they make an exchange. Such people are not seen as anonymous players in one big market but as ethical beings with whom there is an assumed relationship — as family, as community member, as a neighbor or as a friend.

In modern society, however, the localized community ties that traditionally generated such trust have weakened. Despite the essential nature of such trust-forming to the working of the monetary economy, the myriad actions that contribute to trust are often "hidden" since they do not appear in GDP or in other economic indicators of wealth.[32] If the exchange of things, time, services, and so on that takes place within such economies were *valued* in conventional currency, however, they would far outstrip the exchange within the money economy (Zadek & Mayo, 1997: 4–7; NEF, 1998).[33] They are hidden, it could be argued, because the "goods" which are actually circulating — kindness, generosity, solidarity, care and even love — are assumed to be inexhaustible. Market exchange, on the other hand, which is designed to parcel out scarce resources, depends on the existence of this plentiful supply of goodwill. The increased dominance of market exchange within capitalist societies has shown that such social capital (although still plentiful) can be "eroded." The increasing penetration of market thinking into non-market relationships can undermine the trust at the foundation of economic structures: "It is the trust that underpins all the rest, but the international economy tends to drive it out by converting social transactions done by people for each other into cash transactions" (Boyle, 2000: 4).

The Problem of Imagination

Such is the dominance of the notion of *homo oeconomicus* on the human psyche, and such is its reach into so many spheres of life, that it is difficult to imagine an alternative. The pursuit of self-interest in the form of greater wealth, comfort, and luxury dominates the media, particularly through advertising. It provides cultural signposts for life — from the cradle to the grave. In the 1980s, in answer to a question about whether the economy had another way forward besides through unfettered markets, then Prime Minister of Great Britain Margaret Thatcher's famous answer has become the catchword for neoliberal economic thought: "There is no alternative."

We may be uncomfortable with believing that the economy, and hence society, is dominated by the blind pursuit of self-interest, but our temptation is to cut our losses rather than seek alternatives, leaving us trapped in a cycle of self-destructive behavior. If we begin to believe that the economy is actually more complex and depends upon trust in social relationships, however, we begin to focus energy on building and sustaining such relationships. Contemporary economy contains some signs of new approaches that incorporate such elements. It is useful to examine where such alternatives are emerging and which can be applied on a wider scale.

Alternatives can be founded only by looking beyond the mainstream into unusual places. During the 1990s various schools of economic thought began to consider a plethora of "alternatives" for the developing world. Many emerged in reaction to the demise of socialism and globalization's over-emphasis on the "market." Others were influenced principally by the end of colonialism and a desire to assert a different kind of development. Such "alternatives to development" highlighted, in particular, the various modes of economic interaction among communities at the margins of the formal market. Such communities, they argued, have seen the emergence of a new kind of economics, often promoted or instigated by new social movements and other civil society organizations. Such economics based on solidarity, collaboration, and a sense of belonging underline the social, ethical, and cultural dimensions of economic life. Rooted in particular social and cultural understandings, they highlight the existence of different perspectives on economic life within the global market and reflect specific values and behaviors.

Further insights into community economies and the rationale underpinning them come from studies of shanty town communities and social movements in Latin America. Within such communities, people struggle for survival not only economically but also culturally; they strive to define the meaning of life (Routledge, 1990) within a given territory. Esteva's (1987) account of life in the "hammock," a community of peasants in Mexico, highlights how relationships within the community overcome the economic rationality of the market: "*Homo sapiens* and *homo ludens* are celebrating their awareness of having awakened from the nightmare created by the impossible attempt to establish *homo economicus* on earth" (140). In this way Esteva is advocating a break away from the cultural construct that has shaped the Western concept of economic development

— *homo economicus*. His alternative is an economic logic based on sharing, friendship, and good neighbors through which people in the hammock are "rediscovering their space and their present" (142). Friedman (1989) similarly considers the different economic expressions of Brazil's Barrio Movement, which arose in those areas of greatest poverty. The economy within these areas is based on the reciprocal relations among members of a community who have learned to trust one another. The "barrio" economy generates co-operatives that do not have profit as their aim: "Their objective might be said to be the development of a moral economy in which the worker is not merely the embodiment of an abstract category called labor power, but someone standing in relations to others, and thus an ethical being, a person" (226). He asks, like many others in the alternative development school (e.g. Latouche, 1993), whether the moral economies of the poor, which demonstrate the possibility of other economic rationalities, could point the way out of the current domination of the market in Western society.

Through understanding the non-market logics of the moral economies of the poor, the West could perhaps redirect its economy towards a more equitable distribution of wealth. Such alternatives, however, remain marginal and tend to thrive only in times of hardship. During the financial collapse in Argentina in 2001, thousands of local bartering organizations emerged to plug the financial gaps. Many towns and regions invented community schemes to help people through the downturn. The US financial crisis following the turn of the 21st century saw an increase in alternative forms of community-based economic structures like bartering and time banks. Such forms of economic interaction, however, are generally regarded as primitive and essentially a last resort if all else fails. It is difficult to imagine how such alternatives could thrive in a globalized economy. The values upon which they are based, however, point toward alternatives that may have a greater chance of thriving in times of crisis and beyond.

Market-based Alternatives

The first decade of the 21st century saw a growing movement within business towards reconciling some of the ethical concerns that unfettered markets made obvious. Growing evidence suggests that market-based enterprises have begun to address the relationship between the three areas of financial, social, and environmental goals through alternative models. Within certain sectors of the business community such models have begun to gain prestige. The rapid growth and diversification of the ethical investment sector (Hutton et al, 2001) and the growth of the fair trade movement (Ranson, 1999) and social enterprises (Dunford, 2000) in particular point to a change in attitude towards the boundaries between market-oriented enterprises and social concerns. Although still modest, these sectors show clearly that there is an ample space to adhere to the market, in the sense of providing a quality service or product efficiently based on need, while adhering to wider ethical concerns.

At the boundaries of the market and traditional third sector organizations, moreover, another phenomenon is arising: new networks of wealth creation and welfare provision which draw on existing structures within civil society like churches and the business community. These networks draw on the capacity of the private sector to generate resources, harnessing them through innovative patterns of private welfare provision that bypass the state and traditional NGOs. Such networks are based on a different understanding of the relationship between business and wider civil society. Within them, business actors recognize that first and foremost they are *members* of civil society both at a local and at an international level, whether as family members, church goers, charity activists, or simply as citizens of a particular country. As members of civil society, they seek to contribute to the common good, also through their enterprise activities. They realize that they are not partners in some abstract sense, but build where possible on the natural patterns of engagement through existing international community linkages, creating new synergies directed at alleviating poverty, and addressing environmental concerns.

THE ROLE OF RELIGION IN ECONOMY

Even posing the question of religion and economics may seem irrelevant in the modern era, which by and large considers it primarily a matter of personal preference. What have prayers to do with the economy? The profound relationship between religious values and economics, however, dates back to ancient times. Indeed, in its root meaning the Greek *œcumene,* from which the English "economy" and "ecumenism" are derived, signifies "household" and "the known universe." Many economic sociologists contest the view that religion is less influential now than it has been in the past, arguing that modern society underestimates the significance of religious belief. "Despite the fact that the economic organizations have extricated themselves from the direct control of religious functions, traditional teachings continue to exert normative pressure on the way in which economic affairs are conducted" (Wuthnow, 1994: 621). He continues, "The market system is embedded within a cultural sphere of which religion is a significant part. Indeed, few other aspects of culture could be said to have such far-reaching implications as religion, the reason being that religion purports to add and alter the meaning of all realms of human activity including work and money" (640). Although contemporary Western culture seeks to circumscribe the value of religion, it remains a potent source of ethical and moral values. In this sense, religious meaning still shapes the "imaginary universe" and the actual day-to-day experience of individuals and groups.

Although economics and religion may seem to have little in common, in many ways they promote the same ultimate goal: human happiness. Religious texts, in fact, are full of references that directly and indirectly shape the economy: "Why should so much material on Economics be found in Scriptural and Philosophical writings? Because both have the same end, that all may live in happiness. But if a man must scramble continually for the satisfaction of basic needs to ensure his physical survival, he will not have time or energy to address the needs of mind, heart and spirit" (Makewell, 2001: iii). For the most part, the basic tenets for ethical economic action contained in the texts to which Makewell refers pre-date the industrial revolution. At the dawn of industrial society, however, religion in general and Christianity in particular faced profound challenges.

A vast literature by prominent social scientists explores the link between Christianity and economics during the industrial era. The notion of a "Protestant Work Ethic" fascinated Max Weber, who used it to explain why the industrial revolution took hold in some countries but not others.[34] More recently, a controversial scholar like Michael Novak has argued for a "Catholic Work Ethic."[35] Much of the resulting work underlines how Christianity has overcome the apparent tensions between religion and economic action in order to sustain the capitalist economic system. Weber (1958) was fascinated by the Protestant reformation's generation of what he considered several catalysts in the rise of capitalism.[36] Calvinism, by emphasizing the "calling" to work as a way of serving God, as well as by warning against the pursuit of frivolous leisure activities and by dismantling against usury, enabled the accumulation of wealth.

At the heart of this relationship between religion and economics is the question of what "rational" means. Modern economics rests heavily on the concept of "rational economic man." The relationship between religion and economics brings to the fore the contested understanding of "rationality" — of what makes sense. Weber emphasized not the compatibility of religion and capitalism, but the tension between the two due to their presupposition of different notions of "rationality" (Wuthnow, 1994: 628). In religion, rationality is founded on value, whereas modern economics perceives it in terms of means-end instrumentality. Weber notes that the two ought to be incompatible, yet somehow they reconcile themselves. He explains this reconciliation in terms of the "Protestant ethic" that emerged through the Reformation. By breaking down the ethical disapproval of traditional capitalism and by actively encouraging a methodical approach to economic affairs, Weber argues that Christianity played a critical role in shaping the economic and social history of Western Europe and accounts for capitalism taking root in certain countries before others.

Other social scientists expanded upon Weber's thesis. Swedberg (1998) proposes six areas of economic life affected by religious beliefs:

1. Norms about work
2. Norms about wealth and happiness
3. Norms about trade, finance and industry
4. Norms in relation to other economic actors
5. Norms about economic change and technological innovations
6. Norms about those without economic resources (charity).

Believers hold that each of these areas needs to be addressed in terms of their particular religion. In return they gain a "premium" on their actions.[37] These "norms," moreover, differ among different religions or even among sects within different religions. Using the practices and doctrines within Catholicism and Protestantism prevalent at the time of the Reformation, Weber distinguished the influence of beliefs within these two traditions in terms of the "premium" each placed on asceticism. In his attempt to discern a Protestant ethic, however, Weber actually outlines his own understanding of a Catholic ethic. He argues, for example, that what he perceived as an emphasis on "absolution" in Catholicism deterred engaging in economic activities, whereas the emphasis that Calvinism placed on asceticism legitimizes the "philosophy of avarice" that underpins capitalism.

Many contend that Weber oversimplifies the relationship between religion and economics because he does not make direct connections between the actual ways in which religious doctrine becomes economic action, nor does he explain sufficiently how individual application of doctrine comes to be adopted as an "ethic" by a group. As a consequence, they find little power in the Protestant ethic thesis to explain the rise of capitalism (Coleman, 1987).

Others maintain that Weber's analysis lacks empirical evidence. Marshall (1982) questions the evidence that the Protestant ethic influenced the rise of capitalism, concluding that Weber's evidence does not prove the case. For example, Weber maintains that capitalism spread in certain geographical regions due to a dominant Calvinist culture, but failed to recognize that some of the earliest centers of capitalism were not Calvinist but Catholic cities such as Liege, Lille and Turin (Trevor-Roper, 1969: 1–45). Moreover, many of the foremost capitalist families in Europe were not Calvinist but Catholics, Jews, or freethinkers (Little, 1969: 226).

Despite these criticisms, however, Weber's basic intuition that religion and economics are linked has explanatory power. His view is also supported by the growing body of social teaching that has emerged within various Christian traditions over the past century, including the Catholic Church. Catholic social teaching, which covers many areas of social, political, and economic life, sets out basic tenets for how faith applies to contemporary situations.[38]

Studies of how particular religious groups and communities have shaped their economies would seem to bear this out. In his much acclaimed yet criticized study of Buddhist economics in Burma, Schumacher (1973) makes a point similar to Weber's: different worldviews present different visions of economic life. "No one seems to think that a Buddhist way of life would call for Buddhist economics, just as the modern materialist way of life has brought forth modern economics" (Schumacher, 1973: 44). He then goes on to examine various Buddhist teachings and their implications for economic theory and practice. In particular, he examines the size of enterprises and the relationship between the local and the global: "From the viewpoint of Buddhist economics, therefore, production from local resources for local needs is the most rational way of economic life" (Schumacher, 1973: 49). Schumacher calls his economics "Buddhist," but he is conscious that similar "meta-economics" could be derived from other traditions such as Christianity or Judaism.

Recent studies of globalization and theology have examined the appropriate Christian response to ethical issues raised by the capitalist system. These include Ulrich Duchrow's *Alternatives to Global Capitalism* (1995) and Peter Heslam's *Globalization and the Good* (2002), which examines Christian responses to the "New Capitalism." Both draw on biblical perspectives to delineate the contours of a new form of ethically aware global economy. Duchrow emphasizes the importance of grounding concepts that emerge from scriptural analysis in modern day networks of "alternative company structures all over the world, whether or not these are successful" (253). He uses the example of the Mondragon cooperative in Spain, which originated from the work of a Catholic priest and has grown into a multi-million dollar international venture, to illustrate what people working together with alternative principles can achieve. Such structures may seem miniscule in comparison to the global economy as a whole, but their existence does provide an important reminder that "Despite the totalitarian structure of the world economy, it is still possible to reject certain structures and develop small-scale alternatives" (Duchrow, 1995: 274). Such alternatives, in his view, could offer the "germ cells" of a new economic policy. Heslam, meanwhile, returns to the biblical creation story to draw out key economic themes such as property, service, debt and work.

The difficulties of connecting religious teaching and economics are illustrated in the work of Daly and Cobb (1989) and Daly (1996), who examine how Christian teachings offer insights into a more sustainable future, using economic concepts taken from the Bible. In particular, Daly focuses on the cluster of values expressed by "sustainability-sufficiency-equity-efficiency" (220) and how these can be derived from scripture. Although these studies highlight Christian principles and traditions that impact modern economic life,[39] they acknowledge the enormous difficulties in deriving modern economic practices from those preached and practiced in Palestine two thousand years ago. Daly admits, "Everyone claims biblical support for his own pet economic ideas. Like the devil, the economist can quote scripture to prove what he wants to prove" (205).

Religion obviously has something to say about the ethics underpinning economics, but it is less clear how such theoretical knowledge can be translated into an actual "economic ethic." It has yet to be determined unequivocally whether a "religious ethic" has the scope to provide alternatives to the unsustainable models of economic rationality underpinning globalization. In a pluralistic world, moreover, such an alternative vision must have the breadth to encompass more than the religious faithful of a particular belief system. The question to be answered in this regard remains: Can "the economic ethic of a religion" actually translate into a viable alternative?

THE ECONOMY OF COMMUNION

This book examines the origins and development of one initiative which attempts to do just that: the Focolare Movement's Economy of Communion (EoC). The EoC emerged in 1991 in Sao Paulo, Brazil as an attempt to address inequalities in wealth first of all within the Focolare Movement, initially within Brazil. It subsequently has spread worldwide (Lubich 2001). Small commercial businesses were set up or transformed so that their profits could be redistributed to the poor. By 2009, 753 small and medium-sized businesses in 45 countries were participating in the project, redistributing a portion of their profits to promote welfare in the poorest countries and the spread of a "culture of giving" (EoC 2009). The success of this new form of economic activity and the "culture of giving" which it seeks to promote has generated interest both from within the academic community and from governments and non-governmental organizations (NGOs) in different countries. In his encyclical *Caritas in Veritate,* Pope Benedict XVI referred to the experience of the Economy of Communion as one example of a new kind of economic initiative in line with gospel values.

Yet this interest in the EoC could seem disproportionate to the size of the project. In actuality, it has remained small, and detailed analysis of how it is practiced has yet to be carried out. Nevertheless, its very existence and survival within the global market makes it an interesting "laboratory" of alternative economic vision. It raises probing questions about the interrelationship between the cultural, the spiritual and the economic dimensions of life, arguably calling into question the idea that "rational economic man" based on "self-interest" is the only viable principle for a global economy. In the EoC, the economy itself assumes a privileged place, a social space in which the instrumental aspects normally associated with "economy" only acquire meaning if they are carried out in the context of real-world practice so as to promote greater communion within the workplace and between the business and the wider community (Bruni 2002; Ressl 1999). In other words, the EoC frames the "rational" logic of profitability on which the market rests with a greater logic that accords value to every member of the working community as a human person who finds fulfillment, above all, in communion with others.

NOTES

[1]Millennium Report of the UN General Secretary, page 1, www.un.org/millennium. index.

[2]"Economists Brace for Worsening Subprime Crisis," http:www.npr.org/templates/ story/story.php?storyId=12561184 (4 January 2010).

[3]Elliott, L. and Atkinson, D. *The Gods that Failed: How the Financial Elite have Gambled Away our Futures.* London: Vintage, 2009.

[4]Statistics for GNI based on the most recent available data ranging from 1999–2004 (calculated using $ US Altas Method), http://siteresources.worldbank.org/ DATASTATISTICS/Resources/GNIPC.pdf.

[5]Statistics for education, health and life expectancy based on the UNDP Human Development Report 2005. Available at, http://hdr.undp. org/statistics/data/indicators.cfm?x =3&y=3&z=2.

[6]Dollar, D. and Kraay, A. (2000) Growth is Good for the Poor, World Bank Research paper, http://www.worldbank.org/research/growth/pdfiles/growthgoodforpoor.pdf.

[7]Milanovic, B. (2009) Decomposing world income distribution. Does the world have a middle class?, http://econ.worldbank.org/view.php?type=18&id=3442.

[8]According to the World Bank, the GNI of 719 million people living in Sub-Saharan Africa is $432 billion US. This is roughly equal to the combined worth of Bill Gates, Warren Buffett, Lackshmi Mittal, Carlos Slim Helu, Prince Alwaleed Bin Talal Alsaud, Ingvar Kamprad, Paul Allen, the Albrecht family, Lawrence Ellison, the Walton family, Kenneth Thompson, Liliane Bettencourt, Bernard Arnault, Michael Dell and Sheldon Adelson at $432.2 billion, http://devdata.worldbank.org/external/CPPProfile.asp?PTYPE= CP&CCODE=SSA and www.forbes.com.

[9]See FAO report 20.6.09.

[10]*Ibid.*

[11]World Bank estimated cost of meeting the MDGs is $50 billion; Global GNI in 2003 was $34.5 trillion, http://devdata.worldbank.org/external/CPPProfile.asp?SelectedCountry= WLD&CCODE=WLD&CNAME=World&PTYPE=CP.

[12]Based on WHO SOFI Statistics, http://www.fao.org/newsroom/en/focus/2004/51786/ article_51791en.html.

[13]Based on Euromonitor statistics, http://www.in-cosmetics.com/files/Euromonitor. pdf and Human Development Report 2004.

[14]*Market failure* occurs when free markets do not lead to an allocation of resources that is best for society, as when decisions lead to a situation in which marginal social cost is not equated to marginal social benefit.

[15]UNDP's Human Development Report, published annually, ranks the world's nation states in a Human Development Index, http://hdr.undp. org/statistics/data/indicators. cfm?x=1&y=1&z=1.

[16]OXFAM (2004) Guns or Growth "In 2002, arms deliveries to Asia, the Middle East, Latin America, and Africa constituted 66.7% of the value of all arms deliveries worldwide, with a monetary value of nearly US$17bn; the five permanent members of the United Nations Security Council accounted for 90% of those deliveries, *http://www.oxfam.org.uk/ what_we_do/issues/conflict_disasters/downloads/guns_or_growth.pdf.*

[17]The theory of resource curse is based on economic analysis of economic performance of resource rich poor countries. It concludes that "An *abundant* natural resource endowment provides more scope than resource-paucity does for cumulative policy error. Resource-abundant countries are more likely to engender political states in which vested interests vie to capture resource surpluses (rents) at the expense of policy coherence. The economy is increasingly distorted and manufacturing is protected so that development depends upon commodities with declining competitiveness." Richard Auty, WIDER University, http://www.wider.unu.edu/research/pr9899d2/pr9899d2s.htm.

[18]Studdard, K. (2004) *War Economies in a Regional Context: Overcoming the Challenges of Transformation* International Peace Academy Publication, http://www. ipacademy.org/PDF_Reports/WARECONOMIES.pdf.

[19]See article by Shattuck, A. 2008, *Financial Crisis and the Food Crisis — Two Sides of the One Coin,* http://www.stwr.org/food-security-agriculture/the-financial-crisis-and-the-food-crisis-two-sides-of-the-same-coin.html.

[20]Unless otherwise stated, statistics in this section are taken from the Report of IPCC available at, http://www.ipcc.ch/.

[21]See UK joint NGO group on development and climate change Up in Smoke? Africa and Climate Change, http://www.neweconomics.org/gen/uploads/4jgqh545jc4sk055sof fcq4519062005184642.pdf.

[22]Fields, S. (2005) "Continental Divide — Why Africa's Climate Change Burden is Greater," *Environmental Health Perspectives,* Vol.113 (8), pp. A533–537.

[23]*Ibid.*

[24]Smith, A. (1981) *An Inquiry into the Nature and Causes of the Wealth of Nations* (Indianapolis: Liberty Classics).

[25]Mill, J. S. "On the Definition of Political Economy, and on the Method of Investigation Proper to It," *London and Westminster* Review, October 1836. *Essays on Some Unsettled Questions of Political Economy,* 2nd ed. London: Longmans, Green, Reader & Dyer, 1874, essay 5, paragraphs 38 and 48.

[26]Oakley, A. (1994), *Classical Economic Man: Human Agency and Methodology in the Political Economy of Adam Smith and J.S. Mill,* Brookfield, Vermont, Edward Elgar, p. 155.

[27]Sen, A. (1987), "Rational behaviour," *The New Palgrave: A Dictionary of Economics,* v. 3, pp. 68–76.

[28]Gui, B. (1996), On "relational goods": strategic implications of investment in relationships, *International Journal of Social Economics* 23 (10/11): 260–278.

[29]Pelligra, V. (2007), "Intentions, Trust and Frames: A note on Sociality and the Theory of Games," Working Paper CRENoS 200702, Centre for North South Economic Research, University of Cagliari and Sassari, Sardinia.

[30]Embeddedness is defined as "the fact that economic action and outcomes, like all social action and outcomes, are affected by actors' dyadic relations and by the structure of the overall network of relations" (Grabher, 1993: 4).

[31]There is some contention over the validity of the approach that Polanyi took in his research. Some anthropologists and historians (e.g. Latham, 2000) disagree with Polanyi's interpretation of primitive economies as being "free" from market economies. In their view, such societies were just as dominated by markets as in the present day.

[32]To highlight the indispensable nature of this economy, the futurist Alvin Toffler, for example, asked executives what it would cost big business in hard cash if their new recruits had not been toilet-trained (Boyle, 2000: 4).

[33]Such "non-market" economies have been theorized in different ways by social economists and economic sociologists. Thompson (1966) makes reference to the "moral economy" whereas Putnam (1993) refers to the "civil economy."

[34]Work done by NEF has highlighted the close links between social capital and local economic development. Putnam (1993), in his book on associative democracy in Italian regions cites membership of choral societies as one of the three best predictors of a robust and effective local democracy and economy.

[35]Weber, M. (1958) [1904–5], *The Protestant Ethic and the Spirit of Capitalism.* Translated by Talcott Parsons (New York: Scribners).

[36]Novak, M. (1993), *The Catholic Ethic and the Spirit of Capitalism* (New York: Free Press).

[37]A comprehensive overview of the various debates surrounding the thesis of Weber can be found in Swedberg (1998). In this book Swedberg discusses the various critiques to which the Weberian thesis has been subjected. He concludes, however, that the central ideas of the thesis can still be used in the analysis of religion and capitalism.

[38]Weber, M. (1978: 54–56) termed this premium "Heilsgüter," which has been translated into English as "religious benefits" or "religious goods." Weber uses the term to cover a range of "religious desirables" (Swedberg, 1998: 109) in a similar way that the term "goods" is used in economic theory to mean anything that is required or wanted. Such benefits can be this-worldly or other-worldly, material or spiritual.

[39]Pontifical Council for Justice and Peace (2007), *Compendium of the Social Doctrine of the Catholic Church,* Vatican Press.

[40]For example, their books highlighted the idea of the "Jubilee" as a year of deliverance from debts — a concept which has been central to the Jubilee 2000 campaign for the cancellation of unpayable debt.

CHAPTER 1

2
A Global Community:
The Focolare Movement

Once upon a time, there was no home, no matter how poor,
without a hearth.
I would even say that the hearth was the symbol of home.
There, meals were prepared, you were warmed.
Seated at the fireside you rested your weary bones, chatted,
told stories, dozed off.
You met with each other, with family and friends.
Those times have gone. It would be hard to bring them back
completely.
But something can be done.[1]

INTRODUCTION

F*ocolare*, the Italian word for "hearth"[2] is more than just
the description of a physical space within a house. *Focolare* is the
symbol of "hearth and home," the most intimate image of family,
love, security, warmth. Within Italian culture, it summons the image
of a bygone age, when poverty was widespread and life was harsh
but nothing could take away from the closeness of family and friends
huddled together around an open fire, telling tales and sharing food
in an atmosphere of serenity and peace. The *focolare* was a way of
life, especially in northern Italy, where bitterly cold winters meant
that the fireside was a welcome sight at the end of a hard day's work.
At the *focolare*, all cares would disappear, and the darkness of the
night would be dispelled by the caress of a mother and the intense
heat of the fire. It is by no coincidence that the spatially intimate
focolare first became the nickname and eventually the title of a
global movement for the promotion of peace and unity in the world.[3]

The economic, cultural and historical geographies of the Focolare
Movement are bound up in this image of the *focolare*. The Movement
is global, with universalizing tendencies, as this chapter will
demonstrate, but its ideals, aims and overall organizational structure
all recall the ideal of the *focolare* as the intimate place of sharing; its
dream is to rekindle that intimacy of human friendship and family

39

on a global scale. The Focolare Movement was founded by Chiara Lubich and her friends in the 1940s. Its aim right from the start was to bring about solidarity and mutual respect among all members of the human family. As Lubich underlines: "We would have to live for a high ideal: to bring about unity among all people, considered as brothers and sisters."[4] It does not propose bringing this about through a new religion, but through a renewal of a basic principle to which many world religions subscribe, the "golden rule": "Do to others what you would like them to do to you" (UNESCO, 1995: 36). The Focolare started in Italy within the Catholic Church but has spread into all of the main Christian denominations and to other religions, uniting people worldwide in a common commitment to promote peace and justice. It has developed an increasingly public profile, particularly in Italy and Brazil, where Chiara Lubich has received many awards for her work for human rights.

The various initiatives and projects of the Focolare Movement all share one principal aim and objective: promoting greater unity within the human family at all levels, calling for social integration among races, between rich and poor, between different sexes, different age groups, different political groups, and so on. The Focolare spirit and message rests on the belief that greater social integration will not come about from the top down, as through the action of governments alone. It will come about, above all, through the transformation of interpersonal relationships between individuals and groups, from the revival of those kinds of caring relationships found within the *focolare*. To this end, over the years, the Focolare has developed initiatives and projects geared toward the promotion of a humanistic cultural vision rooted in values such as peace, solidarity, respect and sharing, which it sees as necessary to build a more caring and united world.

How the Focolare Spread

The origins of the Focolare can be traced back to the city of Trent, Italy, during the Second World War (Gallagher, 1997). The Focolare being born in Trent is highly symbolic. Trent sits at the northeastern extremity of the Italian peninsula, in the region of Trentino-Alto Adige, in the shadow of the Dolomite Mountains. In the course of its history, Trent has been invaded many times by the Slavic nations and also by the Austro-Hungarian Empire. Its position as a natural meeting point between the peoples of eastern and western Europe, as well as between the southern Mediterranean peoples and those of the Germanic north makes it a region of territorial conflict.

Trent's symbolism for the Focolare, however, reaches far beyond the city's being a cultural meeting ground in the heart of Europe. Within the history of Christianity Trent is a contentious geographical symbol, the place where Reformation divisions were codified during the sixteenth century. As the Reformation was unfolding in northern Europe, the nineteenth ecumenical council opened at Trent on 13th December, 1545 and lasted for eighteen years. Its main object was to determine Church doctrine definitively in answer to Protestant heresies (Knight, 2000).[5] Trent, therefore, came to represent the failures of Christianity to overcome its internal divisions.

The political, economic and human costs of such divisions were once more played out in the city of Trent during the Second World War. Historians note the "brutal friendship" between Mussolini and Hitler that proved fatal to Italian fascism after Italian troops were humiliated in Greece and Africa and the fortunes of the war swung in favor of the Allies (Ginsborg, 1990: 10). Within Italy this change of fortunes led to the Allied aerial bombardment of the country and the invasion of Sicily in the summer of 1943. Allied forces made their way north, but it was to be several months before they liberated the entire peninsula. In the north, Nazi rule prevailed,[6] and the underground resistance movement came into being, especially in the mountains surrounding the city of Trent. Even though the many independent bands of partisans could mount only token resistance to the Nazis and suffered high casualty rates, the Nazis responded with brutal reprisals: "Partisans and their sympathizers were treated with the utmost savagery by the Nazis and the blackshirt troops of the Republic of Saló. In September 1943, the Germans committed their first atrocity against the civilian population, reducing the village of Boves in Piedmont to ashes, burning alive many of its inhabitants" (Ginsborg, 1990: 17). The prolonged warfare devastated the industrial and agricultural infrastructure, leading to widespread poverty and near starvation, especially in the north. Life in the north of Italy in the 1940s, therefore, was characterized by dire poverty and brutality, and the shadow of suspicion of neighbors and friends led to the destruction of many communities.

Against this backdrop, the Focolare emerged in Trent as it was bombed continuously throughout the summer of 1943. Chiara Lubich and her companions were caught up in the tragic circumstances of war on a personal level, through the destruction of their homes and the death of friends and family. [7] Witnessing the futility of the war, they decided together to counter the hatred and division by beginning to live out the Christian message of concern for others in a radical way, starting among themselves. They had no intentions of starting a movement, but through their actions a small community came into being (Robertson, 1978). This community was dedicated, above all, to relieving the sufferings of those hardest hit by the war.

By 1949 the Focolare numbered just over 3,000, mainly in the north of Italy. Since then, it has expanded both geographically and in terms of its kinds of involvement. By the year 2000, the Focolare included four million adherents, a quarter living in Latin America and another quarter in Western Europe. Even though the Movement is now "global," it nonetheless has several strong concentrations of development: Italy, Brazil, Argentina, and the Philippines, where it is most developed. It is interesting to note at this stage that these countries also count a high proportion of Catholics among their populations. At the same time, relatively high numbers of people in Eastern European countries participate in the Focolare.

SPREADING BY EXAMPLE

The Focolare has spread across the world almost entirely through word of mouth and through the personal witness of those involved in the Movement. The story of its spread through Brazil epitomizes the development of the Movement in many countries. The Focolare arrived in Brazil almost by chance in 1959. In 1957, a monk from Recife had met some members of the Movement during a trip to Italy. On his return to Brazil he wished to spread this new vitality, showing that the gospel could bring about an effective social revolution, one based on dialogue and understanding rather than conflict and hatred. Within a few months, this new vitality became collective action among the rich and poor. The Movement set up its roots in *Ilhâ do Inferno* [Island of the Inferno] (Calliari, 1991), a notorious shantytown in Recife. Several people of the Focolare gave up their modest standard of living to live there. Their motive was simple: to offer the island's residents a credible and real example of Christian love. In order to do this they realized that they had to take on the conditions of the others fully, holding nothing back for themselves. So they too set up shacks similar to those of other residents and set about integrating themselves into the community. It was not easy, as one local resident recalled: "There was suspicion on the part of the locals: they could not understand why these people had come to live with them. They were defiant of any attempts to help them better their situation. Yet the local community did gradually begin to accept them because of the practical help that they offered and their shack became a center where everyone was welcome, regardless of who they were." People began to talk to one another and began to share ideas, talents and material goods.

The local community accepted the Focolare's gesture of solidarity and situations began to change throughout the shantytown. In a spirit of co-operation, they began to bring about small changes: removing garbage heaps and digging trenches. They formed a credit union and through the proceeds set up a brick factory, AMT. One 80-year-old completely paralyzed resident said, "I have lived here for a long time … Before the Movement came my situation was dire. With the help of the community I have been able to rebuild my house." Eventually, they formed an association of shantytown dwellers and were able to demand that the authorities supply the island with basic infrastructure. The spirit of co-operation became the distinguishing feature of the shantytown, so much so that they changed its name to *Ilhâ Santa Teresinha* [Island of St. Teresa]. Forty years on, Santa Teresinha now has, among other amenities, a school, health center, a pediatric hospital, a sewing workshop, and a brick factory. The Focolare community is still present, but no longer as an "outside" presence. Most of those who co-ordinate the various community projects, as in many initiatives of this kind, are Focolare members who come from the shantytown itself.

Since the 1950s, the Focolare has spread across Brazil, almost entirely through chance meetings and personal contacts. Wherever it arrived, the same pattern of change generally followed; members of the Movement now conduct over 100 social welfare projects (Focolare, 1994). The Focolare did not restrict itself to changing the situation of the poor. Its message of solidarity was just as relevant (if not more so) to other social classes. Consequently, people from the most diverse backgrounds and from the most different places began to become part of the same "family," united by a common desire to bring about a social revolution based on solidarity, dialogue and love. Those with money and resources put them freely at the service of the poor, bringing about a "gift relationship" in which those who give and those who receive are respected on equal terms.

Likewise, when the Berlin Wall came down in 1989, the extent of the Focolare Movement in Eastern Europe became apparent. The Focolare had been present in Poland and other Eastern European countries since the 1950s working alongside Church organizations undercover — or so they thought. In 1991, when many of the Stasi documents were released in Ex-DDR, it became apparent that the police had been gathering detailed information about the activities of the Focolare since the arrival of the first members in 1958 (Gallagher, 1997: 120). Two of the founding members of the Focolare went to the Leipzig fair as tourists and met there with some friends of the Movement, including Fr. Hans Lubsczyk, whom some Focolare members had encountered the previous year in Munster. For the next two years they made several trips to Berlin with Chiara Lubich, always as tourists. Then, on 13 May 1961 two of them, Enzo Fondi and Giuseppe Santanche, took positions at St. Elizabeth's Hospital in Leipzig. During the first few months they laid low, trying not to attract attention to themselves nor to the numerous friends they already had through the Movement.

In August that year, as East Germany faced a mass exodus, the Berlin Wall was thrown up. More Focolare people decided to enter the country to provide humanitarian assistance. Suspicious of their motives, the police held them in a detention center at the border and interrogated them for a week. Eventually they were allowed in but the secret police kept them under surveillance. Over the following years the Movement spread into all of the Eastern European countries almost entirely by example and by word of mouth. The Movement could not hold any large scale meetings, but the people in the communities met in each other's houses and occasionally arranged holidays together in the mountains.

Despite this intense surveillance, the extent of which only became apparent after the fall of the Berlin Wall when Stasi documents were released, the Focolare managed to get off the ground in Eastern Europe. Throughout the 1950s and 1960s, the number of people participating in the Focolare grew, and communications between the communities in the East and West were kept open. The "underground" nature of the Focolare's activities in Eastern Europe in many ways reflects the hidden, underground geographies of social movements that have been written about within human geography (Routledge, 1992). Within the context of the communist regimes, the Focolare was resisting the domination of the state in the everyday life of people and articulating an "alternative."

The activities of the Focolare, although sharing a common aim, are diverse. Greater social integration can be promoted at various levels and in innumerable ways. The range of activities that have emerged within the Focolare reflects this variety. A summary of its main activities during the 1990s is provided in Table 3.1. Its social and economic development initiatives promote the integration of people at a grassroots level. Such projects are regarded primarily as a way of overcoming barriers between rich and poor. The Focolare, however, also works increasingly on a political level, through the *Movimento per l'Unità* [Movement for Unity]. Through this initiative, which has taken off particularly in Italy, Brazil and Hungary, politicians of different traditions aim to generate greater unity within their own party and between parties, based on the promotion of human rights. The Focolare has resisted the temptation to form its own political party (or to influence the way people vote); instead, it urges all parties to promote social justice and human rights.

Igino Giordani, the Italian politician who influenced greatly the development of the Focolare Movement's political dimension, is considered a co-founder (Robertson, 1989). Prior to meeting the Focolare in 1948, Giordani had written prolifically on such topics as the social message of the gospel and the relationship between church and state. He was actively involved in founding the *Democrazia Cristiana* and was a close friend and colleague of De Gasperi. "Giordani gave the Party its basic principles and De Gasperi gave it its policy" (Robertson, 1989: 114). The two men, however, often differed on principles and policy. De Gasperi was regarded as a man of action, ready to adapt his ideology to fit the situation, whereas Giordani, who insisted on definite moral values, came to be regarded within the Party as somewhat "ingenuous" (Robertson, 1989: 115). Giordani died in 1980, but the tension between ideal and practice in public life which he experienced first hand, the way values can be subsumed within "Party" structures and ideologies continues to have a strong influence on the way the Focolare regards political life.

The Focolare, however, continues to work on a cultural level to promote the values for which it stands. It spreads its ideas through a network of "New City" publishers throughout the world, as well as media centers in Italy and Brazil. On a more subtle level, these values and ideas reach new audiences through music, dance and artists' groups that convey the Focolare's message of unity.

Table 3.1: Main Sectors of Focolare Activity

Sector	Nature of Activity
Social and Economic Development	1,000 development projects run by Azione per un Mondo Unito (AMU), New Humanity (NH), and the United World Fund (UWF); Adoptions at a Distance (AD), sponsoring around 15,000 children; Economy of Communion project (753 businesses) School of Social and Political Formation, Araceli Brazil;
Publishing and Communications	27 publishing houses in 4 continents publishing around 300 titles yearly; 37 editions of *Città Nuova* magazine in 23 languages with subscriptions of around 200,000 2 multi-media communications centers (Italy and Brazil); Regular world-wide TV coverage of large scale events (e.g. Genfest);
Cultural Activities	Sofia University Institute, Loppiano, Italy; International Groups (theatre, music, dance) — *Gen Rosso* and *Gen Verde;* Centers for artistic excellence e.g. *Centro Ave*, Loppiano; *Casa Clara*, Buenos Aires; Conferences for artists; Film industry study group in Hollywood; Incontri Romani Tourism Group in Rome;
Political Activities	Cross party group called *Movimento per l'Unità* working in 7 countries to promote greater co-operation in favor of human rights; Represented at UN ECO/SOC by New Humanity, which has Category 2 consultative status;
Religious Formation	Publication of "Word of Life" commentary each month. Estimated distribution: 3,000, 000 copies; Courses (from 1 day to 1 year) in various aspects of spiritual formation in various Focolare Centers and Mariapolis Center, Rome; Dialogue with approximately 300 Christian churches via the Centro Uno center for ecumenical dialogue; Inter-religious dialogue including the Center for Buddhist Dialogue in the Philippines; Istituto Mistici Corporis College, Loppiano.

Source: Focolare Information Service, Rome, 2009

Ever since its inception the Focolare has emphasized the translation of its spiritual vision into practical action on behalf of those in need. During the Second World War, it strived to help the needy within the immediate community and the poor in and around Trent. By doing so, they extended their ideal of "hearth" to an ever greater number of people. As the Focolare has spread, it has had to attend to the needs of a vast and constantly changing international community while retaining that intimacy of the hearth. The concerns of the Movement have led to the multiplication of local initiatives to promote social integration and to eradicate poverty. In addition to these micro-projects, it has also developed internationally recognized NGOs.[8] These help to secure the long-term funding of the various projects, forming a transparent and accountable institutional framework, through which the projects can receive private and government funding. Table 3.2 presents a summary of some of the main projects run by these NGOs.

Table 3.2: Human Development Projects Promoted the Focolare Movement

Project Name	Nature of Project	Location
Bairro do Carmo	Multi-sectoral: health center, primary school, co-operative, church, bakery, sewing workshop	Sao Roque, BRAZIL
Bukas Palad	Multi-sectoral: health center, social services, carpentry workshop	Manila, Cebu, PHILIPPINES
Fontem	Multi-sectoral: hospital, primary school, college, social services	Fontem, CAMEROON
Magnificat	Multi-sectoral: agricultural, artisan and social services (school, doctor) project	Pernambuco, BRAZIL
Santa Maria di Catamarca	Artisan workshop (indigenous textiles workshop)	Santa Maria di Catamarca, ARGENTINA
Santa Teresinha	Multi-sectoral: health center, primary school, nutrition center, day care center, building project, social work	Recife, BRAZIL
Adoptions at a Distance	Monthly donation of money to support a named child in a developing country with basic needs	Various
Bobo Dioulasso	Multi-sectoral: literacy project, health education, center for disabled people, Center for the promotion of women	Bobo Dioulasso, BURKINO FASO
Tailor workshop	Provision of machinery for sewing workshop	Chiguayante, CHILE
Thika	Agricultural co-operative	Thika, KENYA
Youth Center	Social center for young people	Urpay, PERU

Source: Focolare Center, Rome, 2009

All of the Focolare's multi-faceted projects share the same vision of integral human development that seeks to put the welfare of the individual at the center, balancing the need for a personal approach against the needs of the wider community and limited resources. This vision is incorporated into the statutes of AMU: "The inspiration for AMU comes from the spirituality of the Focolare Movement and proposes to co-operate in the development of countries and peoples, with special reference to developing countries and to spread a culture of dialogue between peoples" (Art. 2, AMU Statute). The basis of all AMU development projects is "dialogue and reciprocal listening in order to establish the needs of the local communities with which it is in contact so as to define objectives and methods of the programs together." In this process, the most important factor is respect for specific communities' cultural and social circumstances. Through respect, the members of the local communities are encouraged to participate in the decision-making process and become protagonists in their own development. This vision echoes the integral human development outlined in Catholic social teaching.

ECUMENICAL DIALOGUE: "A DIALOGUE OF LIFE"

Globalization today demands inter-faith dialogue and global perspectives on problems. Such demands require that the world's religions consider the possible overlaps and convergences in their thinking, rather than the conflicts that divide them. Such an approach, which lies at the heart of the Focolare's vision, has led Chiara Lubich and her followers to work with all people of faith and those of good will to further the vision of unity in diversity. From the start, Chiara Lubich was convinced of the universal relevance of the message she and her friends had adopted. The question of ecumenism, however, only arose within the Movement in the 1950s when some Lutheran sisters visited one of the summer gatherings of the Focolare in the Dolomites. Despite the difficult ecumenical situation of the time, they invited Chiara Lubich to Darmstadt, Germany to speak to a group of their sisters about her spiritual experience. As a result of this first meeting, the Focolare began to enter into the Lutheran Church (Reindl, 1992). During the Second Vatican Council, Chiara Lubich became a close friend of the Anglican Observer, Archdeacon Bernard Pawley. After their first meeting, 19 May 1961, the Archdeacon arranged for a group of Anglican clergy to visit the Focolare center in Rome (Back, 1988). This meeting, first held in 1964, became an annual event and has since expanded to involve members of over 300 Churches who wish to witness their unity in love and their Christian faith. Chiara Lubich also played an instrumental role in fostering closer relations between Pope Paul VI and Patriarch Athenagoras of Constantinople in the 1960s and 1970s (Gallagher, 1997: 133).

Although as a charismatic leader Chiara Lubich has played an important personal role in fostering greater understanding between leaders from different church traditions throughout the 20th century, the emphasis of the Focolare's work remains among the ordinary lay members of different churches. Through fostering a greater communion among people of different Christian traditions, the Focolare has given rise to a new form of dialogue, the "dialogue of the people," borne out through shared activities rather than discussions. A dialogue of the people that emphasizes what various traditions share arguably forms an indispensable foundation for theological dialogue (Back, 1988).

Likewise, the question of the involvement of other religions within the Focolare became relevant when it began to spread where Christianity is a minority religion, such as Japan and the Middle East. In such countries, religious prejudice and intolerance can cause unrest and hatred, much of it based on the fear that others (of a different religion) might impose their vision of the world and their truths onto ideas and practices regarded as sacred. Authentic dialogue, on the other hand, has to be free from this fear of an ulterior motive and rooted in a belief that, despite the differences that separate the various religious traditions, there is always common ground. For this reason, the Focolare has been working since the 1980s to generate dialogue between people of different religious traditions. In 1997, Chiara Lubich was appointed an Honorary President of the World Council for Religions and Peace. At the 1999 conference in Amman, in the closing address she was invited to deliver, she underlined the shared values that underpin all world religions and the need to stress these in a common commitment to work for peace.

This dialogue is based upon a shared commitment to put into practice the "golden rule" at the heart of many great traditions — "Do to others what you would like them to do to you; do not do to others what you would not like them to do to you." The dialogue that the Focolare seeks, as with the other forms of social action, emerges from the local circumstances in which the people of the Focolare find themselves. Thus, dialogue between Jewish and Christian communities may be prominent in areas such as Israel and Argentina, whereas in Thailand and Japan, there is a strong relationship between Buddhists and Christians. For several years the Focolare has been working together with other groups within different religious traditions to foster greater understanding and co-operation in favor of the poor. One of the Focolare's earliest contacts with other religious groups was with the Buddhist *Rissho Kosei-Kai* Movement in Japan. In 1980 Nikkyo Niwano, at that time leader of *Rissho Kosei-Kai*, invited Chiara Lubich to address 10,000 Buddhist followers in the Golden Temple. This initial step has led to years of mutual collaboration between the two global movements. In Thailand, collaboration between members of the Focolare and the local Buddhist community has led to the development of a model town of the Movement in Chang Mai, which has both a Buddhist temple and a Christian church.

One particularly significant event in the history of the Focolare's inter-religious dialogue took place on 18 May 1997, when Imam Warith Deen Mohammed invited Chiara Lubich to address his congregation at the Malcolm Shabazz Mosque in Harlem, New York. Her address to over 3,000 Muslims and Christians stressed the need to work together to promote the human values shared by Christians and Muslims and to combat any form of fundamentalism. This meeting, reported in the Muslim press as "historic" (Lateef & Lateef, 1997), has led to ongoing and mutually enriching collaboration within the Focolare between people of Christian and Muslim traditions. The Focolare now hosts regular meetings for Muslims who wish to deepen the Focolare's spirituality within the Islamic tradition and from an Islamic perspective. Such open statements of unity between leaders of different religions have also been met with fierce opposition from those on either side who hold a more fundamentalist position.[9] Despite this opposition, Chiara Lubich is convinced that *this* kind of dialogue is the only way to deeper awareness and understanding of the values that can lead to a more peaceful society.

The various branches and groups of the Focolare share three principal structures: the local Focolare centers, the model towns and the global Focolare Center in Rome (Johnson, 2002). These places on the Focolare world map are regarded not as mere organizational structures but above all as spaces in which the Focolare spirit is put into practice. They are "hearths" in action. They may differ in size and shape, but their main function is always to generate a welcoming atmosphere and environment.

Local Focolare Centers

In the network of Focolare spaces throughout the world, the local "focolares," which take the form of houses or conference centers, are the focal points. These consist of small communities of 5 to 8 people who make a life-long commitment to work for the Focolare. Most of the "focolarini" have jobs outside the Focolare and share all of their possessions in common (a practice to be discussed further in the next chapter). The focolarini facilitate meetings and activities for the various community members, usually based on age or personal circumstances. Above all, however, the Focolare houses maintain the warmth of a family atmosphere within the community. These houses are generally located within major cities that have concentrations of people involved in the Focolare. Their location makes them easily accessible for visitors from a wide range of regions. Some are located within the "model towns."

Model Towns

The second main Focolare space is the model town, the first of which was set up in the late 1960s. Given the depersonalized urban setting in which many now live, the ideal of a close-knit community can seem remote or even impossible. It is reminiscent of another era when people knew each other and had many opportunities for conversation. To give witness to the possibility of a city rich in interpersonal relationships, over the years the Focolare has developed 33 of such permanent communities throughout the world. They are more or less self-sustaining, and to a greater or lesser extent take on the functions of small towns.

There is a long tradition of religious communities establishing clearly distinguishable communities in the form of villages. Monastic traditions like the Benedictines were formed on a similar basis of living out their spirituality together. Likewise, the Focolare towns aim is to make the high ideals of the Focolare — unity among all people — accessible, as ordinary people live it out. Such projects bring to mind other attempts throughout history to build egalitarian societies, such as Kibbutz in Israel or the Distributionist Movement in England. In its heyday New Lanark Village, set up by the philanthropist Robert Owen, was a radical statement of an alternative way of thinking about human relationships in the workplace (Gatrell, 1970). Parallels can also be drawn with the quasi-religious communities that have emerged through the New Age movement, such as the Findhorn community. All of these communities have set themselves apart as micro-alternatives to the dominant social, economic and religious norms.

It is important, though, to highlight the differences between Focolare model towns and other examples of utopian societies. First, they do not see themselves as places closed off from the rest of society. They are open to a high number of visitors who come for a time to meet the inhabitants and to experience the atmosphere of sharing and trust that exists there. The town of Loppiano in Italy has around 750 inhabitants and receives on average 40,000 visitors each year — a trend that could possibly indicate the emergence of a new kind of "spiritual" tourism, corresponding to the "eco-tourism" of the 1990s. Second, even those towns that serve as focal points for the global Focolare Movement at large have frequent turnover in the majority of their inhabitants. Third, these towns have modern economies that are inserted in local economic structures, and compete in global markets, as will be discussed later. They have a complex division of labor ranging from agriculture to industrial activities to services. Many utopian societies have relied on a high degree of economic and social closure for their communities' growth and development. The Focolare businesses compete freely with those outside the towns on equal terms and so have to be as profitable as any other business.

These "model towns" are founded on the principle that everyone strives to live out mutual love and respect each day. Despite the many difficulties encountered in relationships, they persevere so as to make the ideal of mutual love and respect the law or the norm of the town. As a result of many years of commitment to this genuine ideal, trust, honesty, generosity and sincerity have become central to the social interactions within the community as a whole. This gives rise to new cultural practices called the "culture of giving," the spiritual and cultural soil out of which the EOS grows. The differences between peoples are not annulled in a forced attempt to create equality, but are cherished and become mutual enrichment between people in a culture. Certain shared values such as honesty, truth, and trust transcend all barriers and become predominant. Brazil has three of these towns: Santa Maria lies about 20 miles from Recife, Gloria lies just outside Belem in Para, and Araceli, the largest, acts as a focus for the whole of the Focolare in Brazil. In 1995 it received 29,000 visitors. Through these towns, the ideal of the Focolare becomes accessible and credible. Such towns, as later chapters will show, now form a natural focus for the development of EOS businesses.

Global Focolare Center

The central international offices for the Focolare Movement, located near Rome, acts as a central co-ordination point for all of the Movement's activities around the world: gathering and circulating news and information about the Focolare in different countries, planning major initiatives for the Movement on a global scale, making major decisions especially regarding structural growth and organizing large-scale events in Rome that involve the whole of the Movement. Less important decisions that relate to the everyday running of the Movement in individual countries are taken by the people in the countries themselves, often in consultation with the Movement's delegates. The delegates of the Focolare and the positions of responsibility at the head of the various branches are elected during the General Assembly of the Focolare every four years. The General Assembly consists of local representatives from each Focolare region plus the members of the Central Coordinating Council of the Focolare in Rome.

The Focolare, therefore, has an institutional dimension reflected in well-defined organizational structures at local, regional and global levels. These structures, however, as discussed above, are not an end in themselves. They have meaning only if they are able to reflect a global "hearth" in which the principles of caring and sharing are lived out in a radical way. In other words, the structures serve to facilitate the growth and development of a global community that has its own cultural vision. For this reason, the growth of the structures of the Focolare has been "organic" to some extent — adapting and growing to fit the needs and circumstances of the Movement at each stage of its growth and in each particular location. No one sat down and wrote a master plan for the development of the Focolare; it has emerged over the years through the commitment of many individuals, and in particular through the work of Chiara Lubich. In this way it is highly flexible and adaptable to the changing regional conditions over time.

The physical and organizational structures of the Focolare are regarded as places in which the spirituality of the Movement is lived among two or more people with the greatest intensity. Within the Movement, specific Focolare terminology can relate to its local and global geographies. In many ways, they represent a world-wide spiritual homeland for those who participate in the Movement. When this notion of homeland is invoked, it therefore designates not some imaginary place as in general speech (e.g. "in the ideal world no one would have to work") but refers to actual physical places in which the Focolare spirit is lived out by communities of different sizes. The Focolare's "ideal world" is not simply "utopian" in the conventional sense but is worked out on a day-to-day basis within real spaces and by real people. This is reflected in the way that some spaces are made over in order to reflect the Focolare ideals: the towns, the houses, streets and other shared spaces are often named after either important aspects of the spirituality or people who were part of the Focolare and who have died. One example of this is Araceli, one of the first people to bring the Focolare to Brazil, who died at a young age. The town of the Movement near Sao Paulo is now named after her.

A TRINITARIAN PERSPECTIVE

The starting point for defining a possible "Focolare ethos" is the common spirituality from which the Movement emerges. It is this shared understanding of the nature of the world on an ontological level that binds the Focolare together in different parts of the world, enabling it to develop into a global *community of meaning and action* with a common lifestyle. The spirituality of unity is centered on the belief that the essence of every human being lies not in any ultimate material reality, nor in their holding an overly spiritualistic understanding of the world, but on their *being love.* Such an all-embracing vision could arguably be interpreted in an infinite number of ways, many of which do not correspond with what the Focolare understands to be *love* (Cambón, 1999: 35).

Before considering the wider implications of this vision within social and economic fields, therefore, it is first necessary to clarify the epistemological roots of the Focolare spirituality in the Christian tradition and the ontology that emerges. Although the Focolare is now beginning to emerge within various religious traditions, the essential principles of its spirituality remain rooted in a Christian worldview, and this study draws on this perspective. Studies on other religious traditions, examining the way that various aspects of the Focolare's perspective have been integrated within other religions and the implications for dialogue, are essential. Throughout the history of Christianity the doctrine of the Trinity[10] has often been deemed an unfathomable mystery beyond human reason, with little or no connection to human life. Kant once wrote that the doctrine of the Trinity does not mean anything in practice. Karl Rahner said that if the doctrine of the Trinity was to be eliminated from theology nothing would change in theory — nor in the practice of Christian life (Cambón, 1999: 16). Hans Küng said that, sadly, when the Trinity is discussed the conversation either turns to abstract discourse or ends in silence. The Trinity, however, is at the heart of the Focolare spiritual vision.

Although the Focolare accepts that the Trinity is a mystery of faith, it nevertheless has grasped the far-reaching implications of Trintarian doctrine not only as a matter of faith, but as model for interpersonal relationships[11] and for society as a whole.[12] Through a "Trinitarian perspective," Chiara Lubich, like many theologians, argues that all social relationships, including the economic, can be re-interpreted in such a way as to cast light onto the interpersonal dimension of human existence (Hemmerle, 1995). The Trinity is regarded as the perfect model of a united community (Boff, 1990) with both perfect freedom and respect for the identity of the other. Three key concepts are used within theology to describe the nature of the Trinity. The first is *pericoresis* — which names the way in which there is "mutual in-dwelling" of the three Persons of the Trinity. Although there is indwelling, however, the Persons remain distinct and are not mixed up with each other: "they are united but they are not confused, they are in one another, and this inter-penetration (*pericoresis*) comes about without fusion or mixing" (Damasceno, 1998 in Cambón, 1999: 31). The second term is *kénosis*, the "total emptying of self," exemplified in the Person of Christ who died on the Cross. The third term is *agàpe*, the reciprocal Love that binds the Trinity together, in which people also participate and that comprises their ultimate vocation. To say that human relationships are "Trinitarian," therefore, is to specify that they have these three dimensions: *pericoresis-kénosis-agàpe*. The life of God is thus a perennial and total gift of self to the other.

As St. Augustine said: "They are three: the lover, the loved, and love" (in Cerini, 1992: 45). This Trinitarian perspective at the foundation of the Focolare spirituality reflects a move within academic theology in the past thirty years and in the teachings of the Catholic Church.[13]

From an existential point of view, therefore, the Focolare vision necessitates an implicit rejection of materialism and the anthropology of the "individual" as a being in isolation from others. Rather, within the *Trinitarian anthropology*, existence is defined by the free choice of individuals to recognize their personhood through offering themselves to others in loving service: "The more you give, the more you are fulfilled, the more you are you; since you have what you give, what you give makes you be."[14] This dynamic of "being love," the central motivating force, translates into a desire to bring about unity through dialogue. As a consequence, social behaviors and attitudes take on a new meaning within the context of a Trinitarian anthropology: solidarity, participation, freedom, pluralism can all be redefined as central concepts within this Trinitarian anthropology.[15] Human beings are longer seen in isolation as "individuals" but as "persons-in-community."

The idea that the essence of the person lies in "being love" is further bound up in Chiara Lubich's personal experience and understanding of the mystery of the abandonment, death and resurrection of Christ (Lubich, 2000). In Chiara Lubich's understanding, in the cry of abandonment from Jesus on the Cross "My God, my God, why have you forsaken me?" (Mt 27: 46), God (in Jesus) experienced the terrifying sensation of being abandoned by God (the Father), the culminating point in the suffering of Christ (Lubich, 1985: 50). In this way, at that point when he cried out, he experienced the greatest negation of his humanity (physical and mental torture) and his divinity. At the same time, however, in that negation he reached the greatest expression of love in giving his life for others. Through this mysterious co-existence of the greatest suffering and the greatest love, he assumed all human failings within himself and thus assumed the mysterious paradox of human suffering. He did not annul all that is negative or non-existence, but through his actions showed that "existence" is not necessarily determined by the absence of all that is negative — suffering, pain, hurt. Existence is rather determined by the ability to "be love." Being love, as demonstrated in the death of Christ, is *kénosis*, the complete giving of self. This involves suffering and sacrifice to the point of being ready to die for others, but being love also brings the greatest fulfillment.

"Non-existence" in the Focolare spirituality may have two meanings. On the one hand, in one kind of non-existence a person accepts[16] to "not exist" for self out of love so as to live for others. Such a non-existence is actually the fullness of existence in the Christian mystery (Coda, 1984). Through accepting suffering, humanity participates in the mystery of the redemption within the Trinity and is in communion with that life. On the other hand, there is another kind of non-existence that is derived from the refusal or denial of the freedom of others in order to assert the self. This kind of non-existence is seen as a nothingness that conveys an illusion of freedom. As subsequent chapters will show, such an understanding of the human person also forms a powerful basis for a theological critique of "free" market individualism.

The spirituality of the Focolare, although highlighting the need to recognize suffering as a pre-condition to love, sees this as a starting point rather than an end in itself. Other more individual spiritualities highlight ascetic practices such as self-denial, isolation and penance. Here, though, the individual person is not seen in isolation from the community, which is viewed as both the means and the end of life. This emphasis on "togetherness," on sharing, mitigates isolationist social and spatial practices. Where two or more people try to live in this way, both accepting the suffering implicit in loving one another, it is possible to create the conditions where Jesus himself is mystically present in the community. Through the presence of Jesus in this love, unity can be achieved between human beings.

The gospels report that Jesus said that he would be present where two or more are united in his name (Mt 18:20). Throughout its history, the church has taken this statement somewhat literally to mean that people had to recognize the name of Christ. Through the Focolare, the phrase "united in my name" is understood to mean "being united in my love." Rather than being a question of semantics (understanding and accepting Jesus), it becomes an existential question (does love exist or not?). For those who share the Focolare spirituality, the main concern in life is not that of converting others to a particular belief pattern or symbolic universe. It lies, above all, in being love for other people and where possible creating the conditions where reciprocal love can generate the presence of God, regardless of creed or race.

The main principles of the Focolare spirituality, hence, can be interpreted as an explanation of the nature of this *agàpe* and how this translates into different aspects of human life, forming a lifestyle of love. Chiara Lubich sums up the particular characteristics of Trinitarian love in her book *Charity* (Lubich, 1981). This kind of love is universal, in that it is *open to everyone*, excludes no one, and is capable of loving those who do not love in return, even enemies. It is willing to *take the initiative* and does not wait to be loved. It *listens to others* and puts them first, trying to do to others what you would like them to do to you. It is rooted in the *present moment*, not in the past or future. In this way, it is a love that can be experienced here and now, regardless of the conditions. In order to do this, it is a love that knows how to accept failure, to forgive and to *start again*.[17]

Likewise, the whole of creation is seen as a reflection and outpouring of this love that exists in the heart of the Trinity. The world and everything in it is viewed as the work of a creator who has not abandoned creation, but is mysteriously present in it.[18] Creation, therefore, bears the imprint of the creator since everything is seen as being in a relationship of love. The Focolare therefore has a great sensitivity toward caring for the environment and promoting environmentally sustainable practices. Such practices are not seen as ends in themselves but as an expression of love for God and for others. The earth, moreover, is not seen only as a temporary abode for people, (like a hotel), but as a home — even a hearth — in an intimate relationship with heaven. It is regarded as a home that, although inhabited by individual people for a short time, is also transcendent through Christ.[19]

This underlying humanistic vision of the Focolare, although founded on a renewal of principles at the center of Christian thinking, is not the exclusive domain of Christians. The practice of the spirituality of the Focolare, as outlined in the first part of this chapter, has brought about greater collaboration and understanding between peoples of different religious traditions, highlighting many aspects of this Trinitarian perspective that can be shared by people of other faiths. Many of the aspects of the Focolare spirituality are accepted equally by Buddhists, Hindus, Muslims and Jewish people, who translate the basic principles of love into their own theological traditions, developing their roots therein. Common to all is the aim to increase love and understanding in the world. Likewise, some people who are part of the Focolare do not share the religious perspective that underpins the Christian vision, but who accept the application of that vision in practice and identify fully with the aims of the Movement.

What has been said above illustrates how the Focolare contains strong undertones of civilization as an ideal, a notion also at the heart of the "modernist" project. The unifying vision of humanity and of the world of the Focolare is largely the same one upon which other global institutions like the United Nations are based, though achieved in different ways. In an address at the UN, Chiara Lubich stressed parallels between the two institutions. Both share the aim of promoting the development of a global society founded on peace and security. In contrasting the Focolare with the UN, she said: "It [the Focolare] proposes and promotes peace, not from the top down, as in the UN, but in humanity, among the people, between peoples who are different in terms of language, race, nationality, faith."[20]

There are parallels, therefore, between the notion of universal culture that the UN has been promoting and the vision of the unity of peoples that is part of the Focolare vision. The Focolare contains a heightened sense of being *world citizens* with duties and responsibilities within an international community. This corresponds in many ways to the *global civic culture* that the UN sees as one sign of hope for the future (UNESCO, 1995). Whereas the UN seeks to achieve this primarily through inter-governmental co-operation, the Focolare seeks to bring this about from the "bottom up," through a grassroots transformation of cultural consciousness that can also influence economic and political structures.

As a global organization the Focolare shares many traits reminiscent of modernism — in the ideal of civilization and equality of all peoples, and in the desire to universalize its message of peace and unity. The Movement also shares the Christian roots of colonialism, as did missionary movements that have had arguably detrimental effects on the development of non-Christian ethnic groups and religious traditions, what Spivak (1987) has called "epistemic violence." Such missionary movements are deeply implicated in political and economic power structures, and often facilitate the dependency of developing countries (Câmara, 1969). The Focolare likewise, wherever it arrives, advocates a Christian ethos. In its advocating unity and universality, it also advocates an underlying morality clearly in line with Christian thinking. The case could be made, therefore, to hold the Focolare suspect because of its global missionary tendencies.

Holding the Focolare suspect because it is global and has Christian roots, however, has to be seriously questioned. The obvious parallels with colonialism must not be overstated. The two differ profoundly. Colonialism was founded on the doctrine of racial superiority, rooted also in a Christian belief in salvation bound up with Westernization discourse. It was imposed on peoples, often forcibly, at a time when communications and information about alternative ways of thinking were arguably restricted. This doctrine is far from the Focolare's vision. The Focolare does not impose a vision from above, but proposes certain human values that emerge from a spiritual vision of the world. These values, rooted in a particular understanding of Christianity as a radical cultural and social revolution, are also widely held by people who are not Christian. Many aspects of the cultural vision of the Movement, therefore, do not fit neatly into a modernist vision.

Moreover, the Focolare's notion of global culture does not deny or annihilate diversity. Rather, it views global culture as the foundation of a civilization in which diversity and cultural pluralism can flourish against a background of shared values. Its spiritual basis lies in diversity based on oneness through openness to difference. Without shared universal values such as mutual respect and tolerance, diversity will inevitably give rise to hatred based on prejudice and fear of the unknown. In this way, the Focolare demonstrates that cultural differences can be positive and enriching if welcomed in the context of universal human values. In many places where the Focolare has developed, the Movement's presence has led to the revival of often forgotten or neglected cultural traditions, such as those of the Bangwa tribe in Fontem, Cameroon (Focolare, 2000c). Within Focolare gatherings, celebrating diversity is regarded as an integral expression of unity. This dialectic of diversity and unity, which can be only maintained through love, lies at the very heart of the Focolare vision.

The Focolare itself contains a characteristic understanding of culture rooted in its specific vision of the world, one which stresses the historical process of dialogue. This process does not require a clear-cut choice between difference and similarity, but recognizes and highlights common human values, through which differences and similarities can be expressed. The Focolare, however, also stresses the transcendent nature of difference and similarity, the human reflection of the mystery of the Trinity. According to the Focolare, the mystery of the Trinity allows authentic understanding of unity and diversity. As Marco Salvati has said, "The life of the Trinitarian God, in other words, appears to be a perennial 'making space' for the other" (Salvati, 1990: 156).

CONCLUSION

This chapter has presented an overview of the Focolare as a global religious and social movement, outlining its historical geographies and aims. It shows how the ideal of the *focolare,* rooted in an image of intimate family harmony, is at the heart of the Focolare's message and also its cultural geographies, which now have created distinctive Focolare spaces throughout the world. It has also underlined some of the critical questions that arise when attempting to define the Movement as a "global culture" that is the portent of universal human values. Although it may be argued that, on the surface, the Focolare demonstrates certain colonial tendencies, such parallels are open to question. A global population striving to face up to the ecological limits of the biosphere must consider the human values that the Focolare advocates. The critical question is whether such values, translated into action, can create social conditions that enable the human race to co-exist. In a world of neo-colonialist international financial structures and capital, is it not perhaps necessary to make space for a different kind of "colonialism" based on solidarity and sharing, "alternative" human geographies with global economic, political, social and cultural implications?

NOTES

[1]Anonymous poem.

[2]Harrap's *Shorter Italian Dictionary* (1989) offers four meanings to the word *focolare:* "hearth," "fireside," "furnace," and "home."

[3]General references to the Focolare's aims and objectives are taken from the Focolare Movement's website (Focolare, 2000a).

[4]Excerpt from Chiara Lubich's address to the Council of Europe on the occasion of the European Human Rights Prize, Strasbourg, 22 September 1998.

[5]The choice of Trent as a location for this meeting was itself highly contentious: "On 28 November, 1518, Luther had appealed from the pope to a general council because he was convinced that he would be condemned at Rome for his heretical doctrines ... Owing to the feeling prevalent in Germany the demand was dangerous. Rome positively rejected the German national council, but did not absolutely object to holding a general council. Emperor Charles V forbade the national council, but notified Clement VII through his ambassadors that he considered the calling of a general council expedient and proposed

the city of Trent as the place of assembly," *The Catholic Encyclopaedia, Vol. 15* (Online Edition Knight, 2000).

[6]This came into effect through Mussolini's puppet government at Saló on the shores of Lake Garda. From there, he acted as a figurehead for the Germans, who gave him orders to round up as many Italian Jews as possible for deportation to extermination camps.

[7]On 13 May, 1943, the home of the Lubich family was destroyed and the family had to take refuge in the mountains (Lubich, 1987).

[8]The Focolare runs around 1,000 social projects mainly under the auspices of the NGOs New Humanity (Category 2 consultative status in the UN Economic and Social Council since 1985) and Azione per un Mondo Unito (AMU — recognized by the Italian Government in 1987).

[9]Warith Deen Mohammed had several attempts made on his life and any public appearances, such as his presence at the Focolare town of Luminosa in 1998, always required heavy security.

[10]The doctrine of the Trinity is summarized as the belief in three Persons in one God: the Father, Son and Holy Spirit (Forte, 1986). It is central to the Christian faith since it rests on the belief that humans are "Made in the image and likeness of God" (Jn 1: 26).

[11]Some theologians have been reluctant to adopt such a perspective as it could bring many dangers. St. Thomas Aquinas stressed the fundamental difference between human relationships and God; people have relationships — in God, the relationship is the Person (Di Meana, 1992: 30). St. Augustine refused to accept the analogy of the Trinity for interpersonal love to explain the life of the Trinity since, in opposition to what happens in the Trinity, in human relationships the person does not proceed from the other who loves but already exists as a subject (Mura, 1995: 204). It is therefore essential when talking about the "Trinitarian perspective," to first accept that "no analogy can 'explain' the Trinity" (Cambón, 1999: 53) and that concepts can only allude to an inexpressible mystery which is.

[12]Cambón (1999: 195–198) underlines that the persuasiveness of this idea could also lead to serious errors in thinking. The idea of the "Trinity" as a social model can be regarded as a style of relationships, a provider of ideal motivations and priorities but not a provider of technical "guidelines" that can replace specialist knowledge. At the same time, the idea could be used to promote "an absolutist style of authority which is dictatorial or the most absolute anarchy, justifying every kind of oppression." Here, too, therefore, the need to guard against fundamentalist ideas — whether based on naiveté or control.

[13]The idea of a "Trinitarian Perspective" permeates all levels of the Focolare spirituality, centered on Christ's prayer for unity (Jn 17:21). This shift toward a "Trinitarian anthropology" reflects a trend within the Catholic Church since Vatican II and in the wider ecumenical movement. The idea that the Trinity could be considered as a model of social and economic action is found in many Church documents in Vatican II (*Gaudium et spes,* nos. 21, 24, 40; *Unitatis redintegratio,* no. 2; *Lumen gentium,* nos. 4,47; *Perfectae caritatis,* no. 1). Pope John Paul II has spoken and written many times about the Trinity as a model of communitarian and social life, in particular, the social encyclicals *Sollicitudo rei socialis,* no. 40 and *Ut unum sint,* nos. 8, 18, 19, 31, 52. The spirituality of the Focolare Movement is cited as an example of this perspective in action in several texts including Cambón (1999) and Cerini (1992).

[14]Chiara Lubich, Genfest 1995, Rome, 31 May 1995.

[15]Cambón (1999: 75–100) provides an overview of the various possible implications that the Trinitarian perspective could have for these concepts. Those aspects most related to the EOS will be explained in subsequent chapters.

[16]The word "accept" here has to be read with caution. It is not to say that the Focolare "accepts" suffering in the sense of resignation or indifference to it. Rather, it "accepts" that suffering is an inevitable part of the human condition and experience, and works to alleviate it in whatever way possible.

[17]There are parallels here between the principles which Chiara Lubich terms the "art of loving" and the "art of loving" outlined by the psychoanalyst Erich Fromm (1957). Breaking from the Freudian psychoanalytic tradition which focused largely on unconscious motivations, Fromm held that humans are products of the cultures in which they are bred. In modern, industrial societies, he maintained, they have become estranged from themselves. These feelings of isolation resulted in an unconscious desire for unity with

others. The difference, however, is that whereas in psychoanalysis, the pursuit of loving relationships is ultimately personal happiness, within Chiara Lubich's perspective, seeking unity is answering God's will.

[18]Chiara Lubich calls this presence of God within the whole of creation, the "silence that speaks" (Lubich, 1995: 8). Cambón (1999: 69) says that this silence of God can be understood by starting from the perspective of the Trinity: "If Trinitarian relationships mean complete reciprocal giving so that the other can be itself, it is logical to think that God, having given himself totally in creation 'withdraws' in order to make space for it, he 'disappears' from creation so that it can fully be itself."

[19]The book of Revelation refers to the "new heavens and new earth" (Rv 21: 1), in which the whole of the cosmos and creation will be recapitulated into the Trinity.

[20]Press release about Chiara Lubich's address at the UN, Focolare Information Service, 29 May 1997.

3

An Alternative Economic Vision

> Human beings, made in the image of God, who is Love, find their
> fulfillment in loving, in giving. This is a need which is at the center
> of their being, whether believer or not. (Lubich, 2001: 51).

INTRODUCTION

The origins of the Focolare Movement's economic vision date
back to the experience that Chiara Lubich and her companions had
during the Second World War in the city of Trent in northern Italy. It
was an experience that altered their deepest perceptions of who they
were in relation to God, to other people, and to their place in the cosmos (Zamonini, 1991: 45). During the war, Chiara Lubich understood
in a new way, through a series of personal experiences that have since
been confirmed by several theologians as "mystical insights" (Cerini,
1992), the immanence of God's presence in human existence. She
began to perceive the infinite God as being within the realm of human
experience. Perhaps Chiara Lubich's experience is most striking in that
it generated a new understanding of God's personal love for her and for
other people.

Amid the destruction of war, Chiara began to see God "present
everywhere with his love" (Lubich, 1984) in the minute details of
life. Above all, she understood that the core of the gospel message
did not relate primarily to a series of moral directives, but in
the revelation of God's love as a father who is very near to his
children. In wartime, when God was being blamed for the causing
or not preventing atrocities, she seemed to discover a different
God present in every circumstance, even in suffering. She called
this profound experience/belief in the love of God the "inspiring
spark" (Cerini, 1992: 11). It challenged her perspective on every
aspect of human life, including economic and social realities.
Every circumstance, every meeting, every happy and painful event,
was willed or permitted by God. The other people to whom she
communicated this new understanding were so convinced by her
personal experience that they too began to change how they viewed
reality, and to follow her (Zambonini, 1991: 161–2).

Unbounded trust in God's love and providence, a defining feature of the early experience of the Focolare Movement, had practical implications on its emerging economic and social vision. The roots of the term "providence" can be traced back to classical Greek and Latin thought. In the Bible, particularly in the Old Testament,[1] it signifies that God, the Creator, did not merely decree what should be, and then "retire to heaven" to watch what inevitably must come to pass in the created universe. Rather, in infinite wisdom and power, God mysteriously governs all circumstances, making all things work together to accomplish the divine will. Whereas the Old Testament emphasizes providence as God's blessing of the good and punishment of the wicked, the New Testament, emphasizes the mercy of God who makes the sun rise and set on everyone. Many texts from the early days of the Focolare underline the revival of a profound belief in providence.[2]

The war forced the initial group associated with Chiara to give up their ordinary occupations and to earn their living in temporary jobs. Their rediscovery of the gospel led them to give away all of their possessions to the poor, keeping only the essentials for survival. When they did this, they started to receive items of all sorts from other people who had heard about how they were trying to help the poor in the city. People arrived at their flat with bags of food, clothing, firewood and other items, a pattern of donation and distribution that continued throughout the war. This help, which seemed to always arrive at the right time, was seen as Providence: a visible sign of God's blessing on the work being done. Several stories about providence form the oral history of the early days of the Focolare. The first story is about a pair of "size 42" (European size) shoes:

> Jesus assured us: "Ask and you will receive" (Mt 7:7; Lk 11:9). We asked for the poor and we were filled with every good from God: bread, powdered milk, jam, firewood, clothing … which we took to those who were in need. One day — and this is a fact that is always told — a poor man asked me for a pair of shoes size 42. Knowing that Jesus identified himself with the poor, I asked the Lord this prayer in church: "Give me a pair of size 42 shoes for you in that poor person." I came out and a lady gave me a packet. I opened it: there was a pair of shoes, size 42. Millions of similar episodes have occurred like this through the years. (Lubich, 2000)

This episode demonstrates how, from the very beginning of the Focolare, the spiritual and economic dimensions of life became intrinsically bound together in Chiara Lubich's understanding. Economic facts were interpreted as signs of God's intervention in human life. They viewed their action to help the poor not as an optional appendage to the "religious" act of praying, but as an expression of spiritual life into social and economic life. They believed that if they did their part through living evangelical poverty and giving themselves to their neighbors, God would fulfill the gospel promise that whatever is necessary to help the poor would be provided. God himself would be present through their love for each other. Their part was to trust in providence and to create the underlying "conditions" of mutual love so that gospel promises could be fulfilled. In this way, through the various experiences in the war, they began to understand that the gospel contains a unique "economic logic." The amount given away to the poor corresponded with what they received in providence. They understood this to be as a consequence of Jesus' promises, not simply coincidence:

> There were eight of us focolarine and every afternoon we went with lots of suitcases to take things to the poor. Someone could wonder: but where did so many things come from? I had nothing and my companions, the first focolarine, were more or less like me. But providence kept arriving and in such quantities! The corridor of my house was always full of sacks of flour and potatoes. And there we were, distributing the goods to one or other of the poor people, according to their needs. (Lubich, 2000)

Such belief in God's providence continued throughout the history of the Focolare and still remains a key point in understanding the relationship between economic affairs and spirituality. Within the Movement as a whole and in the individual focolare houses, providence (in the form of unexpected gifts and donations) is even calculated formally as a part of the overall budget. Calculations and decisions regarding future developments are made on the basis of such providence arriving.[3] Necessary resources not arriving signifies that a given development is not in God's will. In this way, Focolare institutions have evolved without accumulating debt.

Such a belief in providence, which contradicts a rationalistic mindset, raises some important issues. In particular, how does such a deep-rooted belief avoid association with superstition, magical tendencies, luck, or fantasy? How does it avoid association with an Old Testament mindset that sees riches as a blessing and poverty as a curse? A strong belief in providence carries the risk of reductionism, accompanied by positive re-enforcement of a selective reading of historical facts. In particular, analyzing the relationship between economic action and spirituality carries the risk of seeing providence as a magic formula, a mechanism for guaranteeing success. The risk of such a mindset within the Focolare, particularly in the EOS as will be seen further on, has not escaped the attention of those studying this phenomenon. The dominant vision underlying the Focolare spirituality, however, considers providence a sign of God accompanying his people.

The "Communion of Goods"

Another phenomenon from the early history of the Focolare is the formation of a community from a disparate group of persons in which everything was shared out according to each individual's needs. The unity of heart and soul produced by reciprocal love among the community generated a communion of material goods. The first Focolare community, fascinated by events in Jerusalem just after the death and resurrection of Christ, consciously started to mirror their life on the passage from the Acts of the Apostles that describes the nature of that first Christian community.[4] In a commentary on this passage, Chiara Lubich highlighted a connection between material giving and living the gospel. She also outlined many of the key ideas on which the Movement is based:

> While reading these words, we might begin to think that everything worked perfectly in the community. In fact, it is Luke himself who points out that there are incidents in which members of the Church of Jerusalem failed to live up to this standard (see Luke, 6). However, despite these failures, the tone of the community was set by this effort, which animated everyone, to achieve the Christian community. It is this effort that Luke wants to emphasize. The examples of those who sold their property show the revolutionary power of the Gospel, i.e. its capacity for creating totally new social relationships with concrete effects on an economic level.
>
> Nobody was forced to dispose of his or her goods. Luke wanted to show how the Gospel, while respecting each person's

individual freedom, is able to make us overcome all the barriers that divide us, and of these barriers, the selfish use of private property is one of the most serious causes of division. Naturally, the social revolution starts from an inner power, from faith in and love for Jesus. For Luke, this practical sharing is the unit of measurement for meaningful authentic Christian love. No matter what economic system the Christian finds himself in, with the power of this love he will be called first and foremost to overcome every form of attachment to earthly goods, in which fear, greed and selfishness continually tend to imprison him.

The examination of conscience, which these words invite us to, covers a very wide field of values. We need to review our relations with the political community as a sign of solidarity by paying taxes. We need to review our relations with the social community by committing ourselves in a responsible way to building a more just society. We need to review our relationship with our church community, by giving our spare time, energy and material goods in order to help our brothers and sisters who are in need. We need to review our relations with our neighbors whose difficulties are perhaps known to us alone. In the first Christian community in Jerusalem, no one said that any of the things that he possessed was his own. This is the heart of the problem. What we must ascertain is whether we feel we are absolute owners or we feel we are children of God and brothers and sisters in Christ who act as administrators of the goods they receive and keep others always in mind. In the first centuries love for Jesus, by inspiring consciences, transformed pagan society, opening up the progressive liberation of long-standing situations of institutional injustice (slavery, the exclusion of women from society, poverty, the position of the defenseless and children in society, etc.). Why should our love for Jesus not do as much again today in the face of serious situations of injustice in the world? (Robertson, 1993: 57)

The radical vision of gospel living that emerges is not only a form of spiritual edification, but also a means of emancipation for the poor. Living the gospel had far-reaching social and political implications that led individuals to "review" their relationship with the various institutions and to make concrete changes in how they live.

The "heart of the problem," in Chiara Lubich's view, was the desire to claim possessions for one's self as opposed to feeling connected to others as a family. The distribution of wealth is perceived as an economic matter, but the question of being brothers and sisters is regarded as a spiritual one.[5] The gospel offered a means of bridging this divide and bringing about a peaceful social revolution that would achieve greater equality through the charity that imbued people's hearts. In this way the "evangelical poverty" that traditional spiritualities considered a form of asceticism took on a new function within the Focolare. It was not an end in itself but a means of serving other people and creating greater equality. Reaching this equality became the main aim of the first Focolare community in Trent.

Redistribution in the Trent Community

So how did the first Focolare community live out this vision? Not long after the start of the Movement, Chiara Lubich explained in detail how this redistribution took place in the community of Trent:

> The spirit of unity in charity was the ever living flame which kept this fraternity alive … In some ways it was similar, in others dissimilar, to that first Christian community. In fact, while having the same aim, it did not require everyone to sell all that they had and to bring it to unity, but rather, that everyone gave what they possessed, depriving themselves of what they could without causing themselves harm … This was possible among us who are already trained at living out in a radical way the first great principle "You shall love the Lord your God with all your heart" (Lk 10:27). Everyone brought the extra that they had, above all in money, and committed themselves to giving a monthly sum. The donor and the amount promised remained secret. With the money received, the Committee would help, month by month and in secret, those families in the community in need, carrying out this delicate task with the greatest charity and discretion. This was our aim: to reach the point where there would be no more people in need, and that everyone would have enough to live on. (Lubich, 1948)

This article reveals how even at that stage the community of the Focolare was structured so as to help those in need while protecting the identities of those who were helped and those who gave. People were primarily helped via the Focolare house itself, through a central fund, since those dedicated to the community were arguably in the best position to know the needs of people in the community as a whole. Even at this early stage of the Focolare, the key was *trust* in the people who were carrying out the redistribution based on their total commitment to the community and their understanding of the needs of the various members. This image of the first Focolare community, mirrored on the life of the first Christians, has remained like an icon for Focolare communities all over the world.

This "communion of goods," as it was called, became a prominent feature of the life of the early Focolare community. It was not limited to the people who were part of the Focolare community itself. Right from the start, the first group were aware that the problems of inequality could not be solved unless the rich could be made to realize in some way the injustice of the situation. In the Focolare's guidelines on economy and work, Giosi Guella recalls their ideas of a social revolution at the beginnings of the Movement:

> We wanted to solve the social problem of Trent ... our reasoning was simple: we have more and they have less; we will raise their standard of living so as to reach a certain equality. We even thought of ousting the rich, not through violence, but through our ideal that would burn the hearts of those who have more and the communion of goods would be spontaneous. (Guella, 1983)

What is striking about this passage is how the group of the Focolare recognized creating greater equality in society required the active participation of all people — not just the poor. It was not enough that they themselves give away all that they had to the poor: they had to "oust" the rich through winning them over to the ideals of the Movement. The strong parallels between this way of thinking and the communist doctrine so prevalent in the city of Trent at that time led to several brushes with the Fascist regime, which was suspicious of their activities. Chiara Lubich's brother was an active member of the Communist Party, on the editorial team of *Il Popolo*, and a partisan (Gallagher, 1997). Both were advocating a radical redistribution of wealth. Although it is right to say that the ultimate aim of greater equality was the same, the means suggested and employed in order to carry out this goal could not have differed more. For the communists, the end of equality justified the means — even violent repression of those in control of the means of production, resulting in revolution.

For Chiara Lubich and her companions, the rich could be ousted mainly by "burning their hearts" with the ideal that they themselves had discovered and begun to put into practice through giving away all of their possessions (Lubich, 1984). By seeing and learning from their example would the rich themselves be moved and become personally involved in the redistribution of wealth, since they too would feel that the poor were their brothers and sisters and that they had a duty to share their possessions with them. Rather than alienating the rich, their way would create greater participation of all, fostering greater social integration and narrowing of the gap between rich and poor. On several occasions, however, the Focolare group was mistaken for communists, as recalled in a biography of Chiara Lubich:

> Word went around that they [the Focolare] were communists ... In those days, remembers Chiara, only the communists spoke about "unity." It was not something that you heard preached about in Sunday sermons. So they were communists, then? Either that or Protestants! All this reading of Scripture and living of Gospel phrases! (Gallagher, 1997: 42)

This strategy of overcoming the rich through engaging them is arguably more effective in the long term than using force, since it is a personal practice that touches individuals in a real way. It does not replace the law or the role of the state, but provides "a more solid foundation of all other good and lawful means of guaranteeing an honest and dignified livelihood for all" (Movimento Umanità Nuova, 1984: 31). Perhaps for this reason, two communist activists who had noticed the effectiveness of what the group was doing in the city of Trent, approached them:

> One day in May 1945, two communists came into our little focolare and said to me "Look, we've been watching you. We've seen the way you girls share everything and how you give it away to those in need."
>
> Chiara remembers the meeting very clearly because the two communists asked her, "What's going on? Why on earth are you doing this? Tell us the secret of your success."
>
> She says, "I pointed to the crucifix on the wall, because he is the one who is love and who taught us to love. They lowered their eyes."
>
> One of them said to her, "What you're doing on a small scale, we will do all over the world."
>
> Chiara challenged them: "We are few, we're young, we're poor. But God is with us. Let's see who gets there first, shall we? (Gallagher, 1997: 43–44)

The fall of communist regimes in the early 1990s and the start of the EOS within the Focolare seemed to be a response to this question. In the 1950s and 1960s, however, the radical approach to wealth redistribution that they were advocating and the parallels between their message and that of the communists (and Protestants) led to lengthy investigations by the Holy See (Zambonini, 1991: 63; Gallagher, 1997: 78–89). The Vatican could find no evidence of infiltration of ideas not in keeping with the message of the gospel, though, and approved the Focolare in 1963 for the first time. Final approval in 1990 provided an opportunity for the Focolare to expand further.

A "Culture of Giving"

This economic and social vision has generated many specific practices within the Focolare, some of which have already been mentioned (communion of goods, trust in providence). The wartime practice of giving everything away to the poor is no longer literally applied to the range of circumstances in which people within the Movement find themselves. Several thousand people still feel called to take on the commitment to sell all that they have and live a celibate life in community. Others prefer to remain in close contact with the Movement but cannot actually leave everything behind, either because of their commitments as married people or their responsibilities in society. Instead, such people, who now make up the vast majority of the Focolare Movement, change their lifestyle so that it reflects their commitment to put the fundamental Focolare principles into practice.

The first practice, present right from the start, is that of sharing material goods. As the Movement has developed this practice has evolved, enabling people from different social categories to participate in some form. Some give all their possessions to the poor via the Focolare and adopt the community based on the first Focolare community in Trent (the focolarini). Each month their salaries are deposited in a central account from which the individual community houses receive an allowance, with the rest being used to fund Focolare communities in developing countries and to help fund the international center of the Focolare in Rocca di Papa, near Rome. The focolarini bequeath all of their present and future possessions to the Focolare. Over the years, these bequests have enabled the Focolare to grow and to develop at a substantial rate. Many of its pieces of land were bequeathed by focolarini or well-wishers. For example, the land in the Chianti hills near Florence on which the town of "Loppiano" has been built was inherited by the Folonari children (a famous Milanese family of wine makers), three of whom joined the Focolare.

Others connected to the Movement commit themselves to sharing what is superfluous to their immediate needs, basing their "need" on the measure of their brothers and sisters who do not have enough to survive. In a 1992 address to a group of teenagers, Chiara Lubich highlighted this choice of sharing as a lifestyle that could overcome the tendency in Western society to focus on consumption and "having" rather than "being" or "giving":

> You should keep for yourselves ... only what you need, as the plants do. They absorb from the earth only the water, salts and other things that they need, and not more. Likewise, each one of us must have what he or she needs. All the rest should be given away and put into common with the others.[6]

This comparison with the natural world may seem prosaic but it illustrates how the children who participate in the Focolare are educated in a lifestyle that emphasizes sharing with others as well as for the environment. Children are encouraged to live simply, to avoid unnecessary attachments to material goods and, above all, to think of others before themselves. Focolare communities share things in several ways. On a local scale, individual communities try to be constantly aware of the needs of those within the community. People with specific needs are encouraged to communicate those needs to others through the small groups in which the Focolare members meet, through the Focolare houses or through contact with other people within the Focolare.

One practice that dates back to the origins of the Focolare in Trent, still carried out in many Focolare groups, particularly among young people, is known as the "bundle." It recalls how the first group of focolarini piled up all of their possessions in a room so as to give them to the poor (Zambonini, 1991: 43). At least once a year, members of the Movement from the oldest to the youngest re-assess their personal possessions and make a "bundle" of everything that they no longer consider necessary. This bundle is then shared out with the local community. If all of the needs in community are met, the remaining articles are sorted out — some sent to charity shops, others given to the Focolare house in case they need them or know of others who do. Occasionally, items are sent abroad to the center of the Focolare in Rome, to victims of disaster or war. Focolare communities also share money on a local scale. This takes place through donations by

CHAPTER 3

individuals who wish to contribute to the Focolare's activities. Within the smaller groups, the common practice is to keep a common fund administered by one of the group to meet any immediate or future needs. A portion of this money is also given to the international center of the Focolare to fund the infrastructure of the Movement across the world and to support community members in other countries.

Sharing within the Focolare is not limited to material possessions, but includes the material, social and spiritual. In many cases sharing may take the form of an offer of help that involves time, skills and energy. In other cases sharing may involve offering advice or a listening ear. Material sharing reflects the spiritual communion between people — their awareness of being brothers and sisters — and not simply a charitable action. The kind of giving advocated by the Focolare cannot easily be reduced to philanthropy, although elements of philanthropic giving are in it. In an article on the different kinds of giving, Araujo highlights what is called "evangelical" giving, which the Focolare aims to promote:

> The "culture of giving" qualifies the human person as a being that is open to communion, to a relationship with the Absolute — God, with others, and with creation. Individuality and sociality converge in the gift of self, the gift of one's being and in the circulation of material goods, which are needed for the development, and growth of everyone.
>
> Not every kind of giving therefore results in the culture of giving. There is a kind of giving which is contaminated by a desire for power over the other, a search for dominion and even the oppression of other peoples. It only has the appearance of giving. There is a kind of giving which seeks satisfaction and pleasure in the act of giving itself. Deep down, it is an egoistic expression of the self and, in general, this is perceived by the person who is on the receiving end as a humiliation or offence. There is also a kind of utilitarian giving which has an ulterior interest. This is present in the current forms of neo-liberalism, in which there is a search for a payoff in terms of profit. This kind of giving does not create a new mentality.
>
> Last of all there is the giving which we Christians call "evangelical" because it is an integral part of the personal attitudes of those that welcome and commit themselves in the construction of the kingdom that Jesus brings ... This giving is open to the other — individual or people — and seeks out the other in respect

for their dignity, which includes traditions, customs, culture, etc. It is an expression of our deepest being. The word "to give" is synonymous with loving in a practical way. (Araujo, 1994a)

Within the Focolare, the person in need is accorded a high position. Since possessions hold secondary importance, individuals are valued not for their capacity to have or give materially but for their capacity to give of themselves to others. In this respect, even someone with no possessions has something to give. Need is not something inherently negative, something of which to be ashamed, but rather a situation that allows sharing to be put into practice among the community. Offering a need to the community is therefore a positive action; people are encouraged to "offer" their need in order to give others the opportunity to help. This in turn empowers the community, creating greater solidarity among the members. The act of receiving is therefore transformed into an act of giving.

A NEW ECONOMIC ETHIC

The root and the first consequence of this economic vision, a renewed awareness of the ethical content of the Christian message and its relevance to economic action, has led to millions of people across the world adopting a spirituality rooted in communitarian values, especially the value of trust. Such an application resembles strongly the Weberian idea of the "economic ethic of a religion." According to Weber, as discussed in Chapter 1, individuals attach to economic action meanings bound up with their religious beliefs, making it possible to discern different economic rationalities deriving from religious belief systems (Weber, 1958). Weber, for example, distinguished between the rationalities in operation within Catholicism and Protestantism by the premium each tradition placed on ascetic lifestyle at a given time. In his view, the Catholic emphasis on "absolution" deterred engagement in economic activities. The premium Calvinism placed on asceticism legitimized the "philosophy of avarice" that underpins capitalism. Weber's approach has been criticized, particularly its logic in relation to the rise of capitalism (Marshall, 1982).

Despite its limitations, however, Weber's concept allows much scope for development, especially the way he relates economic rationalities to specific religious beliefs (Novak, 1993). In some ways, the strength of Weber's thesis lies not so much in his attempt to connect the rise of capitalism with religious traditions as his development of intermediate concepts that link culture and economic action. They provide a useful framework for understanding how the deep structures of spiritual understanding and symbolism alter perceptions, and ultimately choices of economic life.

Economic Ethic of the Focolare

This framework makes it possible to discern certain principles that appear to have governed the Focolare vision over the past 70 years and that form the cultural matrix against which all other dimensions of human life, including the economic, have to be measured. An instrumental economic rationale, in a sense, is subdued or "framed" by the communitarian ethic in practice. This gives rise to new concepts and principles that shape economic choices. It is interesting that, unlike certain fundamentalist forms of Christianity, the Focolare's vision does not negate the capitalist system per se. It represents both a radical critique of the unsustainable dimensions of the current capitalist system, and a positive vision of the place of wealth and business. Rather than basing itself on puritan vision that rejects money, it is directed out toward the world in a highly positive vision of the redemptive power of Christ working in the community. In a way similar to Weber's analysis, the Focolare Movement conveys powerful signs of an economic rationality framed by important religious principles that drives a new form of capitalism. At the same time, the Focolare's economic vision brings to the fore certain elements and concepts not so obvious in Weber's original thesis:

Work: Because people are *co-creators* with God, their creative capacity has to be advanced. Work is a source of personal fulfillment and service, and plays an important function in building the community. It also entails sacrifice, which can be united to the abandonment of Christ. Work represents the principal Will of God.

Trade, finance and industry: Christians and people of good will ought to actively seek to appropriate the means of production to be used to good ends, such as the redistribution of wealth to the poor. Debt is generally avoided within the institutional structures of the Focolare Movement, and is strongly discouraged for all members of the Movement. Abandonment to God's will also means trusting his ability to intervene in the practical circumstances of life, as well as in having the material resources to carry out that will. Nevertheless, certain forms of low interest micro-finance are valued and alternative financing structures have been promoted.

Wealth and possessions: In general there is a positive view toward wealth, with people expected to maintain a living standard and level of security appropriate to their function in society. Possessions, however, are generally put at the disposal of the common good. Poverty has value, both positive and negative. On the one hand, the involuntary deprivation of essential basic needs is an injustice that must be addressed. At the same time, it is a virtue, an essential prerequisite to spiritual fulfillment. Material attachments can form an obstacle to one's relationship with God and neighbor. The voluntary deprivation of surplus resources is encouraged through the communion of goods. This encourages simple living and the avoidance of clutter, with important environmental implications. Trusting in providence means that God will accompany people on their journey, using circumstances to reveal the divine will.

Relations with other economic actors: The market retains its basic function as the most efficient form of exchange in an open economy. This, however, is set within the wider framework of the market as a "meeting place" between two or more ethical subjects. The highest function of economic interaction is social, the normative aim of every economic encounter being communion. Within the Focolare, economic activity serves to build up the human community.

Economic change and technological development: As stewards of God's creation, protection of the environment is an essential part of personal and corporate economic activity. Progress and technology derive from the innate creativity of the human person, made in God's image.

Relation to those without economic resources: Those without economic resources are *brothers and sisters*. The redistribution of wealth ought to occur from the grass roots upwards, as well as from the top down, emphasizing the importance of subsidiarity. Sharing is a practical sign of love for Christ and for neighbor. Revived through the EOS, the practice of *tithing* is an essential component of building God's kingdom in a world envisaged as a community of love. The practice of a communion of goods, drawing inspiration from the first Christians, is a key part of building the mystical body.

The sense of engagement with the free market economy crucial to this spirituality, moreover, in many respects corresponds to Novak's (1993) understanding of a "Catholic ethic," that draws on Catholic social teaching. Novak notes that the teaching of Catholicism on "creation" makes it compatible with an economic system that emphasizes free enterprise. He argues that Weber was right in his understanding that religions can give rise to a particular economic ethic, but his understanding of "rationality" and how it gave rise to capitalism is inherently flawed because it does not recognize the value of creativity. Economic thinkers throughout the twentieth century such as Schumpeter, Hayek and Kirzner have repeatedly stressed creativity as central to maintenance of the market. Novak's understanding of the Catholic ethic draws on the rich theological anthropology of "creativity" within the Catholic tradition. He says that the moral strength of capitalism (and democracy) lies not so much in its ability to distribute wealth fairly, but in its ability to promote human creativity. Interestingly, Novak also predicted that such an ethic would be most likely to appear in Latin America since it has traditionally been the source of progressive Catholic thinking.

CONCLUSION

This chapter outlines the main ideas that sustain the Focolare's vision of economic life. Consideration of the ideas that emerged at the historical origins of the Focolare and tracing their development reveals the interrelationship between the "spiritual" and the "economic" within the context of the Movement and the practices that have derived from it. Such practices and ideas represent a radical departure from orthodox economic thinking about the mechanisms that operate within the market economy and to some extent mirror the more recent literature emphasizing the socio-cultural dimensions of economic action. The Focolare, however, adds to this literature the spiritual dimension of human life, raising new questions about the place of religious concepts such as "communion" within the context of economic life. There are strands of thinking that can be drawn on when talking about the economic vision of the Focolare, such as the literature of Catholic social teaching based on the theory of human rights and the promotion of peace. Subsequent chapters will explore these in depth.

NOTES

[1]See, for example, Daniel 4: 32, 35; Psalm 139: 7–18; Isaiah 41: 21–31.

[2]Many of the original sources such as personal letters have since been lost or destroyed. Edited versions of the remaining original sources from 1943–54 have been published in Chiara Lubich, *Essential Writings: Spirituality, Dialogue, Culture* (New York, London: New City Press, 2006).

[3]Giosi Guella and Oreste Basso, "The Communion of Goods and Work Guidelines," Part 1, Internal Focolare Document, Focolare Center, Rome, 1984.

[4]Acts 4:32; 34–35.

[5]Chiara Lubich, "Letter to the Focolare communities in Italy," *Gen* 6: ([1944] 1968): 1.

[6]Chiara Lubich to the *Supercongress*, Marino Ice Stadium, 12 June, 1992.

4

The Evolution of the
Economy of Communion

INTRODUCTION

Over the years, the Focolare Movement has developed a distinctive vision of economic life. This vision, which can be traced back to the experience of Chiara Lubich and her companions during the Second World War, demonstrated a heightened awareness of the inter-relationship between economic life and spirituality. It led to the development of many economic practices, such as the "communion of goods," in which there is an intimate relationship between the symbolic language of spirituality and economic action. As outlined in previous chapters, this emphasis on the practical application of a shared spirituality also gave rise to local and global networks consisting of 1,000 well-established initiatives and projects to alleviate poverty. These networks now constitute a dynamic global community based on a shared sense of belonging.

In general, however, this distinctive vision of economic life tended to be applied to the *personal economy* of individual people, families and local communities. In the early days of the Focolare, the circulation of personal possessions among the various members of the community was based on the common bond of the shared Focolare spirituality. In some ways this could be seen as the first stage of widening out from the "hearth" of the Focolare by extending it into the family and then the local community. Over time, it began to be supposed that these larger "spaces" could also become "hearths" of sharing where the "culture of giving" might be lived out among small groups of people who share everything that they own.

One of the critical questions raised in Chapter 1 is whether or not such alternative visions of the economy based on community and sharing can be extended into the still more extensive *public economy*. Such economies emphasize the values of co-operation, caring and sharing, which are normally assumed to reside within a more personal sphere, based principally on face-to-face communication. Moreover, could the "hearth" of the Focolare be effectively operationalized at the scale of the institutions of the *global economy*? In a certain sense, this is precisely what the EOC does indeed seek to do, through the logical extension of the Focolare's spirituality into the realm of business. This chapter will consider the context in which the EOC first emerged and provide an overview of the global dimensions of the project.

GLOBALIZATION AND THE "COMMUNION OF GOODS"

From the very beginning of the Focolare, as outlined in Chapters 2 and 3, the economic vision of the Focolare revealed a strong emphasis on equality. The foundation of this equality, however, is radically different from dominant forms of egalitarianism that have emerged in the last 40 years, based on the idea of "rights."[1] To talk of "rights," in relation to the first Focolare community during the war, clouds the central point of what was happening within that community. The absurd violations of war, in which there was an endemic climate of violence, stripped everyone of what could be called their basic rights. At the same time, this absence made the restoration of those rights an urgent necessity. One could say that in certain ways, the emergence of the Focolare in Trent led to the restoration of rights for some people, but that the way in which this happened had nothing to do with the discourse of rights itself.

Rather, the equality of the Focolare derived substantially from the understanding that human dignity derives first and foremost from the belief that all people are children of the one God, who loves each one with infinite love (Lubich, 2001: 95–106). This renewed awareness of the oneness of the human family was the fundamental point that transformed their particular "communitarian" spirituality into economic and social action. This intimate relationship between spirituality and economic action, epitomized in the model of the first Christian community in Jerusalem, was the powerful force activating a sense of family within the emerging movement. Within this "family," equality was based on an "ethic of care" in which each one recognized their responsibility to care for the others. In a similar way to Simone Weil's (1951) emphasis on attending to the needs of others, the Focolare's spirituality opened people's hearts to recognize and to attend to the needs of others, regardless of who these others may be.[2] Reaching greater equality was bound up in the ability to hear the cry of those who were hurting and to ask "Why are you hurting?" not "That's terrible — your rights have been violated." Through attending to the needs of those who were hurting, they could offer care in a personal and direct way.

This mutual attending also gave rise to the acceptance of a degree of natural inequality within the Focolare. Since equality within the community was not so much based on the possession of rights, but on the growth of ever greater mutual attending and therefore of spiritual communion, there was also the recognition that different people have different material needs. What mattered was not so much inequalities on some arithmetic scale by which individuals were measured against each other, but the extent to which the communion among the members of the community was able to fulfill specific needs as they arose. Things were privately owned by individuals or families, but there was a strong sense that private ownership did not exclude the possibility of others having access to goods, whenever necessary. Ownership, therefore, was regarded as "stewardship" on behalf of the community rather than as an end in itself. At the same time, the sense of responsibility toward those who were in material need — lacking food, clothing, work, and shelter — remained the strongest sign of the active life of the community and the greatest witness of Christian love (Johnston, 1981).

"No Poor among Us"

The EOC emerged in 1991 as a consequence of the desire to make this ideal of communion within the Focolare work on an increasingly global scale. As the Focolare grew and developed, it became an international movement. Since the late-1970s, the number of members of the Focolare grew disproportionately within the poorest communities of Latin America, Asia and Africa, as did many other radical religious groups (Gutierrez, 1984; Slater, 1985). For many of these groups, such as the Christian Base Communities of Brazil, religious affiliation was also seen as a means of emancipation from poverty (Wirth, 1987). During this same period, Pope Paul VI launched his Encyclical on the "Development of Peoples," in which he drew attention to the desperate inequalities throughout the world and the Christian challenge of responding to these. While this internationalization gave rise to many initiatives to attend to the needs of people linked to the Focolare throughout the world, by the early-1990s there were increasing strains on the capacity of the Movement to create equality on a global scale.[3] In particular, the fall of the communist block in 1989 revealed entire Focolare communities numbering several thousand behind the Iron Curtain who were in desperate need of basic food and shelter.

This situation came to a head in May 1991, when Chiara Lubich visited the Focolare communities in Brazil. While she was there, she saw for herself the extent of the inequality that is so apparent in the city of Sao Paulo and its surrounding areas. The scale of the poverty caused her to reflect on what action the Focolare was taking in order to alleviate the problem. In a sense, her visit was an opportunity for everyone in the Focolare community in Brazil to reflect on how they were attending to the needs of the poor. She was moved by the commitment that the Focolare people had in starting and running a range of projects to improve the living conditions of people in the poorest areas. She visited some of the projects to see for herself the work being done. She became all too aware that the efforts of the Focolare were just one drop in the ocean faced with the scale of the poverty in a city like Sao Paulo. She asked herself whether the Focolare, as a group, could make a greater contribution to resolving this entrenched social and economic inequality.

The launch of the EOC can also be interpreted as recognition that the "communion of goods," as a strategy to overcome the inequalities on a global scale, was no longer sufficient. Thus, although the communion of goods works as a powerful strategy of wealth redistribution at a local scale, it had obvious limitations in the context of the inequalities seemingly endemic within a globalized economy. The communion of goods said nothing about the nature of work and how value is created and distributed within an industrial (or post-industrial) society. In a sense, the practice of communion of goods is a kind of *post hoc* redistribution that may have a profound spiritual meaning, but does not have a direct impact on the public economy. It emerged during the War, at a time when there was no alternative to sharing since the normal patterns of work had been suspended. In the context of the economic imbalances within countries such as Brazil, the communion of goods did little to address the root causes of inequality: economic rationalization, low wages, and unemployment. In a sense, the Focolare, like other civil society organizations in Latin America, was picking up the pieces left by both an economic system that thrived on inequality and a government which was unable to cope with the rising social "fall out" from economic crisis (Green, 1996).

In Chiara Lubich's view, it was no longer enough to sit back and watch as the economy created ever greater inequalities. The principles of the Focolare spirituality had to be extended into the realm of business and industry. The communion of goods, which the Brazilian members of the Focolare practiced with great generosity, was certainly one part of the solution — this had to continue. But the scope of this communion had to be recognized and the root causes of the inequality on a structural level had to be addressed. Chiara Lubich suggested that the Focolare in Brazil was perhaps being called to start to live the communion of goods in a "superior way," what would later be called the EOC. The thinking behind the EOC is clear in a speech that she gave in Araceli on 30th May 1991:

> This is the novelty: in the Movement we have always practiced the communion of goods; the focolarini do it in a complete way, because they give everything; volunteers give what is superfluous, families also share out their surplus among themselves. Now we would like to propose a communion of goods which is at a superior level, that is, to give rise to businesses and industries here around the Mariapolis, which would be run by our people, who would put all the profits in common for the poor, having kept what is necessary to keep the business running. With these profits we will live the reality of the first Christians in the twentieth century: they brought all that they had to the feet of the apostles and distributed it to the poor, so that there was no one in need, there were no poor.[4]

What was new about this communion of goods, therefore, was that it would involve the participation of legally constituted commercial enterprises and not just individuals, who would choose to share what they regarded as superfluous or to proceed with social projects aimed at providing welfare for the poor. People were encouraged to start enterprises that would generate profits to be shared for predetermined aims. The EOC hence aimed to make the communion of goods productive, generating new wealth from the existing communion between the people of the Movement.

At the same time, the businesses themselves would create a new space in which the "hearth" of the Focolare could be extended out into the realm of the public economy. Through creating businesses run by people who lived out the Focolare ideals of caring and sharing, the actual causes of inequality would be addressed in a radical way. It was a simple, but extremely challenging proposal. The principles of caring and sharing can arguably be easily applied to the realm of the *personal economy*, where there is a high degree of clarity and choice on how goods can be distributed due to the rights of ownership of private property. Within the sphere of the more *public economy*, however, the application of such ideas is not so straightforward, as will be seen from the case studies on the emergence of the EOC. Nevertheless, the members of the Focolare in Brazil grasped the challenge wholeheartedly.

The Challenge of Centesimus Annus

The texts relating to the launch of the EOC also reveal another strand of reasoning. In 1991, the aftermath of the fall of the communist regimes was reaching a critical point. There was euphoria over the triumph of capitalism, but also a profound and growing sense of disillusionment over the collapse of the communist states and socialist ideals. Many social critics were beginning to discuss the possibility of a "third way" and some even pointed to the new social and religious movements, including the Focolare, as the protagonists of economic alternatives (Secondin, 1991). In the spring of 1991, moreover, Pope John Paul II had published *Centesimus Annus*, celebrating a century of Catholic social teaching. The focus of this letter, in the aftermath of the fall of the Iron Curtain, was an in-depth critique of communism and also of the free market. While restating the Catholic principle of the right to own private property and individual freedom, in this letter he stressed the need to highlight the universal ownership of all goods and social responsibility. Although not explicitly advocating a "third way," the letter threw down the challenge to all people (and Catholics in particular) to engage with the capitalist system and use the freedom of the market to serve the common good.

Within the Focolare, the proposal of a radical alternative to the capitalist and communist models had never been far away. As discussed in the previous chapter, right from the beginnings of the Movement Focolare leaders had advocated the Christian principles on which the Movement rests as an alternative that had far-reaching implications in the social and economic field. Yet this alternative had always been seen as a matter of personal choice, and until this point had not been advocated as an institutional alternative set apart from either capitalism or communism. But in 1991, Chiara Lubich seemed to recognize that the Focolare could perhaps point to a "third way," also in the public sphere, which would address the inequalities that she herself had seen.

The idea was extremely simple and the immediate response to it was one of excitement (Gallagher, 1997: 160). News of it spread through the existing local Brazilian and global networks of the Focolare rapidly[5]. Within hours of the launch of the idea, there were offers of participation pouring into Araceli from Focolare communities all over Brazil. Within a matter of days, the idea had spread to people all over the world and there were numerous offers of participation. From reading the documentation on the launch of the project and from watching footage of the meetings, the feeling one gets is that the EOC was viewed as a response, perhaps *the* response, to the urgent need for greater equality in Brazil and beyond. The following are extracts from letters from communities in different parts of Brazil that arrived at the Focolare Centers in Rome and Araceli, following the launch of the EOC. The first extract comes from a family who lived in the city of Sao Paulo, offering their participation in the project:

> 1 June, 1991, Sao Paulo … We have a small business which makes office furniture and we would like to offer to equip the office which will be used for the secretariat that will administer this new reality [the EOC]. This is what we have available: an Olivetti typewriter, Olympia calculator, 2 desks, 3 seats, 1 computer table, 1 stamping machine, 1 cupboard. We are also able to buy objects from the factories that work with us at factory prices.

The most striking thing in this letter is the practical nature of the help offered. There was nothing abstract about the idea of the EOC, and the response to it reflected this clarity through concrete offers of help. At the same time many people readily grasped the potential of the idea to transform the economy. In another letter, from the Focolare community in Manaus, the writers reflected on the spiritual significance of the idea and how it had changed their own attitudes toward the economy:

> Manaus, 2 June, 1991. We have contemplated the project [EOC] for building of a new society based on Trinitarian relationships! … In their desire to give life to the EOC, simple and poor people have offered the little money they had saved for their vital needs with extraordinary generosity, in order to participate in this great project in an unconditional way. Several communal and personal enterprises have already come about. These include: the opening of a bank account where the money for the capital

will be deposited, jewelry, objects, availability of people to move house, offers of sales points for the produce of Araceli here in Manaus.

The first reaction of those who heard about it, therefore, was to intensify the communion of goods that they were already putting into practice in their communities. People offered whatever they could — even wedding rings — so as to make a contribution toward building up the EOC. People began to talk of a "third way" between capitalism and communism (Sorgi, 1991b), and many people who had little or no experience of business felt "called" to leave everything and to dedicate their lives to building up the project. People began to offer their services to assist the project in Sao Paulo and declared their availability to move to Araceli to start up businesses. The news of the EOC was not confined to Brazil. Responses to the idea soon began to arrive from around the world. In particular, a group of business people belonging to the Focolare were participating in a meeting on the social and economic implications of the Focolare vision in Rome when news of the developments in Brazil reached them. Such was the enthusiasm for the proposal that several decided immediately to start businesses or to "convert" the businesses that they had for the EOC. Within a matter of weeks, the EOC had emerged all over the world through the Focolare networks.

"Creating" a New Economy

The basic principles of the EOC were laid out in a series of talks that Chiara Lubich gave during her trip to Brazil in 1991. Subsequently, these principles have been deepened, elaborated and discussed by other leading members of the Focolare, as well as by economists and other professionals working within or alongside the Focolare Movement (Bruni, 1999; Bruni & Pelligra, 2002). This body of literature now forms a growing reference point for those engaged in the development of the EOC.[6] From this work, several key ideas relating to the nature of the EOC emerge.

Profit Sharing

The main principle that underpins the EOC is that of increasing equality through making the communion of goods productive. People linked to the Focolare were encouraged to set up businesses as a means of increasing the overall amount of resources available to help those in the community who were in desperate need of food, clothing and shelter. The novelty of the project was initially seen as the division of the profits of the businesses into three parts (Lubich, 2001). One part was to be given to the poor, one kept for re-investment in the firm and the third part for creation of educational structures to promote the "culture of giving," as shown in Figure 5.1.

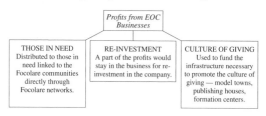

Figure 5.1 Sub-division of EOC Business Profits
Source: Adapted from Gold (1996)

There are some similarities between this method of profit sharing and the tradition of "tithing" in some churches. Within the EOC, however, this desire to generate profits to share became one of the chief motivations behind starting up new businesses. Within the EOC, donations of profits were not seen as a benevolent afterthought — what to do when excess wealth has been accumulated — but as an integral part of the business mission. The administration of the project would take place through the Focolare centers, which were the focus of the communion of goods, and that the same structures in place for the communion of goods would be able to fulfill the functions of the EOC. The idea seemed simple, yet it had the potential to redirect wealth in a way that was much more productive than the communion of goods alone.

Based on the underlying vision of the human person within the Focolare spirituality, a key element of the project from the start was that participation in the EOC and sharing had to be entirely *voluntary*. If the sharing was not voluntary, but the result of pressure or coercion, it would result in the person who was giving being denied the possibility of granting consent. Without consent, the possibility of reaching "communion" between people is taken away, given that the freedom to say "no" is what makes authentic communion possible (Catapan, 1994). The act of giving within the EOC has to be the result of recognizing the needs of others and freely choosing to attend to those needs through practical assistance (Araujo, 1994a).

The logical extension of this freedom is the fact that the businesses wishing to participate in the EOC remained in the direct management of the people who owned them. The Focolare did not create some kind of overarching communal ownership: the statutes of the Focolare state that, as an organization with charitable status, it cannot own or directly manage commercial activities except for where they directly relate to the more spiritual and educational functions of the Movement. Such centralized ownership of the businesses, apart from not being in keeping with the statutes of the Movement, could arguably lead to the development of a communistic mentality of central planning and could be highly bureaucratic. According to the EOC principles, the businesses should be managed and owned by private individuals who participate in the Focolare and live the culture of giving, not by the Focolare as an institution. Private ownership of the businesses, therefore, and all of the legal responsibilities that ownership brings, was seen as a prerequisite to the donation of profits.

The business owners/shareholders have no legal obligation to give profits to the EOC. The choice to share profits (and the proportion) comes primarily from the people within the business itself, based on their professional assessment of the needs of the business. Nevertheless, the business people are encouraged to bear in mind their responsibility to others in the context of living out the "culture of giving." On the one hand, this affords the businesses the freedom to participate in the EOC to whatever degree they feel they can without having to fit into some rigid scheme. It also makes it possible for the range of businesses wishing to participate to be as wide as possible. On the other hand, as will be seen further ahead, the interpretation of this freedom has led to difficulties that were perhaps unforeseen at the beginnings of the EOC. For example, if the businesses are granted the freedom to give as they please, how can one set criteria for those wishing to participate broad enough to include many kinds of businesses, yet tight enough to avoid possible misuses of the name "EOC"?

Widespread Ownership

Another key principle that emerged at the beginning of the EOC is the idea that ownership of the businesses should be widespread, giving as many people as possible the chance to participate in the project in some form. This idea of diffused ownership raises the question of the responsibility and rights of shareholders, and places it at the heart of the EOC. If the business involved aims to redistribute its profits outside the company, the shareholders must receive less. Such a decision cannot be forced on shareholders, but has to be based on a conscious choice. As a result, one of the initial objectives of the EOC had to be that of making sure that the majority of the shareholders in any company shared in the ideals of the Focolare and were prepared to forgo their dividends in order to help build up the EOC.

Business Parks

One of the key points that emerged right from the beginning of the EOC was the importance that special business parks linked to the Focolare little towns would have in the promotion of the project (Boselli, 1991a). The idea of the "model towns" was at the forefront of Chiara Lubich's mind when she launched the EOC in Brazil. While visiting Brazil in 1991, she recalled how she had always imagined these places as industrial places with full integration in the local economy. She recalled an event that had taken place in the 1960s, in which she had the impression that the Focolare was being called not only to put into practice a spirituality of unity, but to create social structures and institutions that reflected this vision of the world. While she was on holiday in Switzerland, she came across the Benedictine Abbey of Einsiedeln and was struck by how the spiritual vision of St. Benedict *"Ora et Laborem"* (prayer and work) was reflected in the buildings of the abbey and the surrounding village that had grown up around it. She had the impression that the vision of the Benedictines "lived on" in that place and was inspired to think that, in a similar way, the characteristic spatial structures of the Focolare would entail model towns wherein the ethos of the Movement could be developed and put into practice. These towns would also act as models of how society would be if all people were to live out the ideal of mutual love:

> At one point, it was as if that very beautiful sight of the church and fields in the dazzling sun was dissolved, and I felt that I understood that God wanted something similar from us. Einsiedeln appeared almost like a little city, because of its vastness, and it seemed that God also wanted a little city from us, but not like that one. He wanted a real and true little city, with houses, especially little houses, but also larger ones, with pavilions, with factories, with businesses and industries. This image has remained so deeply impressed that it is as if I can still see it, even now.[7]

Part of the vision of the towns, therefore, would be an economic dimension that would also reflect the Focolare spirituality and culture. The towns of the Movement could not remain spiritual enclaves, but had to exhibit the features of a modern town. As a result, the business people in Araceli, in response to this vision, decided to start up an industrial park near the model town of Araceli, in which all the businesses would share the vision of the EOC.

The creation of business parks, as will be seen in the following chapters, would serve several purposes. Firstly, since the businesses would be located within the same area, this would facilitate the growth of linkages between the businesses. Secondly, the creation of an actual physical space in which the idea was being applied, not only by an isolated business but also by a group of diverse businesses, would offer a credible example to others who were more skeptical about the viability of the project. It would therefore have a demonstration effect that could be imitated by others, as an economic parallel to the social exemplar set by the model towns.

GLOBAL NETWORKS

Although the EOC began in Sao Paulo, Brazil in 1991, the project spread rapidly throughout the world and permeated a wide range of sectors of the economy through the Focolare networks. In the first four years following the launch of the project, there was a rapid increase in the number of businesses participating. This early exponential growth rate of the numbers of businesses across the world participating in the EOC reflected an initial phase of enthusiasm within the Focolare and among others who heard about the EOC and wished to participate in it.

The second phase of development of the EOC could be termed one of consolidation. The growth rate began to slow down in 1996 and since then the number of businesses participating in the project seems to have leveled off around the 753 mark. The rate of growth thus appears to have slowed down, suggesting that the EOC is entering a new phase of development.

The geographical distribution of the businesses throughout the world correlates closely with the diffusion of the Focolare Movement. The first concentration is in Brazil, with 84 businesses (11 per cent of the total). The second such concentration is in Western Europe, and in particular Italy, with 242 businesses (33 per cent) and Germany, with 53 businesses (seven per cent). There are also relatively high concentrations of EOC ventures in Argentina (four per cent), Ex-Yugoslavia (four per cent) and in the USA (five per cent).

There are several regions with few or no EOC ventures. The most noticeable absence is Africa, north and south of the Sahara. In North Africa there is only one EOC business in Egypt. In the whole of Africa south of the Sahara there are 11 businesses in total. In part, this absence could be the result of lack of communication between the Focolare communities in African countries and the Focolare Center. The more likely explanation, however, relates to the inability of those who would like to participate in the EOC to generate adequate funds to start businesses. Likewise, there are few EOC ventures in former Soviet countries. In this case, the main reason is the limited presence of the Focolare Movement within the former Soviet countries.

How EOC Profits are Shared

One of the main aims of EOC ventures is to help create greater equality among all those linked to the Focolare across the world. An important element of this is the redistribution of profits, which are shared in three ways, as outlined above. The portion of profit for re-investment is kept within the business itself. The amount is at the discretion of the business owner. The other two parts are divided equally between assistance to those in need and formation activities for a culture of giving, and are channeled through the central Focolare Center in Italy. Since 1994, the business profits given to those in need have been supplemented by personal donations from people within the Focolare Movement. The redistribution of these profits and donations is carried out in two ways. First, direct community assistance, as described below, is provided through the community network structures of the Focolare Movement. Second, a portion of the profits is directed toward more structured development projects via Azione Mondo Unito, which has been running projects based on the Focolare's principles since the 1980s.

Geographical Redistribution

The 2009 EOC Annual Report provides a comprehensive overview of the project. In Table 5.1, the geographical breakdown of income and disbursements is provided, as is the actual amount of profits and donations redistributed through the EOC.

Table 5.1: Summary of EOC Accounts in 2009

REGION	Income (€)			Outgoings (€)		
	Profits	Personal Donations	TOTAL	Those in Need	Formation Activities	TOTAL
Sub-Saharan Africa	759,79	3.093,00	3.852,79	108.404,14	8.500,00	116.904,14
Central America		12.335,00	12.335,00	65.592,71	7.000,00	72.592,71
North America	52.621,41	10.073,32	62.694,73			
South America	85.554,00	75.121,25	160.675,25	536.266,60	39.319,43	575.586,03
Asia	41.456,00	35.837,65	77.293,65	125.414,12	7.000,00	132.414,12
Eastern Europe	20.355,73	19.971,27	40.327,00	153.352,00	31.700,00	185.052,00
Western Europe	180.187,05	208.231,61	388.418,66		28.000,00	28.000,00
Italy	189.368,35	161.244,61	350.612,96			
Middle East and North Africa	3.340,00	7.788,00	11.128,00	23.052,00	7.000,00	30.052,00
Oceania		3.481,75	3.481,75			
Carry over from 2008	104.768,54	153.287,34	258.055,88			
Focolare Centres		49.289,03	49.289,03		10.300,00	10.300,00
Newsletter			0,00		11.117,00	11.117,00
Sophia Cultural Institute			0,00		200.000,00	200.000,00
Administration					349.936,43	55.791,24
Total	678.410,87	739.753,83	1.418.164,70	1.012.081,57	349.936,43	1.417.809,24

Source: EOC Annual Report 2009, available at www.edc-online.org

In terms of geographical patterns, the donations of profits into the EOC came mainly from countries in Western Europe, South America and North America. The countries contributing the most were Italy, followed by Belgium, Brazil, Switzerland and the USA. Personal contributions to the EOC also came predominantly from the same regions.

In terms of disbursements, the vast majority of the funds for those in need went to developing countries and Eastern European countries. The greatest amount went to Latin America, where the Focolare community is large. In relation to formation funds, a large proportion of the funds in 2009 (€200,000) was directed toward one specific international project, the Sophia Cultural Institute, based in Loppiano, Italy.

Despite the low level of donations redistributed to African countries, the actual number of requests and the percentage of requests satisfied were high. On the one hand, this suggests that those linked to Focolare communities who would be eligible for help through the EOC are actually more self-sufficient in Africa than in other parts of the world. It also reflects the variation in living standards and the relative value of the Euro in different regions of the world.

Through the EOC, the Focolare Movement has generated a positive monetary flow from the wealthy North/West to poorer nations, albeit still on a limited financial scale. In itself, such an achievement only scratches the surface of the global economy, but does offer a model of global sharing that could arguably be applied on a wider scale. This has been possible by attending to the actual needs of individuals and families rather than through remote decision-making.

Local-Global Distribution Networks

The data presented above highlights the global scope of the EOC. Through the EOC it is clear that a small-scale global "communion of goods" is already occurring within and through the Focolare Movement. At first glance the Focolare decision-making processes seem rather centralized: there is one main fund based in Rome and decisions on the needs of remote communities across the world are taken there. On the surface, there are strong similarities between the EOC and other international NGOs that are continually faced with the problem how to distribute funds world-wide.

When the decision-making processes of the EOC are examined within the context of the wider Focolare structures, however, a different picture emerges. Although the EOC results in one central fund, decisions on the amount of money required from the central EOC fund and on how it will be used remains with the local Focolare communities. This process of decentralized decision-making is operationalized through each local Focolare community working out in real terms what its particular needs are on a regular basis. Each year in June a "census" (commissioned by the Global Center) is carried out in order to establish the needs of all those linked to the local Focolare communities. The emphasis that the Focolare spirituality places on attending to the needs of others makes this task relatively straightforward. In order to avoid such needs being overlooked, everyone is invited to present them directly to the Focolare houses, which act as central co-ordination points in the process. Thus, this primary stage of decision-making in the EOC is at the most decentralized, local level and is based on a kind of community self-assessment. Although this system is based almost entirely on trust, since those who are being helped actively participate in the life of the community, verification of circumstances would be relatively straightforward due to the high level of face-to-face relationships.

Once established, every attempt is made to cover the needs of the community, first using resources available on a local level through living the "culture of giving" which is the basis of the Focolare spirituality. In many cases, especially in Western nations, this communion of goods is enough to cover all of the needs of the immediate community and to generate an additional surplus that can be shared for other communities. If the needs of the local community cannot be met through this local communion of goods, they are put forward to the regional Focolare and the same process occurs. If the regional Focolare centers are still unable to cover the requests, the needs are then communicated to the International EOC Commission. In this way, requests that reach the International EOC Commission have already been verified by means of the communion of goods.

The responsibility for verifying the needs of the community on a regional level lies with the regional delegates of Focolare communities.[8] In a sense, the task of discerning who needs what lies with them more than with the International Commission. Delegates from Latin America, Italy and the Philippines explained how they reached decisions regarding who to help, and whether there were general guidelines on what help could be given. They revealed a range of interpretations of "basic needs" and diverse ways of attending to those needs in different countries. One delegate described how the Focolare in his region reached decisions on who to help and how:

> We don't define it [help] by the amount he or she receives. It could be, for example, that you receive 100 and I receive 100 … but you have five children and I only have one, your father is sick and you have to care for him, or you have to pay for your house … So we define this in a personal relationship, so that the person can reach the end of the month … we define it personally, in a personal relationship.

The decision on how to help, therefore, is based on a personal relationship between the person in need and a responsible member of the Focolare community. It is not based on some predetermined criteria of need on a global scale, but on the actual needs that are brought to the community and in particular to the attention of the delegates. The help, when it arrives, goes through the same channels of personal relationships. It is a result of attending to the particular needs of the individual or family. The census means that how much each one will receive is decided prior to receipt of the money. One delegate said: "This is all carried out beforehand. First we find out what the needs are in a personalized way, with great discretion and charity. Then, after we have this list, we give it to the Center." This takes away any possibility of disagreement within the community when the help arrives. Hence, the task of the Center is more that of administering the distribution of funds that have been already allocated than deciding how money should be spent.

DIRECT ASSISTANCE TO THOSE IN NEED

Given the highly personalized nature of these EOC networks, there could be discrepancies in what constitutes a "basic need" within the project as a whole. The global scope of the EOC could give rise to questions regarding the nature of poverty in different parts of the world. Recent academic texts have raised the issue of distinguishing "relative" and "absolute" poverty (Foster, 1998; Yapa, 1996). Such work has highlighted the social construction of poverty and how it differs according to cultural settings and geographical locations. For these reasons the Focolare Center was reluctant to set fixed standards at the start of the EOC, as it was thought that establishing needs was best left to those closest to the individuals who required help.

As the EOC has developed, however, they recognized that discrepancies did exist in what different countries defined as poverty. In order to avoid disagreements and misunderstandings, a working definition of what constitutes a "basic need" within the context of the EOC was established. The basic needs covered in practice by the EOC fund are listed in Table 5.2.

Once needs have been established, the total amount of money required to satisfy them in the local communities is added to the totals from the other regions each year in October, when the 300 regional Focolare delegates hold their annual meeting in Rome. In the course of the month, each pair of regional delegates meets with the International EOC Commission to resolve any discrepancies arising from the information that they had provided and to discuss the progress of the EOC in their region.

Table 5.2 Basic Needs and the EOC

Type of assistance	Nature of EOC assistance
Shelter Help with rebuilding a house Help with accommodation expenses	Direct financial contribution; Participation in existing house building projects;
Education Help with the cost of school fees Help with the cost of school equipment	Direct financial contribution; Placement in Focolare school; Payment of fees to a non-focolare school;
Household expenses Help with the cost of groceries Help with the cost of school meals	Direct financial contribution; Provision of groceries from the Focolare house; Payment to school;
Employment Assistance in finding employment	Help with cost of preparing letters, applications, attending interviews; Placement in an EOC firm; Financial contribution toward training courses;
Healthcare Help with the cost of urgent medical expenses	Financial support for families if breadwinner is ill; Direct financial contribution for medical expenses.

Source: Fieldwork at Focolare Center, Rome

How to share the money is then determined by means of a simple calculation based on the total funds received in the year. If the sum received for the year is the same or exceeds the amount requested by the various communities, then everyone receives exactly the amount requested. If the amount received is less than the amount requested (as has been the case since the start of the EOC), then each region receives a proportional amount based on this overall sum. For example, in 1997 the amount of EOC funds available fulfilled around 80 per cent of total requests. In that year, each region received 80 per cent of what they had requested.

This method of calculating each region's share has only been in effect since 1995; prior to 1994 the EOC contributions from businesses were allocated on a regional basis without passing through the Focolare Center. Those countries that had the highest level of EOC profits distributed them within that particular country. In 1994, however, the system was globalized. This decision came partly from the realization that the businesses were still not managing to produce enough profit to cover the needs of the Focolare communities throughout the world. A global structure, it was thought, would enable a more comprehensive distribution of the profits and therefore a more widespread communion of goods among countries and not just within the countries themselves.

In order to do this, in 1994 the Focolare adopted a calculation based on the cost of living in different parts of the world in order to bring about a fair distribution. In a sense, this can be seen as an attempt to acknowledge the pattern of global inequalities in an objective fashion. The different regions received help in proportion to the cost of living in that particular region, based on the number of people within the Focolare in need. This calculation, however, proved laborious as it did not relate directly to the needs of the individual communities in the countries that had requested help. As a result, the proportional calculation was adopted, which proved much quicker and more effective in achieving the aims of the EOC.

The greatest benefit of this procedure of profit distribution is the clarity of the system on a global scale. As a result of globalizing the EOC, the Focolare Center has achieved a system through which it can oversee distribution of EOC profits without assuming responsibility for deciding precisely how the funds are spent in the different regions. The regional delegates and local communities make those determinations according to the needs within their communities. This relieves the EOC of time-consuming bureaucracy. At the same time, the EOC's use of established networks within the Focolare and established meetings means that the EOC *per se* has almost zero administration costs. The profits collected specifically for the EOC can be given directly without any percentage being siphoned off to satisfy overhead expenses.

ASSISTANCE VIA *AZIONE MONDO UNITO*

A new element introduced in 2006 to the EOC has been a partnership with the NGO *Azione Mondo Unito* (Action for a United World). AMU, started by members of the Focolare Movement and run according to the same principles, has been running development projects throughout the developing world since the mid-1980s. When the EOC started in the early 1990s, the work of AMU and the EOC were regarded as separate entities and operated in parallel. As the EOC has evolved, the necessity of expertise in development assistance management has become clearer because of requirements that the use of funds be transparent and that they be used not only to meet immediate needs but also for long-term development work. Partnership with AMU provided a workable solution.

In 2009, AMU administered €202,000 of EOC funds on behalf of the project. The role of AMU has consisted in vetting and providing support to those in the developing world seeking EOC funds. A distinctive contribution of the projects supported via AMU has been in the provision of sustainable livelihoods through small productive activities. In 2009, projects funded through this scheme have been carried out in Argentina, Brazil, Chile, Colombia, Mexico, Paraguay, Peru, Uruguay, Cameroon, Ivory Coast, Kenya, Ethiopia, Uganda, Bosnia, Bulgaria, Croatia, Macedonia, Romania and Serbia. This partnership with AMU looks set to become a growing element of the EOC in the coming years.

Centrality of Trust

The system of profit-sharing within the EOC on a global scale depends upon high levels of trust within the Focolare at every level. Such trust is normally assumed only in face-to-face, everyday community relationships at a local level. There is limited internal scrutiny of documents from the delegates on the part of the Center and profits are shared in the total trust that all the money will be well spent. In this way, the process is quick and efficient with paperwork kept to a minimum. Such a system could seem inappropriate within the dominant market economy, where everything spent or requested has to be justified through a laborious system of accountability. The EOC appears open to corruption, fraud, and misuse of funds. The nature of the Focolare spirituality that underpins the system, however, makes it difficult to abuse the trust on which it is founded. At the same time, it discourages questioning others' trustworthiness. Those in roles of responsibility, for example, have given up all their possessions to live in the Focolare houses and do not have access to personal bank accounts. Nevertheless, given that the EOC is working at the intersection between the normal public economy and the distinctive economic vision within the Focolare, this reliance on trust could present difficulties. The nature of such difficulties will be considered in relation to the case studies.

CONCLUSION

This chapter has provided an overview of the evolution of the EOC and its development on a global scale, highlighting the evolution of various local-global networks. It showed how the EOC emerged from the practices of sharing already present within the Focolare and gave these practices a more institutional presence within the context of the global economy. Structures within the Focolare, which grew out of the "communion of goods," proved an efficient and highly adaptable means of fostering solidarity through sharing. The chapter demonstrates how global movements with a spiritual basis can transform and adapt to the context of globalization and invent new and exciting forms of self-help that by-pass the traditional forms of welfare provision. In many ways, the EOC offers participants a kind of parallel form of welfare, helping them out of poverty.

At the same time, the analysis of the EOC data in its first nine years demonstrates several important features. First, although steady, the amount of profits redistributed by the businesses participating in the EOC project is not growing at the rate initially expected. Since 2000, partly as a consequence of new procedures adopted to guarantee transparency and accountability, the number has begun to rise slightly. Given the high levels of mortality among SMEs in developing countries, this rise demonstrates a high degree of resilience among the EOC companies as a whole. Nevertheless, the question of how to support new businesses has to be considered. Second, the number of new businesses joining the project has slowed in recent years, especially in European countries. The initial burst of enthusiasm in the early years of the project seems to have given way to a slower but arguably more solid rate of growth, as it is based on thoughtful decisions rather than euphoria. Nevertheless, this slowdown of the number of businesses casts doubt over the universal applicability of the EOC on a wider scale.

NOTES

[1]By "egalitarianism" I am referring to the liberal theories of social justice put forward by thinkers such as Rawls (1971), Nozick (1974) and Rorty (1989), which can be traced back to the Hobbes and Locke. Within such theories the dominant civil concept to preserve security and prosperity is that of "rights" (Bell, 1998). Society is viewed as instrumental to the attainment of these rights, which are increasingly viewed in terms of economic goods (Taylor, 1995). These rights are attributed to individuals (although there is an increasing move toward theorizing the "rights" of minority groups), and are not related to society as a whole.

[2]There are striking parallels between the writings of Chiara Lubich and those of her contemporary, Simone Weil. Both Weil and Lubich develop a social and political philosophy centered around what Weil calls the idea of "paying attention" (1951). Through living in the present or paying attention, they see the possibility of seeing through the ideological abstractions that dominated (and continue to dominate) the political and social dogmas of their day. Such dogmas, according to Weil, form a "metaphysical cloud" through which it is difficult to see the all pervasive injustice of the human condition (1968). Both stress the need to start from the experience of people, the "tissue of life" as Weil calls it, in order to understand the human condition. Both advocate an "ethic of care" as the only way to overcome injustice — not only at a personal, but at a political level, through recognizing human responsibilities as well as human rights. Both see *the way* as one that involves the awakening of the human spirit through a spirituality that goes beyond religious dogma and has the capacity to "draw God down" into the realm of human experience. Both recognized the need for "roots," and find these in the incarnational religion of Christianity, but are open to the wisdom of other cultures, especially Oriental religions. According to Richard Bell, Simone Weil's philosophy embodies a position which is both *pragmatic* — in the sense that it is concerned primarily with action — and *idealistic* — recognizing that only through imbuing human action with idealism can injustice be overcome (Bell, 1998: 16). This could also be said about the thought and life of Chiara Lubich. Her thinking is both highly idealistic, urging people to belief in the good of the human spirit, but also profoundly pragmatic. Lubich sees the greatest challenge of human life as that of "rising to the highest contemplation while remaining in the midst of the world" (1981: 56). Only through re-uniting the "spiritual" with the other dimensions of life can social change come about. Finally, it must be noted that both Chiara Lubich and Simone Weil lived and wrote at a time when the male-dominated philosophical systems of Marxism and Fascism were at their peak in terms of political influence. Moreover, neither would label themselves as "feminist," seeing such labels of gender, race and religion as clouding the relevance of their message to humankind in general. Nevertheless, their writing and action clearly shows a woman's perspective, and this has to be borne in mind.

[3]This concern for the poor within the Movement is clear in the inaugural talk that Chiara Lubich gave on the 29 May 1991 in Araceli, Brazil, in which she launched the idea of the Economy of Communion.

[4]Chiara Lubich, Araceli, Brazil, 30 May 1991, page 13.

[5]The Economy of Communion Office in Araceli, Brazil, holds a documentary and audio-visual archive on the development of the EOC. The material in this section is based on primary materials from this archive.

[6]A key reference tool for the EOC is the official website, www.edc-online.org.

[7]See *iv.*

[8]Each regional community is represented within the Focolare at an international level by two regional delegates (one man and one woman) who are both single focolarini.

5
EOC Ventures around the World

INTRODUCTION

Previous chapters have examined how the spirituality emanating from the Focolare Movement has given rise to a new economic vision. This vision, although not limited to the Economy of Communion project, is most visible there. As discussed in Chapter 4, the most striking aspect of the EOC is its attempt to translate universal principles of fraternity, gratuitousness and reciprocity beyond the personal sphere and into the world of business.

The question most asked about the EOC concerns its actual effectiveness in the business world. The project's anthropological and spiritual roots have given rise to diverse expressions in different parts of the world. Although business guidelines have been drawn up to give the project shape, as will be discussed later, the EOC is not confined by a series of rules and regulations. Rather, it is based on a deep-rooted transformation of the place that business occupies within wider human relationships. It has to do with a culture shift — something much more intangible and difficult to universalize. In order to make the step from theory to praxis, this chapter will examine some of the people around the world who have become involved in the project, the businesses they run, and what this means to them in the daily life of their firms. Subsequent chapters will explore the workings of the businesses and their relationship to the EOC project in greater detail.

TYPES OF EOC VENTURES

There are a number of ways to build a typology of EOC ventures. One is to examine the firms from the perspective of the business sectors in which they participate. EOC businesses operate within a surprising range of sectors of the economy, from production/manufacturing, to services, to retail sales. Table 5.1 presents a breakdown. The commercial/retail sector, which accounts for 22 per cent of EOC businesses overall, includes a cross-section of retail outlets. This range of activity within the different sectors, which could arguably be a great asset to the EOC as a whole in the future, is one aspect to be studied in detail in relation to the case study regions.

Table 5.1: EOC Ventures according to Sectors

Retail/ commerical	No	Production/ manufacturing	No	Services	No
Unspecified	59	Pharmaceutical	1	Education	32
Groceries	32	Agriculture	31	Photography	2
Textiles/Fashion	31	Clothing	25	Business Services	71
Home Goods	16	Food Processing	33	Information	25
Medical Supplies	12	Engineering	17	Restoration	5
Books	7	Various Articles	27	Maintenance	22
Computers	4	Graphic Design	17	Planning	13
Vehicles	2	Appliances	18	Legal	10
Photography	1	Furniture	16	Medical	46
Total	164	Fine Art	4	Transport	2
		Total	189	Tourism	14
				Unspecified	59
				Total	301

Source: Focolare Center, Rome

The production/manufacturing sector, which accounts for 25 per cent overall, displays a cross-section of productive activities, from heavy manufacturing to food processing. The sector of "other services" reveals a high number of consulting firms within the EOC, as well as a relatively high number of private medical and educational establishments. These sectors have constituted the highest growth sectors within the EOC.

These particular sectors may have developed because for the most part they have relatively low startup cost. The sectors also offer EOC people an obvious chance to influence economic and social institutions outside the Focolare. Within the consultancy sector, the spirituality of the Focolare can offer new solutions to the problems of interpersonal relationships within businesses. In some, for example, the spirituality becomes an added asset within the firm and even a possible selling point. The same reasoning could also be applied to some extent to the sectors of medicine and education. As the examples below demonstrate, the communitarian ethos practiced within EOC ventures confers considerable advantages. The breakdown of the EOC by sectors reveals an eclectic mix of businesses. The various sub-sections also reveal a variety of businesses, with large- and small-scale firms even within the same sub-sector. This variety of businesses — both in terms of size, sector, and sub-sector — could offer the EOC considerable opportunities for future development.

Some EOC ventures pre-existed the project, and some came about as a result of the EOC project itself. For many, participation in EOC was the principal rationale for starting the business. In a sense, these "new businesses" came about in direct response to the call for a new economy based on gospel values. Other "reformed" businesses pre-existed the EOC, but have been transformed in order to participate in the project.

"New" Businesses

Almost half of the companies listed as EOC ventures fall under the category of "new businesses" — i.e. companies that would not have come into existence were it not for the EOC. These companies responded directly to the idea of making the "communion of goods productive" launched by Chiara Lubich in Brazil in 1991. In the initial phase of the project they generally involved a number of people closely associated with the Focolare Movement pooling their savings to start small companies. The first to do this were Brazilians, as shown in the previous chapter, but others soon heard about the EOC and followed their example.

The Philippines, where the Focolare Movement is well-developed, proved a fertile site for new businesses in the first few years of the EOC. One of the first companies to emerge there was *Ancilla*, a management firm that aimed to incorporate the basic principles of the EOC into its consultancy theory and practice. Since 1991 *Ancilla* has grown into one of the most respected consulting firms in the Philippines with a large portfolio of multinational clients. Since the early-1990s, *Ancilla* has specialized in translating EOC philosophy into good management practice beyond the confines of the project itself.

Another early EOC business in the Philippines was *Giacomino's Pizzas*, which grew out of a small home based grocery store in Manila in 1991. It typifies the new entrepreneurial spirit that took hold within the Focolare communities, particularly among the young people involved in the Movement. Noel Castro, owner and director of *Giacomino's Pizzas,* explains how this happened:

I was inspired by the idea of the Economy of Communion and wanted to play an active part in it. I started with the small family business which we already had (Diversified Foods Inc) and branched out into pizza and pasta with the name Giacomino's. The start of this new enterprise marked a new stage in our family business, giving a new serious commitment and a volume of work which we could never have imagined. We had to face it with courage, tenacity and imagination. This alone, however, cannot account for the survival of Giacomino's in the midst of the well-established pizza giants in the fast food market (*Pizza Hut, Shakeys*) nor the meteoric growth that has taken place so far: 15 restaurants and 40 kiosks in the whole country, 400 employees (direct and indirect), 15,000 slices of pizza sold each day.

This growth, however, presented serious problems:

> What started out as a "home-made" brand has reached the stage of industrial production. This requires high levels of capital investment and the improvement of our organizational structures in order to sustain our growth. It requires a leap of quality of our management and we have had serious doubts whether we are capable of doing it on our own. But faced with growing competition we have realized one thing: either we keep growing or we will die.

They faced the difficult decision of selling the company to their competitors, thus protecting the interests of the employees who they had taken on. In this way they could make a massive profit and invest the sum in a new venture with similar objectives, perhaps in the area of rice (*Rice Time*) or Chinese fast food (*Ho Lee Chow*), two underdeveloped areas of the fast food market. This, however, would mean selling out the ethos of the Economy of Communion to another company that would not, perhaps, share the same objectives. In order to survive, they would have to find capital.

The EOC also gave rise to a number of new businesses in the USA and Canada. There are just over 50 businesses affiliated with the "New Society" Association, which forms the central organizational structure for the EOC in the US. Near the Focolare town of Luminosa, in Hyde Park, New York, several businesses emerged in response to the EOC challenge. One such company is *EOC Finish Line*, a private tutoring service for school-aged children, which was set up by three educators: Joan Duggan, JoAnn Rowley, and Tom Rowley.

In May, 1992, when *Finish Line* started, the local economy was depressed due to the largest businesses in the area cutting staff and closing facilities. But the three educators involved decided to pool their talents and interests to start an educational support center which would both contribute to the local economy and to the global EOC project.

Joan had strong executive experience in a highly successful computer leasing business, as well as university teaching experience. Tom, who had been a teacher for 20 years, wanted to continue teaching; JoAnn had administrative experience in schools. Their objective was to meet the educational needs of students that the public schools could not address adequately due to budget cuts, reduction of personnel, and increasingly large classes. They purchased a building and with the support of friends and neighbors began to set up the rooms in which to welcome the students. Later, they received a gift of desks, chairs, and office material while a press agency helped by promoting their initiative. The business now schedules more than 4,000 educational hours a year and provides steady employment for 13 other teachers. Their total contribution to the EOC fund approaches $20,000 but Joan still cannot forget the joy of writing the very modest first check. In her previous job she had written checks for hundreds of thousands of dollars, but in that small first check she found the answer to what she had always looked for.

Another North American start-up company that came about through the EOC is *Spiritours*, a travel operator based in Montreal, Canada. It came about when Anne Godbout read about the EOC proposal and saw a gap in the market for a tour operator specializing in personal and spiritual development trips and sacred journeys for small groups interested in equitable tourism. Its purpose is to help individuals reflect on their lives and take steps for personal and spiritual growth through local or foreign trips. An experienced travel agent, Anne took a year's sabbatical to examine the possibilities of starting her own company. When she heard about Focolare founder Chiara Lubich's proposal, she took up the invitation to develop a business that could contribute to eradicating poverty and creating a culture of giving. "This way of doing business," she explains, "seemed to me a practical way of helping the needy and of putting my talents at the service of others."

At the end of her year-long journey, Godbout returned to Quebec and decided to start a travel business based on these objectives. After 10 years in the industry, she had both the skills and the passion to launch her idea for a business which would facilitate human and spiritual development. She began to develop the business plan and was offered contracts for group travel, including one for taking young people to the World Youth Day in Cologne. This important contract allowed Godbout to clear her start-up debts and share a portion of her profits with the needy who are part of the Economy of Communion. This philosophy of service extends beyond her clients to her employees, whom Godbout strives to treat very fairly and to her contractors, whom she respects and pays on time. It also extends to her competitors, to whom she often refers clients who want to travel to destinations that she doesn't serve. She is also keenly aware of the reciprocal relationships with her tours' host countries: enrichment for travelers as well contributing to the local economy and fostering sustainable development.

All *Spiritours* excursions subscribe to equitable tourism and ecotourism, which the International Ecotourism Society defines as "responsible travel to natural areas that conserves the environment and improves the well-being of local people." Before departure, Godbout provides *Spiritours* participants a pamphlet that outlines the rules of ecotourism, namely, respect for local culture, minimizing the impact of the travelers' stay and encouraging positive interactions that benefit both parties. Once there, the tour leaders sensitize partakers to their new environment as they visit national parks, deserts, mountains and so on.

Many EOC startups address environmental sustainability. This was a top consideration for John Mundell in 1995, when he started *Mundell and Associates* in Indianapolis, Indiana. The company, which focuses on earth and environmental consulting, specializes in characterizing soil and groundwater contamination at commercial and industrial sites, evaluating the risks to human health and the environment posed by the impacts, and then engineering solutions for cleaning up the pollution. In addition, the company assesses and protects water resources and drinking water supplies for small to large municipalities interested in sustainable water quality practices.

From its founding the large, complex projects *Mundell and Associates* have taken on have required a strong cross-disciplinary approach. John worked alone for a few months, and then hired a part-time employee, a summer intern. Meanwhile, the company John had worked for was sold and one of his former associates, Jim B., had decided to leave it because the new owners were no longer pushing "high tech" environmental projects where his skills were needed. As John's first full-time employee, Jim brought important scientific and technical skills. An Evangelical Christian, Jim also understood and appreciated the idea of the Economy of Communion and wanted to be a part of it.

As new opportunities and more work came Mundell's way, the staff grew. Adding expertise in key areas made it possible to provide clients around the world with teams that had the right mix of knowledge and skills to handle the most challenging environmental and earth science projects. In addition to hiring for strong academic credentials and specialized training, John emphasized quantitative and reasoning skills, experience in project management, and substantial geographic and regulatory experience. Employees were also chosen for their abilities to work well in teams and to represent *Mundell* effectively with clients as "the face and spirit" of the company. Although John explained the Economy of Communion dimension to prospective employees, he did not use their agreement with it as a hiring criterion. John simply wanted them to understand the philosophy of the business so they could make an informed decision. Low turnover and high morale have been hallmarks of *Mundell* staff culture from the start. John regards this as critical to success for a business where people, not capital, are the primary resource. Employee salaries and benefits are competitive.

By 2007 *Mundell* had employed 12 professionals in science and engineering, two technical specialists and three administrative staff. The professional staff included scientists in geology, hydrogeology, geophysics and environmental science, as well as mechanical, geological, civil, biological, agricultural and environmental engineers.

As well as independent EOC startups, a number of businesses to service other EOC ventures specifically have developed where there are concentrations of EOC companies. These businesses form an interesting category in their own right as they often form important links between otherwise dispersed EOC ventures.

One such company is *Comunione Auditoria e Assessorial Contabil Ltd,* which started in 1993 as a direct consequence of the Economy of Communion launch. Three members of the Focolare with actuarial experience saw a need for a reliable accounting firm to serve Economy of Communion businesses. They noted that many of those starting up around the Focolare town of Araceli, near Vargem Grande Paulista, were struggling to find suitable business services in the vicinity. With a small amount of their own capital, they rented a small office on the main street of Vargem Grande and initially began to service other Economy of Communion businesses. Over time, however, their network of customers expanded beyond their original client base.

This expansion presented several problems. First, they faced a business culture in which tax evasion is the norm and payoffs for creative accounting are widely accepted. *Comunione*, however, felt that as an EOC business, they could not operate in that manner. This put them in the awkward position of having to turn down customers, even during a period of economic stagnation. Nevertheless, they persisted and eventually gained credibility from non-EOC businesses and have been able to influence their practices too.

In addition to the many businesses that have come about as a result of the EOC, members of the Focolare as well as people with existing businesses have decided to affiliate with the project. The largest and most established company to join up with the EOC in the 1990s was *Femaq*, a steel foundry in Brazil. The business was founded in Piracicaba in 1963 by Rudolfo and Enrique Leibholz, two brothers of German descent. The business has 60 full-time employees who produce specialized parts for the automobile and paper industries. Over the years, they have gradually become one of the leading firms in its sector not only in Brazil, but in Latin America. In 1994, the firm had an annual gross revenue of US $ 8,200,000. The two brothers are still the majority shareholders and also the managing directors of the company.

They participated in the Focolare for many years and had applied the principles of sharing among employees in the business ever since they founded it. In 1991, when the Economy of Communion was launched in Brazil, they immediately felt that this was a response to their deepest desire to help create a fairer distribution of wealth. As a consequence, they decided immediately to participate and began to share their profits.

The challenge of doing so has led them to a different attitude toward the management of the business itself and toward their employees. They felt the need to pay greater attention to the personal needs of each employee, recognizing that their own particular circumstances could have a bearing not only on their work, but on their general well-being. This change of attitude led to the institution of special health and educational benefits for those who needed them. They noted, despite the turbulent economic climate, a marked decrease in absenteeism and a rise in productivity. They attributed this to their participation in the Economy of Communion.

Participation in the Economy of Communion led them to take a more active role in the industrial institutions to which they belonged. They recognized that as an Economy of Communion business, they could have an influence on the way that other businesses were managed and in local politics. In 1995 they presented a paper at the International Confederation of Foundries (CONAF) on their business philosophy (Leibholz, 1995: 49–61). They also began to participate actively in FEISP, the Federation of Industry in Sao Paulo. As a result of the Economy of Communion, the vision of their industrial activity has changed substantially. They recognize the need to make a profit, but balance that need against their sense of responsibility for addressing inequality within their own community and through the Focolare, on a global scale.

Another medium-sized company that underwent substantial investment and restructuring as a consequence of the EOC was *Webert* in Northern Italy. Emmanuele Webert took over the direction of the family firm at the age of 19. At that time, it was a small artisan activity producing bathroom accessories for large companies, one of over 200 similar small producers of faucets for the home market in the eastern part of Piedmont, near Lake Como. *Webert* had only a handful of employees and was on the verge of closure. In 1991, Emmanuelle heard about the Economy of Communion at a meeting for business people in his region. He decided that it could provide the necessary motivation to invest in the company. Since then, *Webert* has undergone radical transformation and has become a dynamic company designing and producing faucets and other bathroom accessories directly to the consumer and to major wholesalers.

In 2009, *Webert* had 100 employees and had established itself as one of the leading manufacturers in the region. Emmanuele said that the Economy of Communion gave him the motivation to make the business grow. It has also affected the way that he runs the business and, in particular, the investments he chooses to make. For example, he installed equipment to purify the water and recycle the effluent from their industrial processes. Other investments have included the improvement of facilities for workers on the factory floor.

Other smaller companies, such as *Zac* in Piracicaba, Brazil also underwent significant changes through their choice to become affiliated with the EOC. *Zac*, a local business selling religious artifacts and books, was established in the 1970s. According to managing director Maria Ines, participating in the EOC has led to two main changes. The first was a new awareness of the social function of the business. Rather than just regarding themselves as a bookshop, they began to see themselves as a social center — providing a space for people to feel welcome at the heart of the city. This made them change the layout of the shop, put in chairs and tables and alter their approach to people who came through the door. The second change was a renewed desire to grow the business and to generate more profits to share with the EOC. Ever since they joined the EOC in 1992, *Zac* has continued to give 1 per cent of its gross receipts to the EOC.

Another example of a North American "reformed business" is *Sofia Violins*, which manufactures top end violins, violas and cellos for professional musicians worldwide. This Indiana-based company, formed in 1988 by John Welch, maintains a global group of master violinmakers in a vertically integrated production-sharing structure. The privately held company markets its premium quality musical instruments worldwide, a niche market subject to economic upheaval. In recent years the biggest challenge has been finding the market quickly flooded by surprisingly good quality Chinese instruments selling at extremely low prices. Many respected European and American manufacturers quickly scaled back their own production and are distributing instruments sourced in China. By maintaining and enhancing a distinctively high level of quality *Sophia* has managed to survive and even grow. The company's particular character has been deeply influenced by the Focolare mentality, including being part of the Economy of Communion global business network. According to John, these characteristics of operation did not evolve overnight. They evolved step by step, trying to follow what he calls "God's Business Plan" in each moment. It's an adventure that gives them freedom to operate their business without useless manipulations and anxieties. As John says:

> You will not find a sculpture of praying hands on my desk. This vital life that exists within our company is in no way imposed upon our employees or anyone else. There are two of us, (a Catholic and a Protestant), who are committed to quietly trying to live the words of the gospel. This desire is focused by the monthly "Word of Life" sentence from Scripture that is lived throughout the world by millions of people who have been in some way influenced by Chiara Lubich and the Focolare spirituality.

Another large reformed business participating in the EOC is the *Kabayan Rural Bank* in the Philippines. The original bank was founded in 1957 as the Ibaan Rural Bank, Inc. Mr. Bienvenido M. Medrano and the then newly-retired Auditor General Manuel M. Agregado sought to serve the people of Ibaan, Batangas by providing reasonably-priced credit, particularly to small merchants, farmers and traders in the community. With the goal of uplifting the quality of life of the people in the countryside, IRB participated in all the government programs aimed at providing credit to the rural population. Like most rural banks, in its early years IRB operated largely by rediscounting funds from the Central Bank. Aside from the usual savings and loan services, Ibaan Rural Bank also pioneered the use of the checking account as early as 1967.

The second generation of managers sought to move toward placing IRB in a premier position in the rural banking industry. Human resource development was given priority and the first Vision and Mission of IRB was crafted. Inspired by the Economy of Communion, IRB embarked on an expansion program so as to make an impact, both as an employer and as a rural-based financial conduit. Deposit generation became a thrust, in order to wean itself away from the Central Bank and develop its capacity to operate as a stable rural bank. From 1991 to 1996, eight branches were established in various municipalities.

On its 40th anniversary, the bank adopted the business name *Bangko Kabayan*, with the strong will to serve not only Batanguenos but also other communities in the countryside outside of the Batangas Province. During that year the IRB Foundation was established, funded out of the bank's profits, to offer micro-credit and scholarship programs for the poor and to sponsor community-building seminars. *Bangko Kabayan* responded to the financial crisis of 1997 by embarking upon providing microfinance loans in order to reach an even greater number of clients in the countryside. The bank still continues to improve the quality of its products and services to better serve its ever-growing client base, now numbering more than 50,000. With assets of over a billion pesos, *Bangko Kabayan* ranks among the top 3 per cent of rural banks in the Philippines today.

EOC CO-OPERATIVES

The underlying culture of communion within the EOC bears striking similarity to that of the cooperative movement that thrived in certain parts of the world, particularly in Europe, throughout the twentieth century. It then comes as no surprise that a number of co-operative businesses have also affiliated with the EOC. As Economy of Communion businesses, co-operatives are a special case because they are non-profit enterprises.

One such business was *O.V.A* ("Omnia Vincit Amore"), a co-operative that started in 1984 and since 1991 has been part of the Economy of Communion. The hinterland of Brescia where *OVA* operates is a region of intensive agricultural activity and hence, of high competition. The business, which raises around 10,000 chickens — still small by the region's standard, has met the competition by selling directly to around 150 clients so as to avoid paying middlemen. Many of the clients are part of the Focolare Movement in the surrounding area. In addition to the farm, the co-operative now has a retail outlet for many Economy of Communion businesses in Italy and beyond. They sell Economy of Communion produce ranging from organic olive oil to wool fabric produced by nearby yarn businesses. Customers come from all over the region.

Another large co-operative that decided to participate in the EOC is the *Tassano Cooperative* in Liguria, Northern Italy. This consortium is now responsible for managing homes for the elderly, community homes for people with mental illness, and protective structures for people with special needs linked to local industries. Over the past few years, the consortium has grown from a small initiative with a few founding members to 800 shareholders and has been defined as an "enterprise incubator" due to its capacity to stimulate new productive activities.

The consortium consists of 62 cooperatives working together to employ and retrain people in challenged populations. The cooperatives work in partnership with private companies and the local authorities in the Liguria and Genoa provinces to employ people with various disabilities, recovering addicts, and released prisoners. The consortium as a whole employs 1,300 persons. Three of them are "social cooperatives," funded by the rest to employ 130 persons who would find it difficult to find jobs. The entire consortium's underlying philosophy is based on the idea that a protected but productive job can restore a sense of self-confidence to persons who for a variety of reasons have become marginalized from society.

The consortium carries out various activities. Thirteen specialized convalescence homes comprising 700 beds offer care for the elderly and people discharged from psychiatric hospitals. Other activities include a cooperative of people engaged in education, a printing house, and one civil work cooperative that employs 200 partners in assembly activities for third parties. Of the people involved in these activities, 70 per cent have physical or mental disabilities, a history of drug use, or prison records.

The public social service providers of the Liguria Region, together with the Province of Genoa and all the towns in the area, have recognized the social value of this work and the money saved by supporting it. In turn, they created a foundation to help fund the program. They also provide psychological counseling and specialized assistance necessary to help these disadvantaged workers reenter the workforce.

BUSINESS PARKS

As already mentioned in the previous chapter, one important element of the Economy of Communion has been the establishment of dedicated business parks to support a number of the businesses. The first park, "Spartaco," was set up near Sao Paolo, Brazil immediately following the launch of the Economy of Communion in 1992. Entrepreneurs linked to the Focolare Movement who wanted to participate in the project recognized that a lot could be gained from a common approach. Funding for the project initially was generated through the creation of a public limited company, ESPRI, which bought the land, created the infrastructure and then rented out the lots to prospective Economy of Communion companies. Of the 3,300 shareholders in this company, most are members of the Focolare throughout Brazil. Many are relatively poor, but wish to participate in the project as small investors. Currently, nine businesses occupy the business park, some relocations and others startups, which were offered incentives such as rent-free periods from ESPRI in the initial stages of their development. Ideas on who may like to set up in the park generally emerge from within the Focolare Movement. Capital has also come through matching those with good business ideas with other people in the Focolare who have capital to invest. In the Spartaco Park, for example, an Italian financier has set up an investment fund that aims to support the liquidity of the other Economy of Communion businesses. Final decisions on who can set up in the park, however, rest with the ESPRI Board of Directors, most of whom are also Economy of Communion entrepreneurs and members of the Focolare. Other business parks, modeled on the Brazilian park, include Lionello (Italy — Loppiano), Solidaridad (Argentina — O'Higgins), Araceli (later renamed Ginetta) (Brazil — Igarassu — Recife), Mariapoli Faro (Croatia — Krizevci), and Belgio (Belgium). Other business parks are being planned for Benevides in Brazil, the Philippines, and Ottmaring, Germany.

In each case, a holding company has been set up to administer the park. Funds have been generated principally through widespread small donations from people either involved in the Focolare Movement or sympathetic with the aims of the Economy of Communion. More recently, however, the involvement of outside agencies, such as UNIDO, has been sought successfully. Such business parks have proved an invaluable resource for the Economy of Communion both in terms of their capacity to generate wealth, and in their ability to serve as "exemplars" for the whole of the Economy of Communion network and beyond. The existence of these parks has facilitated the growth of sectoral and cross-sectoral collaboration within the Economy of Communion networks both on a regional and international level. They have also fostered the sharing of skills, knowledge, and technology transfer to developing countries.

The flagship business park in Europe, the Lionello Business Park, in Incisa Val D'Arno near Loppiano, Italy, was inaugurated in October 2006. It now houses 22 Economy of Communion businesses from a wide range of economic sectors including financial services (*Assi 1, Banca Etica Popolare*), construction and engineering (*AD Finsimel, Enertech*) and business services (*Unilab Consulting, Xcognito*). In addition, it offers a range of retail outlets and meeting spaces. The park is a vibrant part of the local community, which welcomed the initiative with open arms. Since its inauguration, a distinctive characteristic of this park has been the number of civic and academic personalities who have visited the initiative, including then President of the Italian Council, Romano Prodi. Many other local business associations, particularly cooperatives, often hold their own meetings in its halls. The center is also often filled with people from academic and formational circles, including university lecturers, high school students, entire classes serving internships, and students taking specialized courses given by the EdiC SPA (the association which runs the building), which is accredited by the Tuscan region.

In 2008 the Lionello Bonfanti Industrial Park had 5,640 shareholders, witnesses of how many have believed in the project and in some way have wanted to participate even if they themselves did not run businesses of their own.

CONCLUSION

This chapter has presented an overview of the diversity of businesses involved in the Economy of Communion project. The project includes both large and small companies in a diverse range of economic sectors, new startups as well as older, more mature companies with established reputations. What links them all is their motivation to put the ethos and values of the Economy of Communion into practice within their specific economic operations, within their specific territory. Far from offering predetermined technical fixes to the economic problems in particular regions, each business has found unique ways of establishing a culture of communion. In this regard, there is no "one size fits all" for the Economy of Communion businesses, but rather a rich diversity of experience that has emerged since its inception in 1991.

6
Spirituality and the Economy
of Communion Businesses

INTRODUCTION

Upon its launch in Brazil in 1991 the EOC had one principal aim: to create businesses that would produce profits to share in common. The documentation relating to the launch of the project comes back to this point — the EOC is about making money to distribute to the poor and for the promotion of the culture of giving. In this way, according to an interview Chiara Lubich gave on Polish TV in August 1991, the ideal of communion already in practice among the Focolare members could become productive and could offer a solution to the difficult economic situations in the world. One striking thing about the EOC is the apparent simplicity of Chiara Lubich's idea and how readily it was taken up by Focolare people worldwide in the months that followed the launch. There was little discussion over how the ventures ought to conduct their affairs, except that they should be *"run by competent people who know how to make a profit."* The central point was distribution.

Although it sounded straightforward the proposal that businesses make profits and share them in three parts was laden with assumptions about the nature of profits and as a consequence, the way that profits ought to be made. Within the context of the Focolare spirituality, EOC ventures could not have applied a conventional means-end relationship with regards to profit. Since at its heart the Focolare seeks to create spaces where relationships are founded on love — "Trinitarian relationships" — the businesses had to reflect this spirit in everything that they did. Profits, therefore, could not be the result of efficiency savings borne out of exploitation, coercion or corruption — they had to be the result of a new relationship above all among the people within the businesses. The start of the EOC, therefore, also regarded the nature of the individual businesses themselves and the way they made their profits. This chapter will consider how the aims and objectives of the EOC have been interpreted and applied by examining how EOC ventures in Sao Paulo and Milan have interpreted the relationship between the Focolare spirituality and business.

Ethical Standards

The launch of the EOC assumed that pre-existing businesses had *already* achieved a certain level of ethical practice that would be acceptable on a global scale, and that those setting up would adopt those same practices. In many of the regions where the EOC took off, such as Sao Paulo, such assumptions were far from the reality of existing commercial activity. Business people in these regions considered many of the underlying assumptions of the Focolare spirituality concerning business practice to be uncommon, even unrealistic. Brazilian business directors, for example, highlighted the high degree of informality in certain commercial sectors due to the impossible tax burden that small businesses face. Norms and conventions regarding quality assurance and effects of businesses on the environment exist, but such legislation is rarely enforced (Suzigan, 1995: 134). The businesses in Milan, perhaps surprisingly, faced problems similar to those in the Sao Paulo concerning the earning of profits for the EOC. They were embedded within a business culture of widespread non-compliance and tax evasion. The EOC ventures had to discern to what extent their businesses ought to comply with legislation and risk being noncompetitive.

For business directors who wanted to commit themselves to such a model, the EOC generated the desire to produce higher profits to be put in common, but they had to balance that desire against the available means to do so. In many cases this tension led to the internal transformation of the businesses, as a precondition to giving profits for the EOC. The profits to be shared had to be "clean," as one business director put it. This desire to produce clean profits led to a "cleaning up" process within participating businesses to bring their practices into line with the spiritual ideal against which they measured success.

SPIRITUALITY IN BUSINESS

In recent years, the relevance of spirituality in business has become more fashionable. The various schools of management theory have shifted from the "big is beautiful" doctrine of the 1980s and the "downsizing" of the 1990s to the various schools of "corporate responsibility" in the new millennium that stress the links between business culture, ethics and religion.[1] Yet there is much confusion over what this new awareness actually means. On the one hand, there is a growing awareness that the profits have to be made in ways that harness the inner motivations of people to that end. Increasing numbers of highly qualified people are leaving commercial business in pursuit of more fulfilling jobs, often in the voluntary sector, due to high stress levels and poor quality of life. Spirituality is regarded as a kind of "softener" in the hard-nosed world of cutthroat competition: *feng shui* office designs are said to enable the release of "energy flows" and crystals on desks (pointing in the right direction) are thought to calm stress and enable better working relationships. In this respect, the link with spirituality is viewed more as a means to making profit a feasible long-term objective against the backdrop of increasing competitiveness in which employee and management stress is a major block.[2] Although taken seriously by some sectors of business, such approaches are often ridiculed due to a lack of substantive evidence of their "performance." These attempts to incorporate spirituality into management theory are designed to maximize profit. In many ways this exporting of spirituality into the economic sphere is a good example of how aspects of human life normally unrelated to the utilitarian logic of profitability can be "colonized" by such logic. In this instance, even the "spiritual" is subverted to become marketable.

At the same time, however, the awareness that "corporate responsibility" requires a "necessary altruism" (Wuthnow, 1994) that inevitably limits profitability has caused theorists to rethink the various frameworks of business ethics. In this debate, spirituality is regarded not as a means to making more profit, but as a particular vision of the world, often (but not necessarily) linked to a particular religion, that engenders certain ethical practices. It is about the beliefs and values that frame economic action in a broader perspective. It is important, therefore, to examine how the EOC business directors see the relationship between spirituality and business.

Through the launch of the EOC, the directors wishing to participate recognized that the spirituality of the Focolare could have an impact in the practical running and organization of their businesses. In a geographical sense, they recognized that their businesses no longer stood outside the realm of the spiritual, but through the EOC became part of the "ideal world" as part of the Focolare geographies. Of the twenty-four business directors interviewed, twenty-one responded that the main motivation for their participation in the EOC was "religious." When asked to elaborate on what they meant by "religious," they explained that deciding to link their business to the EOC project or to start a new business was a consequence of realizing that the Focolare spirituality could, and ought to be, lived out within business. One director said that she joined the EOC principally because it granted her "the possibility of giving a new soul to the economy." Another said, "We have seen that being an EOC business means giving a soul."

Prior to the launch of the EOC, many of the respondents considered business to operate within a sphere of action operating according to "cold" laws of supply and demand, independent of the more personal or spiritual. Through the EOC, they came to regard business as intrinsically connected to their religion, as it was founded on moral choices that they derived from religious principles. As such, they came to understand that it could be transformed by the actions of individuals and groups who chose to manage their businesses on principles in accordance with their own beliefs. On the one hand their beliefs gave their actions a new meaning and on the other gave them a moral impetus to change those actions. By doing this they felt that they were giving the economy this "new soul," widening the horizons of the business to the possibility of contributing to a transcendent ideal.

Coming to recognize the relevance of the spirituality in business was a gradual transformation for 36 per cent of the respondents, reflecting many years of experience within their particular field. Some of the businesses, having started in the 1960s, had been attempting ever since to apply the social teaching of the Church in the way these enterprises were run. They took pride in this fact and felt that the EOC served to consolidate the way they had always acted and gave new impetus to those choices, rather than requiring a dramatic transformation of what they were doing. They viewed those years of trying to apply the social teaching of the Church as a foundation for the insertion of the businesses within the EOC. Since the EOC emphasized the commitment of economic institutions to the poor, it renewed their motivation to continue what these businesses were already doing.

A small number of respondents did not understand clearly the relevance of the EOC being launched in 1991. Initially they were a bit puzzled, as they felt that they were already trying to apply the Focolare spirituality in their businesses. In Milan, the managing director of a business that began to participate in 1993, said:

> Since both my parents are … part of the Focolare Movement, at the beginning it was not clear to us why we had to participate in the EOC. Since they … live the spirituality of the Movement, it was normal for them to apply certain values, also in their work. So

at the beginning, we did not understand what we had to do. Then things became clearer.

For 60 per cent of those interviewed, however, the launch of the EOC in May 1991 had crucial importance. It marked a dramatic transformation in the way that they viewed the relationship between economic life, (including work, money and the role of the business) and their spiritual life. They repeatedly referred to this date as a fundamental turning point in their life. Before 1991, they regarded their economic activities primarily as a means to an end — that of making a living — controlled by external market forces over which they had little influence. For some, this sense of working simply to serve another purpose rendered their work meaningless. Their spiritual life and membership in the Focolare were considered personal matters without obvious bearing on the way that they managed their economic affairs within the context of the business. They always tried to maintain good relations with their employees and occasionally offered free services to the Focolare, but structurally there were no linkages between their spiritual lives and the businesses in which they worked.

When the EOC started, they recognized the immense importance that their business activities could have by actively participating in the transformation of market structures through sharing profits and changing business practices. The transformation of existing businesses and the creation of new enterprises became their central focus, not only economically, but also spiritually. It was to become the main motivating force behind their business. This is reflected in how many directors responded when asked what the EOC meant to them. Many responded that the EOC "is their reason for existing." Not participating in the EOC would be like returning to being "Sunday Christians." Through the EOC their businesses could become places where the "kingdom of God" could be spread, based on relationships built on mutual love and respect.

A Spiritual Calling

After 1991, this growing awareness within the Focolare that business was relevant to spiritual life and vice versa is reflected in the spiritual "callings" that many interviewees claim to have experienced when they first heard of the EOC project. In May 1991, several directors from Milan were at a Focolare conference in Rome when they heard about the launch of the EOC. One was so taken by enthusiasm that on his return to Milan after the conference, he and his wife decided to split from the parent company in which he had a large share, and to form his own small firm for the EOC. Had it not been for the EOC, he claimed, "It would not have come about otherwise." It was a risky decision, given that the company he was leaving, one of the most established yarn companies in the district, belonged to his brother. Leaving it and starting another in the same sector put him in competition with his own brother. He recalls the story:

> It started, therefore, at the end of '91 and it came about through splitting from our parent company in which the family had shares. We are four brothers and this business still operates within the field of textiles. Because of different opinions on the way that my brothers were running the business, I wanted to break away. But I would never have had the courage to do this, above all because I have reached a certain age, 50, and I would have had to leave the security of the well-established parent company that had started in the post-war era with a large sum of family capital … so I was prepared to sit around and do nothing rather than taking on the risk of starting over. Then it came to the end of 1991. In May of 1991 Chiara had launched these ideas in Brazil and at that time I was in Rome at a convention for Economy and Work, with all the business people there. We were taken by the enthusiasm and when I returned home I said to G [his wife] that perhaps the time had come to overcome our insecurity, our fears of leaving the company, to put them aside and to do something. I wrote a letter to my brothers who were the other shareholders in the business and I outlined my motives for wanting to start another business. I didn't go into the deep reasons, but highlighted the human motivations for my desire to start something new, yet to continue working together with them. Things were a bit difficult and they did not understand my choice. The legal process took a long time but in the end I left and they paid me off with a large sum of money that we used to plan the factory we are in now.

Despite the difficulties that this choice presented, he was convinced that he had made the right decision, since what mattered most was the possibility of contributing to the EOC by starting his own business. The launch of the EOC allowed him to overcome his fears and insecurities and to risk starting a new company.

CHAPTER 6

Another Milanese lady attending the same conference in Rome invested all her savings in a new metal engineering business. She previously had shares in a similar family business, but the same year as the EOC started she and her husband had decided to sell them. On hearing about the EOC, she felt that the money merely earning interest in the bank could no longer stay there since it was "God's capital." Rather, she felt she had to invest in a small business:

> It started in the beginning of 1991 because we started when Chiara launched the idea of the EOC. It was in May. We started in September, because we were there when it was launched in Castelgandolfo, when the beautiful experience started. We felt right off that the capital we had put aside in the bank from a business we had with my brother ... we didn't know what to do with it. We thought that we could have invested it in houses and lived comfortably, but we felt that this was not what God was asking us. We understood that we had to reinvest the money for God. Immediately, when we came home, we found a building and we started this activity.

The decision was difficult, as many regarded it as imprudent — there were much easier ways to make money. Given that they were nearing retirement age, it would have been more comfortable to invest in a safe fund and live off the interest. Deciding to change their plans because of the EOC met with disapproval on the part of their family and friends: "They said that we were mad. But what is madness for the world is wisdom for God." Their faith in the EOC was even stronger than the opinion of their friends and family.

In Brazil, Focolare leaders from all over Brazil were at Araceli when Chiara Lubich proposed the idea of the EOC. This meeting led to the start of several businesses near Araceli, which is located about 50km from Sao Paulo. On hearing about the project, some left everything and pledged to start businesses. One example of this is an accounting firm. In 1991 its various shareholders were working independently in Fortaleza, over 3,000 km from Sao Paulo, but the start of the EOC changed their plans: "I had already thought of starting a business in my town, in Fortaleza. When we realized the need for a business in Vargem Grande we decided to move here. Three of us moved here from Fortaleza." They had nothing, but saw the EOC as a challenge they had to take up. They also recognized that there had to be a focal point for the EOC near the town of Araceli.

Several local women also present when Chiara Lubich proposed her idea decided immediately to start a small clothing company, locating it at Araceli. They started from modest means: a few sewing machines in the back room of one lady's house. With great enthusiasm, however, they were able to acquire their own premises and within two years they had designed and built their own unit in the new industrial park. In its first year it grossed $6,000 and provided employment for two people. Since then it has grown and in 1994 grossed $115,000 and employed 22 people. When asked what had made them get involved without so much as a thought for the consequences, the managing director answered: "Through this project we believe that we are creating an alternative economy."

Whether the process was gradual, as in the case of *Femaq*, as outlined in the last chapter, or sudden, as in the case of *La Tunica*, all of the directors have undergone a major transformation in how they view the relationship between religious and business ideals. They regard business not as a means of making a profit to serve other purposes, however noble, but as a place where their spirituality can be applied, expanding the horizons of the business as a social and economic institution. All of the EOC business directors shared the belief that there is a specific "divine plan" on the EOC project itself. They viewed their action not only as a personal witness to the truth of the gospel, but an "appointment with history" that could provide a solution to the dramatic inequalities of today.

TRUST IN PROVIDENCE

Since they viewed this project as "divine," business directors believed firmly that God would intervene with providence to help those who risk resources in this project. The idea of providence goes back to the very beginning of the Focolare, as discussed in Chapter 3 in relation to the size 42 shoes and the suitcases of apples during the war. Trusting in providence and relating stories about how it has arrived was regarded as a way of responding to God's love and is central to the Focolare spirituality. Through trusting in God and interpreting events as "providential," God's presence is "drawn down" into human affairs and becomes more visible and tangible to those who believe.

This faith in God's providence that gave many people the impetus to risk all their resources for the EOC is, perhaps, the most sensitive and difficult aspect of the project to examine since it challenges the materialist explanation of economic and social action. Those who participate in the EOC are acutely aware of this challenge and speak about "providence" with reluctance, for fear it could appear that they naively believe divine intervention will save their business from mismanagement or inevitable financial difficulties. One business director was aware of the difficulties that such trust could present to those studying the EOC:

> You have to also believe in providence in this line of work. In effect, one thing that I had never thought about regarding the EOC is this belief in providence ... One can say that it is a coincidence. Sure, but I always feel that it depends on what you yourself have inside. One time you could say that it is a coincidence, but the second time? It could be providence, depending on how you see it. We have never been without work. Whenever there is a hole and I start to wonder how I could provide enough work for a particular employee, someone always arrives to give us enough work to cover that week there. This could be a coincidence or it could be providence. I have learned to see it as providence. It is difficult to say this in the world of business when we are talking about contracts with clients.

He recognized that belief in providence came down to the way that certain events were interpreted — to "what you have inside you" that makes you interpret events in different ways. The directors all expressed a strong belief, grounded in their experience since starting their EOC ventures, that God has helped many of their businesses survive despite turbulent markets. They related providence to many practical circumstances and shared many anecdotes of how it had helped their businesses flourish. For example, one director stated, "Providence helped us to find a marketing outlet that sells all over Italy." Some of such stories can easily be explained in terms of straightforward changes to the businesses that took place as a result of the EOC. Others, however, are more difficult to explain any other way except in terms of their extremely good luck following a high number of coincidences that could have resulted in bankruptcy.

One such story concerns a Brazilian ecological cleaning products company that started up through the EOC and is located in the industrial park near Araceli. It has grown at phenomenal rates following an unexpected break into the market, which the director explained to me as follows:

We are aware of this presence of God within the project. We see this in how the business is run: we run it on the one hand, but on the other hand, it is God who is running the business. We have received immense providence. For example, there was a national fair in which all the big supermarkets networks were represented with displays. We knew a person ... who now works in the area of publicity, who works for a Spanish company that sells kiosks for the supermarkets. Space is very expensive in this fair. This company was preparing its exhibition and selling the spaces within the kiosks for the big companies like Lever, Parmalat at $30,000 per space. This person is highly motivated, she is very young but she knows about the spirit of the EOC, so she said to the director that she knew a business that would like to exhibit in the fair ... but that this business did not have $30,000 to buy the space. So the director asked how much we had and she said we had nothing. It seemed like madness to ask. He said, "They have nothing at all; each space costs $30,000. Get them to bring their products and display them." There are many things like this that give us the certainty that this project is much bigger than we imagine today.

Those participating in the EOC regard this kind of phenomenon as "divine intervention" — God's blessing on their work. They do not regard such intervention as random, but as following a precise pattern. If they take an ethical stance in business affairs — e.g. against corruption, in favor of employees — that results in the loss of orders they feel that they are given a hand in the form of new unexpected orders or information. The story told by the director of a Brazilian clothes manufacturer illustrates this:

A contact in the Town Council phoned us asking for uniforms. He asked us to send a rep so we sent one. They asked us for a quotation for shirts so we prepared it. They liked it and said that they would like to go ahead. They knew that they could find other places that were cheaper, but our quality was better. They wanted something good so they wanted to buy from us. They said: "The only thing is, we have to solicit competitive bids, so we require three quotations. But we would really like to buy from you so do this — make up three quotations for us with three different names and then we will buy from you." This is something that they do at times to make their work easier. Sometimes it is not out of wickedness but simply to make work easier. For me, however, it would not be honest to do this. I can send a quotation from my own business and not from any other. I said this to the rep and he said "But you need this work so much." I said that I couldn't. I could do it if I thought in a different way, but this is the way I think — the way of the EOC. So I couldn't do this. He said "But then I will have to get these other two quotations and you will risk not getting the job." I said "Patience, we may lose out, but this is all that I can do. Don't you agree?" He said he agreed; he is someone who really understands. In the end they did not give the order to us. But the same rep went to a school to whom we had already sold that was seeking a proposal for more uniforms. We presented our proposals and the rep went to show them our projects. Our proposal was accepted and they placed an order that was five times greater than the Town Council's. These two things happened one month apart.

This trust that they will be looked after if they act in accordance with what they see as God's will enables them to make difficult ethical choices. Some even go as far as saying that God is like a "shareholder" in the business who, like the other shareholders, does not want to see the business fail: "Providence is never missing. Work always arrives, so we can see that we have … an 'invisible shareholder.' This is palpable." The business directors said that attempting to live the spirituality of the Focolare together provided insight and intuition regarding decisions to be taken. They explained this insight in terms of the "Holy Spirit" who was able to guide them through difficult moments if they remained united.

By deciding to participate in the EOC the business directors, in the most profound sense, were consciously "re-imagining" their own geographies, challenging many of the common-sense distinctions between private and public space. Through the EOC, their businesses became part of a global network linked to the Focolare. As a result, discourses normally applied only to their private, personal life now came to be applied to the business sphere. On the one hand, this led to a renewed consciousness of the synergy between personal and business attitudes. On the other hand, the business directors recognized that their own perspective was radically different from the dominant view that considers religious beliefs primarily a personal matter. In the EOC, far from being viewed as a simple means to an end, the business itself became the central focus for living out the spirituality. The directors interviewed regarded their businesses as playing a critical role in transforming modern society into one that is more equitable and just.

The majority based this idealistic aspiration to change economic structures, the prime motivating force behind their actions, on a sound understanding of economic action and/or previous experience. Of those who started businesses as a result of the EOC, 83 per cent had previous business experience. Some had left senior positions in finance and banking in order to start their own business for the EOC, their spiritual motivation giving an extra impetus to their previous experience. This meant that the risks the directors were taking in the belief that God would grant them good fortune were not a matter of "blind faith," but generally well-calculated risks based on their experience and spiritual motivation. As a result, this faith in providence did not result in taking risks that, in terms of financial security, could be termed imprudent.

In some cases, however, an over-spiritualistic understanding of the nature of the EOC and lack of business acumen did lead to serious loss of capital.[3] Although such circumstances had not directly affected the businesses participating in this research, many of those interviewed could recall stories of businesses that had failed following the launch of the EOC. They highlighted the fact that such failures were generally not discussed, and several voiced concerns over the way that those who had risked everything for the EOC and lost had subsequently distanced themselves from the Focolare. The loss of capital incurred through failure of the business was compounded by the disillusionment that God had not sent help when needed. Such failures highlight the risks of interpreting the Trinitarian perspective of the Focolare in a way that is too literal and simplistic.[4] Cases like these were more common in the first few years of the EOC; the past few years, however, have seen a growing awareness of the need for proper business training and expertise. Such expertise is now regarded as a necessary condition for God's providence to work.

THE BUSINESS AS A "HEARTH"

As outlined in previous chapters, the spirituality of the Focolare stems from the principle that all people are equal members of the one human family — sons and daughters of the one Creator — and therefore have to be treated as brothers and sisters. This belief in "being brothers and sisters," creates within the Focolare a strong relationship between "being" and "becoming." Although people *are* brothers and sisters, renewed awareness of this fact leads to a greater commitment to *become* brothers and sisters. It engenders a sense of responsibility toward others — both those who are distant, since they are seen as part of the one family, and those nearby. Rebuilding that sense of belonging to one human family requires active participation and conscious effort. The process is regarded not simply as natural, but one that can be learned. It is evolving continually, rooted in the ability of individuals to establish and re-establish everyday life relationships based on solidarity and communion. Achieving such relationships, in view of establishing one human family, becomes the main motivating force behind every action.

The spirituality of the Focolare, therefore, has a distinctive "community-building" dimension, with emphasis on the creation of spaces where this "hearth" can be lived out. As a consequence, understanding the relevance of the spirituality within the world of business led to transformations within the businesses, above all, on the level of human relationships. The first such transformation touched on the business directors' perceptions of their people. Realizing that all those connected with the business were part of one human family and not simply "factors of production" or "human resources" led to a series of changes in management (as will be discussed in the next chapter). According to those who responded to the interviews, the essence of the EOC lay in "treating people as people" or "creating new relationships" in which the economic dimension would be secondary. The EOC was not simply about making profits to share with the poor, but applying the Focolare spirituality in the business, which meant "humanizing" economic structures, starting with the business as the basic unit of economic activity.

This transition from the "spiritual" directly to the "social" within the realm of business itself reflects a strong link within the Focolare as a whole between the idealism of spirituality and the realism of social action. As discussed in Chapter 3, for the Focolare, a spiritual relationship with God is always reflected in the way that others are treated. By humanizing the economy, the businesses recognized that the key to transforming the economic structures was changing the relationships between the people within them. It meant putting into practice within the business, above all, the principles of the "art of loving." Those connected with the business, thus had to be treated as brothers and sisters with equal dignity. The task they were required to do within the business, whether blue collar or white collar, became secondary to this underlying equality. This meant reviewing the distribution of tasks within the business. It also led to the awareness that the relationship with those outside the firm, such as the suppliers and the clients, also had to be reviewed. The creation and maintenance of relationships that transcend the economic function became one of the main objectives of the businesses. One business director in Sao Paulo said:

> What motivates me in the EOC is the possibility of giving a new soul to the economy, a new vision. Not just in the distribution of profits, which is one of the important points, especially at a Brazilian level, but above all, this motivation for a new society, for these new relationships that are built. I feel that this is the most revolutionary aspect of the EOC. These new relationships mean that each person is not only "economic man," but a being who exists. My enthusiasm comes when I see this coming about. It is gratifying when you live this on a daily basis, on a practical level.

For some it is directly linked to the words of Jesus in the account of the last judgment in Matthew's Gospel: "Just as you did it to one of the least of these who are members of my family, you did it to me" (Mt 25: 40). One owner in Milan said: "It means that when they [customers] come in, or when we go to them, you love them right from the first instance. Above all, you see Jesus, a brother, in them, rather than a client who is going to buy something." Being a client, therefore, in the economic sense, is secondary to being a brother or sister to them. Likewise, within the business, the relationship between the employer and the employees was interpreted in the same way:

> What we have seen is that this communion is not only a result of the EOC but it is part of the life of the employees and me too … It is about looking out for personal needs if we realize that someone needs something. For example, one of the ladies had a wedding and another brought in a dress for her to try on. There are many opportunities … Or through making things circulate between us all — food as well. During the lunch hour we do things together. I feel that the relationship of communion between everyone has grown and I would say that this is a result of this harmony and of this search for communion that is put inside us by this project. You don't see "employees" anymore, you see Jesus. You see people who have needs, problems, and you try — without harming the business because you can't just do this and let go of the business — to find a balance between

the human needs and the business needs. The business needs to go ahead and stand on its own two feet.

I would say that there is a brotherly relationship with people. We see our employees, our clients, and suppliers, as people who have to be treated fairly without judging them. It requires a lot of effort since they are business people, clients and so on.

Others did not explicitly make this link to the religious root of the EOC. Rather, they recognized the importance of the EOC as revealing how economic actors could be viewed in a way other than as *homo economicus*. They framed it in terms of humanizing the economy rather than as a question of religion. One business director in Milan said:

The human being is made to be part of humankind and cannot exist as "homo economicus," working only for self. The beauty of the EOC is that it is a distribution of profits that is participative. It is not that we are participating in the EOC only in the moment when we distribute the profits: we are part of the EOC also in our formation [of profits]. It is then that a new way of looking at the economy is spread. This can also have a religious dimension, but above all it is about human relationships.

This idea that the EOC is "participative" also emerged in the various interviews with business directors in Brazil. The interviews drew out how the spirituality of unity can be translated into a business culture that responds to the needs of society today. As Professor Geremias[5] said, "It is a culture which is distributive and participative … For the employers it is certainly participative in the sense that they feel deeply involved in what they are doing. They feel part of a global community that is transforming social structures and not slaves to an ideology that puts profit before people."

The directors did not regard the EOC as an isolated act of "distribution," such as giving philanthropic donations, but as a way of actually doing business. To participate meant applying EOC principles to every action within the business, no matter how menial or trivial. It was about finding intrinsic value — not just instrumental value — in the various actions and relationships that formed the everyday life of the business. This emphasis on participation begs the question of the extent to which employees were aware of the business' involvement in the EOC. Research revealed that only a low percentage of employees in EOC ventures realized their employers' involvement in the EOC. This critical issue will be discussed in a later chapter.

The directors, however, also recognized that the emphasis of the EOC on "becoming brothers and sisters" meant making distinctions between people based on their geographical proximity. If the ultimate aim of the EOC was to generate profits to be shared with the poor and to promote the culture of giving, what about those nearby who were in need?

> For us, above all, being an EOC company is about having a new relationship with people. Above all, there is this fraternal love with the employees, the clients, with everyone. This is what I can see. Then there is also this help for the poor, which will come. It is pointless for me to love the distant poor in Brazil if I do not love the person beside me. They also have needs.

This relationship between the needs of the "poor in Brazil" and the "person beside me" is fundamental to the EOC. The business directors wanted to attend to the needs of both, but realized that the needs of those in the business could potentially be limitless, leading to mounting internal costs. Giving all their profits away, on the other hand, could jeopardize the well-being of their employees and the future of the business. Moreover, within Brazilian business, the *compadrazco* patronage system still remains strong. Through this system it is customary that the employer assumes in part a parental role toward employees, who are helped out with a range of benefits such as housing and education for their children. The EOC is superimposed on this existing network and as a result, attending to those needs limits the possibilities of actually attending to the needs of those far away. In many cases, the directors explained their difficulty in sharing more profits for the EOC in these terms.

BALANCING SPIRITUALITY AND PROFESSIONALISM

This synergy between professional skills and resources on the one hand, and the strong motivations of religion on the other, has given rise to what has been called a "new emerging business culture" within the EOC (Burkhart, 1999). In most cases the development of this new culture in business has developed in ways beneficial to the business itself and to wider society, through the positive contribution that the businesses are making or hope to make in the future. Nevertheless, there is also some evidence that problems could be emerging due to misunderstandings about the different roles that professional expertise and spiritual support ought to play in business management.

Moreover, other problems arose from misunderstandings about reaching decisions within the business. In some instances, the directors of the businesses felt constrained by their participation in the EOC, or mistakenly thought that participation meant that decisions regarding the business had to be taken with the Focolare Movement. This desire to build unity created a situation in which when making business decisions the EOC directors preferred to consult the Focolare rather than independent experts. In a small number of cases, this has led to confusion over responsibility, especially when things start to go wrong.

On the other hand, however, the growing professionalism of the business owners in the EOC has also led to the opposite scenario in which the actual day-to-day running of business has led to the spirituality becoming secondary, if not forgotten. In the interviews, some directors expressed their concern that they were consistently forgetting the ultimate aim of why they were in business. On one occasion, a director was moved to tears when asked what it meant to be an EOC business. He had embarked on the EOC with much enthusiasm in 1991 and had formed a new company specifically for the project, investing his life's savings. Nevertheless, seven years down the line, he admitted that the EOC was not always foremost in his mind: "It ought to be a choice that you make each day, when in fact, as far as I'm concerned, I forget. I am so taken up by managing the firm." The pressures of keeping the business running had become his main concern and as a result he seldom took time to reflect on the ultimate reason why he had started in the first place. This example, though extreme, was not the only one of this kind. Some directors interviewed even said that they had difficulty remembering that their businesses were part of the EOC.

CONCLUSION

Participation in the EOC, therefore, altered the perceptions of the business directors. First, it altered their understanding of the respective roles of religion and business. As a consequence, it shifted the relationship between their "personal," more spiritual understanding of the world and their more "public" rationale within the realm of business. Above all, this led to changes in the way they saw the relationship between themselves and those connected with their business. Through the EOC they came to recognize that spirituality could have profound implications on economic and social structures, providing a strong motivation for positive action in favor of social justice. Through applying the Focolare spirituality in the work place, they began to feel empowered to change the structures of the economy from the inside, transforming their businesses into "hearths" in the public arena. The application of this spirituality in the business, however, also highlighted the relationship between social justice and geography, since the directors were faced with new choices based on their desire to care for those nearby and those far away.

NOTES

[1]Evidence of this shift in thinking is well documented in numerous reviews and websites relating to business ethics. Texts such as Davies (1997) trace the development of the relationship between business, ethics and management theory in the latter part of the twentieth century, highlighting the return to greater emphasis on "soft" subjects rather than economic theory, in the search for greater corporate responsibility.

[2]There is a new breed of consulting firms such as The Domino Consultancy (2000) that offer advice on "spirituality and work" or help with the "alignment between the spirit of the individual and the soul of the organization." "Spirituality," therefore, is fast becoming a marketable product.

[3]In other words, businesses started as a result of the EOC had been liquidated. It is difficult to quantify such failures since the overall number of EOC ventures has continued to grow despite this mortality rate.

[4]The possible dangers of such an interpretation have been discussed by Cambón (1999: 196–7).

[5]Interview with Professor Geremias Oliveira Filho.

7
Transforming Business Space

The previous chapter considered how EOC ventures have recognized the relevance of the Focolare spirituality and have attempted to apply its vision. The interviews with directors demonstrated, above all, that the Focolare spirituality, rooted in the idea of the "Trinitarian perspective," offers a different perspective on the place of business in society. This vision sees the "spiritual" not as an appendage or afterthought to the "economic," but as the main motivating force behind every action. The firm is regarded as a social institution, not just an economic one, in which people can create and maintain relationships based on mutual respect, commitment and understanding. The economic function of producing products, services and, therefore, profits, is regarded as the means by which solidarity can strengthen relationships. By applying this vision, profits can be generated and put to social uses for the common good.

The application of the Focolare spirituality within the EOC dramatizes the intersection of many different social networks wrapped up in the realm of economic action. EOC ventures exist within commercial, legal, political and cultural contexts with established practices and norms. The EOC nonetheless offers a new interpretation of the various networks within which commerce takes place, changing how the directors themselves look at these networks and interact with them. In many cases, they face decisions and dilemmas regarding the relationship between the Focolare's ideals and their firm. This chapter will examine how the EOC is transforming business space, beginning with the application of EOC altered practices within the businesses themselves. Did the application of the spirituality lead to concrete changes in practices? Next, it will discuss how participation in the EOC altered their relationship to the various different social, political and legal networks in which they are immersed.

CHANGING INTERNAL BUSINESS PRACTICES

The main internal change within EOC ventures regarded a new emphasis on building up the firm as a community in which everyone had a stake. The heart of the Focolare spirituality consists in creating relationships based on mutual love and understanding. The directors felt that this "fraternal" relationship had to be expressed in a particular way in relation to their employees. In the course of the research, the directors highlighted four specific changes that they attributed to the EOC: changes to pay structure, changes in recruitment policies, participative management, and action to promote community spirit. Directors who had started businesses as a result of the EOC were asked to compare their current practices with their previous experience of business. If they had no business experience, they were asked to explain the nature of the relationship with their employees.

Pay Structure

The first internal change within the EOC ventures that came about because of this new relationship between employer and employees was a re-evaluation of the companies' compensation practices. A small number of the firms in Milan attributed changes in their pay structure to the EOC. As a result of the EOC, 25 percent of the Italian companies had granted employee wage increases. Most commonly, this was done by introducing end of the season bonuses. This was preferred over other benefits such as making the employees shareholders in the company or alterations to basic pay. "Over and above the pay set down by the unions, we give our employees a bonus that they really appreciate. We give it to them especially for the extra effort they put in to the business." Wage increases within the business were viewed as a way of fulfilling obligations to the "poor" within the business before attempting to help people outside it. One director said, "When I hear that the EOC is about having greater care for the poor, I pay my employees better, since they are my nearest neighbors." This particular director felt justified in not giving profits to the EOC if he had not first fulfilled his responsibility to those nearest to him. It highlights the way that the desire to care for those far away also engendered a stronger sense of justice within the business itself.

In the Sao Paulo businesses, on the other hand, the main change to wages structure was the introduction of sick pay and holiday pay, a break with common practices in small Brazilian businesses. According to the directors, it is normal practice for people to be "hired and fired" according to need so as to maximize the efficiency of the company and to avoid the high costs of mandatory welfare contributions for permanent employees. The decision in 42 per cent of the businesses to change this practice produced a real strain on the companies' profitability. Nevertheless, they regarded it as a first step toward making the business part of the EOC. Those companies that did not make such changes paid wages already above the minimum entitlement, as well as holiday and sick pay.

Some EOC companies made such changes in their pay structure, but many did not. Those directors considered helping the poor a higher priority than increasing wages within the firm itself. They felt obliged to balance the needs of those outside the company who had little against the fortunate ones within the company itself who had a means of income.

Recruitment Policies

The second main internal change was a new attitude toward creating employment. Half of the EOC businesses decided to employ more people. In Italy, 40 per cent of the businesses that had started since 1991 had taken on new staff as a result of the EOC, and one new business had not yet hired employees. Of the businesses that pre-existed the EOC only a tenth had taken on new staff. In Brazil, over and above the new businesses, 17 per cent had reported an intake of staff as a direct result of the EOC. Even if they had not yet taken on new staff, all of the directors regarded the creation of new jobs an important function of the EOC. In particular, they regarded the creation of apprenticeships as an important function for the future of the business. These were offered to a range of people, but in particular to young people with various sorts of difficulties. One director told me why he had taken on a young boy who had had drug problems:

> This year we have taken on two young people ages 15–17 ... We try not to transmit stress to our employees, but to create a friendly relationship and good collaboration. Of course the productivity of the business is important and our employees have to work, but we have to be sensitive, above all with one boy who has problems ... sometimes he doesn't understand what is being said and we have to repeat things ... even if he does not contribute in terms of productivity. Being part of the EOC opens up our horizons — it is not that he has to produce a certain amount otherwise he will be fired. Given that we are a small business, we could just as well leave him at home. But we try to see him new each day and to

give him a chance, even if intellectually he does not seem to have much to offer. For us, however, he is a brother.

They regarded the EOC business as a place where those with difficulties could be accepted and reintegrated into the work environment as a service to the poor. Many of the directors expressed an interest in promoting this kind of initiative in the future. The issue of recruitment, however, also presented some difficulties. After the EOC started, one business in Sao Paulo had become more vexed by the question of when to take on new workers and when to fire them:

There are many things that are difficult to do in a turbulent market. People are employed when there is work and then fired when there is not. If I have work I will take you on and when there is no more work you are fired. This has always been our big dilemma: how to have as big a work-force as possible … Today we are trying as best we can, but there are times when it is necessary to make difficult decisions because the market is not absorbing. But we try our best so that this decision is taken as little as possible, so that it has as little impact on the group as possible. Otherwise it would not be possible to have the chance to train people.

In other businesses in our sector it is not like this — people are hired and fired. I think that the big difference with us lies in this. We only do this as a last resort. This brings many problems in the economic sense, in keeping the business alive. I think that sometimes we can exaggerate in this respect, in our involvement with the people. But we are trying to find a balance — in a way that we will not harm the business and at the same time not harm this long-term plan of work that we have.

In this example, the prospect of laying off employees, perhaps because of a downturn in the market, created difficulties. The sense of closeness to the workers and the strong interpersonal relationships with them made it difficult to make decisions based on financial reasoning alone. The result was that the company often stretched itself to the limits, trying to find work for the employees when there was none, so as to avoid the prospect of laying off staff. In some cases, the directors went without their own salaries for several months to provide the liquidity to pay wages. This gave them time to find creative and imaginative solutions within the business environment so as to keep people at work.

This kind of dilemma, however, also points to something profound about the extension of the Focolare spirituality into the realm of business. Relationships within the family or community can have a degree of resilience based on blood relations or on a common link to a particular group, but the relationships between employees and managers are subject to the pressures of the economic indices that legitimize business as a productive enterprise. In many cases, such indices are governed by factors over which the company itself has little or no control. In some cases, there is no option but to reduce numbers in the work-force, despite the desire to find a way out which does not hurt anyone. This has been one of the most difficult lessons of the EOC in its early years.

Participative Management

The third change that resulted from the EOC affected management structure. Many of the companies in this study had fewer than 20 employees, a factor that made participation in decision making relatively straightforward. Some of the larger businesses in Milan and Sao Paulo said that they had introduced formal schemes aimed at involving workers in decision making within the business. These schemes included workers' councils and formal structures within the business to facilitate greater communication between different levels of responsibility. These changes were instituted to foster a widespread sense of participation within the company.

The main aspects included in this different approach to management included access to training, organization of working hours, and general daily working conditions. As a result of this approach, several Brazilian businesses initiated training courses over and above professional training already in place within the businesses. A Brazilian factory producing ecological cleaning products, for example, introduced a "personal career plan" for each employee. Each was encouraged to come up with a personal development plan to be discussed with the managing director and implemented together:

> This year we began to work out a career plan, investment in training ... but this is still in the early stages. We want to make them employable in the market. We do not want to make them people who can only work within this business, but to make them ready so that if there were no more work here for them or

they felt they should go for a new job, they would be able to go into the market. We want to prepare them for the market.

An interesting feature of this plan is the awareness that within the current market an employee will probably not stay with the company for life. As a result, the firm considered it important for the employee to gain as wide a skill base as possible to be competitive in the market, a way for the company to offer its sector fully trained employees.

Co-operation between employers and employees also brought about the possibility of introducing a rotation within the company so that no one ended up with the "worst" job for any length of time. Employees retained their own specialization in a particular field, but everyone — even the directors of the company — had to take responsibility for a menial task as part of their job. These tasks included administration, answering phones, welcoming guests to the firm, preparing the refreshments and cleaning the office. In Latin America, where the divide between white and blue collared workers is still generally wide, creating the opportunity for employees to carry out a range of blue and white collared tasks could be seen as an important perk. Rotating these "menial" tasks increased morale among the employees.

Action to Promote Community Spirit

The final noteworthy internal change was direct action to increase the community spirit within the business. In a high proportion of the businesses in Italy and Brazil (50 per cent and 67 per cent respectively) management had made changes in order to improve the community spirit. Although levels of pay and changes to management were regarded as fundamental to improving the quality of relationships in the business, many directors decided to take this one step further. They set up initiatives specifically geared toward increasing the quality of social interaction among employees. These initiatives included giving grants to be used for social purposes such as organizing a party for employees' children. Others included the introduction of subsidized shared meals.

One important project, introduced independently in a number of firms, was the creation of special hardship funds for employees. Instituting such funds involved management becoming much more intimately involved in the personal lives and circumstances of their employees and so building up trust and confidence. In this way, employees could feel free to share their personal needs and the needs of their families with the management. Particularly in Brazil, such openness resulted in extra grants to employees over and above their wages for food and basic improvements to their homes.

One Brazilian company introduced a micro-credit scheme to support employee welfare. Through this scheme, which was run and managed by employees, anyone could receive a low cost loan for a variety of purposes. Some had used this extra finance to improve their homes, others to pay for their children's education.

CHANGES IN EXTERNAL RELATIONS

Relationship with Clients/Suppliers

These changes within businesses were also mirrored in the changing relationship with their clients. Participation in the EOC gave businesses an added sense of responsibility toward those they were trying to serve. Over half reported significant changes in the relationship with their clients and/or suppliers. The business was not longer considered only an isolated entity concerned solely with profit. Although survival was still vital, the nature of the relationship with those whom the business served went beyond mere economics. Through the businesses' clients and suppliers, the network of "Trinitarian relationships" extended into the wider economy with which they were engaged.

In practical terms, the new concern for clients and suppliers entailed fulfilling their needs and requests by offering the best possible service or product. Such a proposal not only fulfilled the EOC ideal of serving the other, it also made the firms more economically competitive, reflected in higher quality of service and better value for the price. This change was more prevalent among the Brazilian businesses, although one Milanese business reported a change:

> This means taking care of the product that is produced, making sure that the detail in it is to a high standard … It is not something that can be churned out because it will make us money, but it is something that is going to another person. It is also important for it to be a source of earnings for the person who makes it, but it has to be made with this care because what matters are people. It is a different concept.

This emphasis on service to a person and not a "client" or "consumer" highlights how the EOC companies regarded those outside the company itself as being part, in some way, of their overall objectives. They regarded them as people with whom they had a relationship. It is this sense of relationship, not the desire to make a profit, which motivates EOC ventures. In their eyes, those with whom they are doing business are, in effect, enlisted in the EOC networks, though such participation does not take the express form of some kind of "covenant." As one of the other directors said:

> This idea of giving the best quality service to everyone is not something which is a formality on paper — it is in our mission statement. We wrote that we want to involve everyone — the suppliers and the clients. It is not just that they supply ... they provide the raw materials that are part of a process. So every time that I manage to involve them in this, they too are part of it. We try to do this through the way we act, the way we are.
>
> Behind the functioning of that machine there is something very special that is not just the price or the quality or service — but that there is something behind it that for us is the EOC. He does not know this but one day he will know.

The EOC networks, therefore, are founded on this common agreement that economic commitments and relationships are secondary to one human being who is in a relationship with another. This relationship, if based on the Trinitarian perspective, imbues the relationship with love for the other, and therefore, the desire to serve him or her in the best way possible. Even if geographical distance or the complex chains of manufacture prevent direct contact with the consumer, this relationship can be expressed through the quality of the product or the perfection of the service. In the case of *Ecoar*, which produced cleaning solutions, this relationship was expressed in their desire to produce high quality products that would not harm the people who used them nor the environment:

> The difference lies first of all in the quality of the products. You could say that there are two kinds of clients: there are the final consumers, the ones that consume. We do not have a direct relationship with them — the relationship is through the product, the quality of the product, which we try to ... The only relationship that we have with the client is through the quality of the product and it is through it that they will feel all our love. The other clients

are the networks of supermarkets that buy the products from us … Each day is a challenge with the clients when you decide to put the human person at the center. Before being clients, they are human beings.

Such an approach, however, often means that EOC ventures have to specialize in sectors that place a premium on quality products or services. Giving their "all" to every customer often requires time-consuming and costly attention to detail. In the case of the Brazilian clothes factory, this meant opting out of the general clothing market and finding a niche in the quality clothing market:

Here we try to show our clients the value of the work that we are doing. So in the first place, our clothes have to be of high quality and at the right price. So the price of our clothes is not the "popular" price like those that arrive in containers from Asia and flood the market with very cheap clothes … We could not compete with this. So we need to find the right clients, who want the kinds of clothes that we present and to show them that the price is such because we work in a certain way — look at the quality of our materials, sewing — we have to show them.

The attention to quality meant that the business was able to resist the sudden opening of the Brazilian market to cheap Asian imports in the mid-1990s. The business, however, had other supports, such as dependence on the "internal" Focolare markets that will be discussed in the next chapter.

For other businesses, the EOC meant altering how clients were treated when they came into contact with the business. The desire to build relationships with those who came into contact with the business meant that virtues like politeness, for example, became more important:

With the clients there is always this relationship based on being brothers. I always say to my children that on the phone, what is needed is politeness. You can't do things just because you're asked to do this or that. You always have to be polite because on the other end of the phone there is a neighbor who has to be loved.

The EOC also led some companies to undertake market research to see exactly what their customers wanted — a decision that made good business sense. This was the case with *Zac*, a bookshop in

Piracicaba, which saw a large increase in its gross revenues through changes brought about by the EOC:

> Due to the EOC and the situation in the country we are publicizing our shop much more. Our shop is always busy now. We started marketing research in the bookshop — people were invited to leave their impressions about the shop and we responded to their suggestions: put in new lighting, armchairs, water, electric fans, name tags for the employees — to facilitate a relationship with the customers. We also reached an agreement with the restaurant across the road so that our customers can leave their cars there. There is another bookshop in the town that launched an advertisement saying that it is easier to park your car there. So instead of launching publicity against them, we reached an agreement with the restaurant. We also asked customers to comment on the shop: they all commented that the employees had an "interior peace," they were always happy and ready to help. People come here because they feel good — they feel that the place is different.

Attitudes to Competition

One of the most interesting areas of the EOC is the relationship that the businesses aim to establish with their competitors. Building "Trinitarian relationships" between employees within the business is one thing, but it is difficult to see how such relationships can be applied to competitors. Business literature regards the relationship with competitors either as a matter of mutual warfare or in "win-win" theories a case of mutual advantage through cooperation. Adam Smith, however, would hold such cooperation suspect, since a high level of collaboration between businesses would inevitably lead to monopolies and oligarchies, resulting in a worse deal for the consumer. This negative attitude toward business collaboration has resulted in the widespread implementation of national and international "anti-trust" laws to protect consumer rights.[1] Such legislation governs the agreements and relationships in which companies can engage, ranging from price fixing to codes of ethical practice. Any change in relationships with competitors and potential inter-firm collaboration between EOC companies, therefore, has to be regarded in view of this legal framework.

Over half of the businesses said that the EOC had changed the relationship with their competitors. In most cases, the aim was to create an open relationship in which competition did not degenerate into bad feelings. As in other aspects of the EOC, the "social" dimension of the relationship was stressed over and above the economic function. In some instances establishing such relationships was difficult, especially in economic sectors with cut-throat competition and high levels of mistrust. One example of this is a medical supply business in Brazil, whose director illustrated how friendly relations with competitors can easily be misunderstood:

> When a business starts out in the market, it can be treated aggressively by other businesses. They try to destroy the reputation of the business — we have experienced this first hand. But these problems are overcome quickly, because if you have accomplished a job well and work legally, these things crumble and what is true remains. Many other businesses have tried to copy our way of working. Our competitors are shocked by the fact that we are happy to show them how we work — and they try to do the same. They don't manage to copy our way of working, however, because it is not a formula that says "do this" "do that"... it is a way of being, a way of acting.
>
> Last year there was a competitor who tried to attack us on every corner ... creating a very difficult situation for our business. At a certain point, the law in Brazil changed and it was a very important change. In order to help this other business, we faxed this news to them. The business owner was so struck by our gesture that he not only wanted to re-establish his friendship with us, but he offered to help us in areas that we find difficult. It was through him that we had the idea of getting in a consultancy — the best decision that we ever made. The consultant was so impressed by how we run our business that he goes out of his way to help us in whatever way he can. This all started through responding to the aggression of our competitors with a different attitude.

In some instances, the decision to approach competitors has led to improved relations that benefit both sides and even generate collaboration on certain projects. This is the case with a metal engineering business in Milan. Rapid technological change and high capital investment costs led them to adopt a flexible specialization approach. Through an open attitude with their competitors, they established a consortium of local businesses to share technology and take on larger projects as a group:

With our competitors we are more and more in touch. In fact, we formed a consortium of mould builders in our sector. There was a time when the companies would not even let the others on their premises. Now we receive orders together and two or three companies may be working on the same product. This has made us see that collaboration is the most intelligent solution. We get on very well. There are 15 businesses and we have held fairs together and studied the products together. We build the same product in two or three businesses; then we put it together but the aim is always that of pleasing the client because they are the ones who set the deadlines. They ask us to do something and the part has to be ready straightaway. Also in the investments that we make — we are constantly specializing in our sector so it would be intelligent to use the other's machinery, which are more adapted to the work at hand.

Such agreements are based on streamlining practice within the same spheres of industry but, as outlined above, are subject to EC anti-trust laws. In this case, the nature of the collaboration did not contravene this legislation since there was no evidence that forming such an agreement was creating a monopoly that harmed the consumer. Rather, it enabled the individual firms to specialize in specific areas so as to complement the work of the other businesses. After starting a firm for the EOC, one entrepreneur in Milan faced the difficult decision of having to change the direction of his business or entering into direct competition with his brother, the owner of the company he had left:

> At the end of '95 we were faced with a difficult choice: either we closed, or we entered into direct competition with them. There were no other alternatives … we had left their business and we had a perfect knowledge of all their products. It meant entering into direct confrontation. Instead, we have tried to offer alternatives to them and not competition — it is something completely different — I am proposing something completely different. Clients can choose one or the other freely. Nevertheless, we still are in direct competition on some fronts and this has created problems … Our ex-business had not understood why we are in competition with them.

The decision to start an EOC business, therefore, produced difficult relationships within their family due to the directors' insider knowledge. The situation was clearly damaging the relationship between the business and the family, as well as creating stress within the business itself. It called into question the possibility of the EOC engaging in relationships that are both competitive and "Trinitarian." Although this is possible to some extent in certain circumstances, in this case, the decision to participate in the EOC produced a conflict of interests detrimental to the business and to the families involved.

Environmental Considerations

In particular, in industries where there was a risk of pollution from the extraction of raw materials or toxic waste, EOC ventures put pressure on existing suppliers or switched to suppliers who were known to use technology that minimized environmental impact:

> Our suppliers have changed substantially over the past few years. In the past we had to seek out suppliers. Now the market has changed and they need to sell. They know that these days, many businesses have financial problems … People are scared to buy. So the relationship with them is good. On the other hand, this relationship has become more demanding. If I am more demanding on myself, because of all the aims that are behind my work, I transmit this to everyone and they too become more demanding. For example, I had to buy raw materials and I knew that this process created environmental problems. For me, personally, it is not a problem. But since I have a different mentality, I think about how this problem will affect someone else. So I understand that I cannot do this. So we have to seek out other suppliers who are developing technologies which will not create environmental problems in the future.

Business directors in Brazil shared a heightened sense of responsibility toward environmental concerns. In the industrial park near Araceli where seven businesses were established, one of the prime concerns was to create an *ecologically sustainable* facility. Thus, much effort was made to construct buildings that economized on energy, to plant trees, and above all, to recycle waste from the various factories. *Ecoar*, for example, invested in water recycling and purification technology that minimized its environmental impact. In the region of Sao Paulo environmental concerns are paramount because of the obvious consequences of years of neglect. The Tiete River, which runs through Sao Paulo State, is so polluted with industrial effluent that it resembles tar rather than water and has a layer of foam up to a meter thick. Atmospheric pollution casts thick yellow smog over the city.

Environmental concerns did not feature as highly in the discussions with directors in the Milan region. In the case of the faucet factory, a water purification installation similar to that of *Ecoar* had recently been installed, reducing the level of heavy metals in its discharge. This was done because of its affiliation with EOC, but even more so because in the Milan region, European legislation regarding levels of effluent has brought about more stringent environmental monitoring and enforcement. Since such measures were assumed to be normal business practice, they cannot be attributed directly to the EOC.

Legal Considerations

One difficulty that many businesses have had to face is their relationship with the tax authorities. In the two countries where the bulk of this research was conducted, Italy and Brazil, this issue was pertinent.[2] Both countries have increased taxation on small and medium-sized businesses in recent years, and have attempted to reform their tax systems. The directors interviewed also regarded this as a difficulty that could impede the development of the EOC: "In general in Italy, pressure from taxation is very high and this puts our business and many other businesses at risk. Bear this in mind ..." Likewise, in Brazil, the directors regarded taxation as a major problem:

> The biggest problem is the rate of taxes in place in the country. We still suffer a lot due to this need to keep the country stabilized and its economic plan working, the government has used the weapon of tax increases ... As a result, all of the businesses that require capital investment have suffered. From an economic point of view this has been the biggest problem.

Given that EOC ventures are donating a percentage of their profits to social causes, one would imagine that they place less importance on taxation. The percentage of the profits they give to the Focolare already operates as a kind of "Focolare tax." It would also be rational to assume that, given the strength of the Focolare's message and its all-embracing nature, the legitimacy of legal authorities to constrain business practices would be called into question. One has to consider whether the EOC ventures see themselves as above or beyond the law.

It is significant, therefore, that 59 per cent of those interviewed reported a change in their attitude toward legal authorities, and in particular toward taxation, through their participation in the EOC. One of the biggest changes related to the difficult issue of tax evasion, which the directors perceived as prevalent in Milan and Sao Paulo. Businesses frequently avoid taxes in various ways, such as by not providing receipts for purchases or by marking down the receipts: "Normally it is like this: when they come to pay, they have to be given a receipt. In order to survive under the current taxation regime, they give receipts for a lesser amount, or they do not give them at all." In deciding to participate in the EOC, the businesses felt obliged to put their finances in order and to pay the required taxes.

Some derived the motivation for this sense of duty toward the state from the Bible — "Give to the emperor the things that are the emperor's" (Mk 12:17). "Our objective is clear: we try to obey the gospel. It says — give to Caesar what belongs to Caesar." They regarded this citation in the Gospel of Mark as moral authority for paying taxes and legitimizing the role of the state as an agent of distributive justice. Other directors, however, did not express this sense of obligation to pay taxes in such a biblical sense. They found motivation for paying taxes in terms of social justice among the people, near and far, who had a claim to the profits of the business — workers, shareholders, local community, those in need. They felt that it was not fair to give profits to the poor of another country at the expense of other factors, including duties to the state and their own population. Both of these groups of directors, nonetheless, regarded the EOC as something extra, on top of the normal taxation that all of the businesses are legally bound to pay. As a result, 59 per cent of the businesses said that they were paying more formal taxes now as a direct result of the EOC.

Some of the businesses that cited taxation as a major issue also said that they had pursued a variety of legal measures in order to mini-mize their level of taxation. They regarded their donations directly to the EOC as a particular form of taxation and preferred to maximize these, rather than taxes to the state, since with EOC donations they had more say over how their money was used. Businesses employed a variety of measures to minimize their taxes. Some, for example, had managed to lessen their burden by declaring their contribution to the EOC as a charitable donation.[3] Others found ways of lessening the rates for which they were eligible by moving their head office address to a region with a lower level of taxation:

There are inhumane taxes, they are oppressive. We are trying to look for legal ways of avoiding having to pay. I'll give you an example. We have opened a subsidiary company of this business in Vargem Grande Paulista since there the taxes are cheaper. This is a legal way of getting out of this situation. It is an alternative because this situation is very oppressive. There is pressure from the taxes and sometimes we do not manage to pay our taxes. There are times when I just can't manage it — so we declare that we cannot pay.

The directors in both Italy and Brazil saw levels of taxation as an injustice that small businesses must face because they are competing with large multinational corporations that can avoid taxation through manipulation of their financial assets between different countries' tax regimes. Because small businesses are generally situated in one country by virtue of their size, they have only limited possibilities for transferring funds to minimize taxation. Small businesses, in the opinion of one director in Milan, have to learn to use the same legal loopholes as do the multinationals, otherwise they will not survive:

Our business has developed from the moment that it decided to make out receipts for everything and to pay taxes, within legal limits, not paying what I do not have to. I don't say that I want to pay everything. I use the means that are available to reduce taxes. Above all, here in Italy, we are great at creating laws for the big groups so that they do not have to ever pay taxes. Now I try to use the laws that are made for the big groups also for myself … Everyone should have the same conditions.

Although this director did not specifically state the "loopholes" to which he was referring, the international scope of the EOC and the closer business contacts it could engender may offer some means of overcoming this injustice. All of the directors, despite the difficulties that this approach brought, still underlined "transparency" as the key word for all transactions with the legal authorities. Moreover, many of them said that the decision to tackle this question had positive medium term benefits for the business, especially in times of crisis. The fact that the business knew exactly where it was in terms of cash flow meant that it was possible to survive difficult times: "We can see that when we do things well in this sense, we have an advantage, if only because things are under control. We knew exactly how much we were spending and how much we were earning. It was a guarantee."

Some of the businesses, however, were experiencing severe difficulties in this respect. One director in Milan said that this aspect was the main transformation that had occurred within his business practice as a consequence of the EOC. He said that he came from a large family in which all of the siblings were involved in some kind of commercial enterprise. Among them it was normal not to give receipts, and to engage in practices that were "not above board." Before participating in the EOC, he had been part of this scene. When he decided to participate in the EOC, he realized that these practices would have to change. The choice was not easy and did not occur overnight. The main difficulty was the fact that the other people in his business circle — namely, his family — could not understand the stance that he was taking, especially because that the chances of getting caught were virtually zero. It provoked an angry response from his family since his attempts to do things differently not only meant that he lost many orders, but that their actions would also be exposed. Nevertheless, without wishing to cast judgment on his brothers, he affirmed that he made the right choice, as it has given him a clear conscience:

> There are 11 of us but commerce was always carried out in a certain way ... many of them still carry it out in this way because that is the way it is. It is not all above board, with receipts. This was the change in mentality that took place with this ideal: we try to make the business conform to the law. This business pre-existed the EOC in 1991. When Chiara launched the EOC, we tried to make everything above board. It was difficult and we are still living with the consequences. In these moments of crisis we feel it because we could do a lot more work but it does not respect the taxes that exist which are high, it is true, but ... Others said that when we made this choice we would have to close, but on the contrary, it has increased.
>
> We have tried to do everything possible to make up for the orders that we have lost as a result of this. If someone comes to buy something, it costs 1000 plus 200. If you buy it without a receipt it costs only 1000. So you can see that it is 200 out of 1000 lire but 20,000 out of 200,000 and so on. If you do not make receipts for things then you do not have the proof and that item is not taxed. If it is not written down it is not taxed.

So we could say that we have suffered a lot about this choice that we have made. But now that I have made it I am not going back. Apart from the difficulties that it brings, inside it gives you peace. I don't know if you understand. It is a big effort, but inside you feel you are doing right. It is not that you feel you are better than the others but let's say that I am doing my part … Before I was living a different kind of life and trying to evade the tax man was normal for me. There was this change in mentality.

In this case, the problem arose because the business had existed previously to the EOC and this meant changing practices. The director was caught up in a business culture that saw evasion as normal. It highlights the ethical dilemmas that can arise when trying to foster relationships based on solidarity. In this case, the principles of honesty and legality conflicted with the desire to remain united with the family. The decision to endorse these principles, while strengthening the EOC, paradoxically created conflict within the family itself.

Businesses founded as a result of the EOC have had the opportunity to start out with a clean slate and to govern themselves by certain principles. These new businesses, however, have faced similar problems to those described above:

> It seems like we are always being taken advantage of. Nevertheless, we are very calm. We started out with the idea that we wanted to respect the fiscal laws … There have been opportunities and people advise you to evade taxes, but our experience so far has shown us that this is not productive … We have never … how do I put it … done other things which are done in protest, like not giving receipts or giving incomplete ones.

Thus new businesses come up against advice, often from consultants, that runs contrary to their mentality. The fact that they can see other businesses following such advice has led some of them to question the long-term survivability of EOC ventures. One director, although feeling obliged to pay his taxes as an EOC business, had doubts whether this was the best course of action:

> In some ways the EOC gave us the impetus to do things according to the law, and we did it this way and still do, but these enormous taxes are penalizing us today — in fact today we are trying to put off paying them till later on because we lack liquidity. So, unfortunately, this principle of honesty regarding taxation, which is one of the principles of the EOC, and it is right, but in the actual

reality of our country, it may be better perhaps to rebel against the taxes rather than give money which is pointless. Or perhaps the money could be given in other ways. But this is the historic moment we are living in and we have to respect it.

His desire to "rebel against the taxes rather than give money which is pointless" in many ways is symptomatic of the institutionalized corruption endemic within the Italian political system of the 1990s. The uncovering of "tangentopoli,"[4] which exposed a web of corruption from the highest political levels right down through every level of the civil service, led to a profound crisis in the political system and public disillusionment (Baldassarri & Modigliani, 1995). Given this lack of trust in the state and the pressure to comply with tax evasion, some of the directors did admit that they had resorted to subterfuge so as to save the business. This left them with a deep sense of regret:

> Our intentions have changed a lot in this respect. Now that we have our own business, we can decide what happens ... This "bad habit" [tax evasion] still persists and since I am in control I find myself doing things that go against this total transparency ... We find ourselves reaching compromises with clients and suppliers in order to win a particular order.

In the face of the constant temptation to give in to evasion, it is often the fact of the business being recognized as part of the EOC and therefore having the good reputation of other businesses in the Movement to think about that stops them from giving in. As will be discussed in the next chapter, the EOC offers business directors the support of a like-minded community, but it could also be said that it also puts pressure on them to abide by certain rules even if they feel they could find more expedient ways of achieving their own aims.

These interviews reveal that the relationship between the legal authorities and the EOC ventures is a combination of moral duty, ideological commitment and commitment to maintain the reputation of the other EOC ventures. The directors expressed a firm intention to pay taxes where they were due, but did not regard this as the main distributive function of the business. They recognized that the function of the state in redistribution was limited (and often flawed) and, in a certain sense, this meant that they felt unable to abdicate responsibility for "caring" to the state. Although the state had a part to play, they felt that they had a right and a responsibility to engage directly in the distributive process themselves through the various changes within the business and through sharing their profits.

This question of the spatial relationship between taxation and other forms of "giving" that bypass the state[5] is highlighted through the international nature of the Focolare. The EOC directors regarded taxation as "limited," giving them a sense of responsibility for distribution as well as production. From the Focolare perspective "welfare" is about "attending to the needs of others" and is bound up in the subjective relationship of "caring" implicit in the Trinitarian perspective. In this respect, the state cannot (and in their view should not) be regarded as the sole or main provider of care. Attending to the needs of others is regarded as a responsibility for all and the state has a subsidiary role to play in distributing this care. This position *vis-à-vis* the state might seem to line up the Focolare/EOC with more libertarian, right-wing views (as a final safety net, with most social roles being performed by responsible citizens) and against more traditional, left-wing views (as the organ for collective redistribution). In effect, the Focolare position is neither libertarian nor socialist (though interestingly the Focolare is sometimes placed into *both* these categories), but rather draws on the ideas of a "tripartite" system and "subsidiarity" within Catholic social teaching (John Paul II, 1991).

These ideas emphasize the balance of the state's as well as the individual's responsibility to care for others, but favor the role of the individual in best attending to the needs of others since ideally "needs are best understood and satisfied by people who are closest to them and who act as neighbors to them" (*Ibid* 33). Such a position is tenable only within an open market economic system since it depends upon private ownership (you can only share something if it is yours to give in the first place) and free enterprise. This ideal, however, has to be seen within the underlying concepts of freedom within Christian thinking (freedom to do what one ought, freedom of self-control) as opposed to the libertarian notion of freedom as license (letting go, doing whatever one wants). Within the Catholic tradition, freedom is regarded as the first step in creating relationships built on solidarity (Novak, 1993).

Even where the state assumes responsibility for distributing care, the EOC ethos underlines the fact that care is always administered by people in relationship with others — and not by the state. The desire to attend to the needs of the Focolare community in particular through the EOC highlights the limitations of taxation since it is administered through the government, above all through the welfare system. Nations allocate a small percentage of their budget to international concerns, but spend most of their revenue at home, on behalf of the national community that pays taxes. The Focolare, however, is an international organization and one of the main aims of the EOC is to share wealth on an international scale. A heightened sense of belonging to a "global community" — not just a local one — spurs businesses to assume responsibility to care for it by sharing their profits.

The issue of legality, however, extends beyond taxation. EOC ventures are bound by the laws of their respective countries that cover the various dimensions of employment, including health, safety, and environmental protection. None of the firms saw their decision to become EOC ventures as somehow raising them "above" the law, since they had the greater aim of being part of this project. On the contrary, it gave them a heightened sense of responsibility toward fulfilling their legal obligations as a first step toward other aims. Nevertheless, many stressed that a legalistic mentality is not enough in order to bring about change. What is needed is a "moral conscience" in which legality is a foundation for changes in the relationships that make up the business. One director concisely summed up her opinion on this issue:

> The relationship is one of doing things according to the law — paying our taxes ... Nowadays, great importance is given to the legal situation since there is a crisis of values and identity in the world. I can see that what really matters is that you have a moral conscience. You need a Christian conscience, besides having a legal one. Many things that are legal today, are not moral — like abortion and a whole series of things. But we cannot be extremists on certain issues. We need to use our common sense to see what is best in order to carry ahead the project because there are many laws that harm business. So we have to work within the law and pay all the taxes, but we should not become preoccupied with the legal dimension. We have to look at the ethical, moral, Christian dimension. I think that this is what the EOC is doing in some respects but acting in accordance with the taxes.

THE STRUCTURE OF CORPORATE OWNERSHIP

The past fifty years have seen a dramatic shift in the structure of corporate ownership, especially the separation of ownership from direct management control and the centralization of ownership through takeovers and mergers. The constant need to raise new funds has blurred questions of ownership and control, allowing profitability and efficiency to become the main governing principles of corporate strategy. Within the EOC, most businesses are privately owned by individuals, families or groups of less than ten people (Delia, 2000). None have yet considered public stock offerings. Of the 22 businesses in this study, only one, *Espri*, has widespread shareholders. Ownership of this company, because it raises interesting questions regarding the local-global networks of the Focolare and the EOC ventures, will be discussed in the next chapter. The rest of the EOC ventures in this study were either completely owned by the managing directors of the companies, or partly owned by the directors or close colleagues of the directors who shared the desire to participate in the EOC.

This trend of owner-directorship within the EOC marks a significant reversal from the current well-documented trend toward the disembedding of corporate ownership through which virtual and often physical space separates managers and owners. Within the EOC, re-embedding "ownership" within the location of the firm itself strengthens the trend toward localization of decision making, since the business directors do not have to answer to remote shareholders who expect dividends. To some extent, the pressure for greater efficiency that anonymous shareholders would exert on the business is replaced by the desire to produce more for the EOC.

Remaking the Role of Shareholders

The interests of shareholders within the EOC ventures, therefore, closely coincide with those of company directors, giving them the ability to make executive decisions on the distribution of company profits. In effect, the profits that are distributed mean that the directors themselves forgo dividends that they could receive and invest these in the EOC. There is no conflict of interest in this respect. The prevalence of the owner-director relationship also enables the directors to keep control of the internal workings of the business, meaning that the quality of the EOC ethos can be upheld at all levels. This desire to retain control of the internal workings and the profits of the company could explain why the EOC has not resulted in more people, such as employees, becoming shareholders. Giving over ownership to a "remote" party, such as in stock offerings, would undermine the security of the EOC, above all in terms of its underlying values.

The question arises, though, concerning the extent to which this limited number of shareholders constrains the development of EOC ventures. Two further questions derive from this: how can EOC ventures generate adequate financial resources without the kind of investment raised by stock offerings? Could the EOC be applied in situations in which management is separated from ownership? These questions will have to be considered as the EOC develops. The growth of ethical investment funds within the stock market could provide one avenue for raising business capital in the future. Future listed EOC companies would take this trend one step further by advocating that shareholders forgo dividends altogether and donate them to the EOC. Another possible solution to these problems could come from the growing networks of EOC ventures and groups across the world. These groups could arguably provide opportunities for "internal" collaboration and partnerships in which investors and managers might be separated, yet still set within a global community of like-minded individuals who share the EOC objectives. The prospect for such a future pattern for development is already visible on a national level in Brazil within *Espri*. Through the Focolare, the EOC could offer the possibility of shareholder ownership to a large network of people who share the principal aim of developing the EOC. It is difficult, however, to see how companies could be restricted to working within networks that could jeopardize their stability and strain their relationships.

TRANSFORMING BUSINESS SPACE

Analyzing the relationships and networks in which EOC ventures find themselves underlines the fact that they share at least two essential goals against which to measure success. The first is that of running the business efficiently in current market conditions so as to produce profits to be shared in common. As with other businesses, the underlying rationale behind this process is instrumental. The business, as a "place," exists to produce surplus value to be shared out for other purposes. In the case of the EOC, this surplus value is divided into the three parts according to the aims of the EOC (one for those in need, one for the spread of the culture of giving, and a third for re-investment). The second aim, however, is that of transforming the production process to bring it into line with the spiritual and social ideals of the Focolare. This is about the creation and maintenance of "Trinitarian relationships" within the business at all levels and in the networks through which the business is operating.

The internal space of the business and attention to the needs of those who form the immediate business community, hence, are continuously balanced against the need to make profits and provide for the wider needs of the EOC. This desire to attend to the needs of and within the business prompts questions about the efficiency of the businesses in generating profits to be shared. The primary objective of EOC ventures has to be that of surviving within the market economy; otherwise there will be no profits to share. One of the main issues that an EOC business must face is the extent to which a philosophy that draws so much on altruistic principles is compatible with profitable business practices. Does "love," in the Focolare understanding of the word, limit efficiency? The evidence presented above shows clearly that the transition of conventional businesses to EOC ventures has incurred a number of costs. These higher costs have inevitably squeezed profits. These are summarized in Table 7.1 below.[6] The EOC has also generated many unforeseen benefits which show that the EOC often makes good business sense. Some of these consequences can be quantified financially, whereas others are more social and relate to the underlying spiritual ethos of the company.

Table 7.1: The Perceived Costs and Benefits of the EOC

Costs incurred from the application of the EOC
Investment in the work-force — training courses, higher wages/bonuses, taking on new recruits
Investment in the environment — technology; pressures on suppliers and clients
Investment in occupational health – work safety
Investment in the local community — voluntary services to local organizations, Focolare community
Investment in "global society" through the distribution of profits to the EOC
Payment of taxes
Loss of orders due to stance against corruption
Benefits from the application of the EOC
Increased productivity through greater team spirit
Increased levels of innovation through active participation of all in the business through a shared sense of ownership
Dedication of workers to work extra time to get through difficult times
Loyalty of customers — value the production process and the product
International network of support and contacts through the Focolare — autarkic tendencies, sharing technology
Fiscal transparency enables careful planning during crises
Spiritual motivation to endure extreme hardships rather than see the project fail — belief in providence

Source: Fieldwork in Sao Paulo and Milan, 1997–98

On the one hand, the ethos that the EOC has instilled into the businesses means that greater investment needs to be made within the businesses themselves and certain transactions have to be avoided. This results in the overall costs increasing. On the other hand, the EOC brings about a network of relationships within and without the business that can be relied on, especially in times of crisis, providing a coping mechanism largely absent in conventional capitalist businesses. The quality of the various relationships within the companies and between the businesses can be likened to increasing "social capital" (Coleman, 1988) in which the high levels of trust and co-operation also have a financial benefit. This social capital, however, cannot simply be reduced to "good will" in the case of the EOC. The social capital can also be seen as a network of contacts, of tacit knowledge and moral courage to endure difficulties for the greater good of the EOC.

CONCLUSION

This chapter has examined how the Focolare spirituality has been translated into particular attitudes and practices within EOC ventures. Businesses in Italy and Brazil share strong similarities in directors' attitudes toward aspects such as legality and relationships with employees and with competitors. The overall objective is to improve the quality of the relationships within the business itself as a precondition to sharing profits with the EOC. In a sense, the directors come to regard the business as a "social" place and not simply an "economic" one. This has led to a range of transformations in how the relationships within the business and the variety of relationships associated with the firm as an institution are viewed within capitalist economies.

The picture that emerges, therefore, on the one hand highlights the tensions between the ideals of the Focolare and the perspective of the economy as it functions "on the ground" in Italy and Brazil. In particular, it highlights the way in which the legal system in each country can penalize exactly the kinds of "social" changes that the businesses are seeking to implement. A legal system geared toward enforcing transparent competition and non-discrimination does not encourage reciprocal relationships as they are understood within the EOC. This situation is heightened by a context in which institutionalized corruption and unethical practices are often too entrenched to be challenged. Within such a context, many EOC ventures have had to take a stance against such practices.

On the other hand, the view from within the businesses high-lighted the large overlap between the ethical practices of the EOC and "sound" business practices. The advantages that the directors ascribe to participation in the EOC such as legal tax avoidance, good training, bonuses, staffing policies and loyalty, quality services and reputation, and inter-firm collaboration are all recognized as evidence of good business acumen. Moreover, the decision to give a percentage of profits to "good causes" is already practiced by millions of businesses both individually, or through organizations such as the Rotarians. As an ideal, the EOC is based on the distinctive Focolare economic vision which in practice it shares with other forms of giving already in place within the economy. This overlap could provide possible avenues for the future development of the EOC on a wider scale.

NOTES

[1] Anti-trust legislation has been in place since the Sherman Act of 1890 in the USA and the Clayton Act in 1914 (BOLA Project, 2000). In the case of Italy, the Law no. 287 of 10 October 1990 (Autoritá garante della concorrenza e del mercato, 2000) brought Italy into line with European anti-trust legislation governed by the EU Commission competition directorate (EC Directorate-General for Competition, 2000). In Brazil, competition law is governed by the Ministry of Justice CADE (Ministério da Justiça do Brasil, 2000).

[2] Further information from Brazilian Business Council (2000). Kinzo and Bulmer-Thomas (1995) examine the various attempts of the Brazilian government to reform the country's fiscal system since the introduction of the Real Plan in 1991. For up-to-date information relating to the Italian fiscal situation refer to "Italy" at Price Waterhouse Coopers (2000).

[3] Declaring their contribution to the EOC, which through the Focolare is a charitable institution in both Italy and in Brazil, enabled the businesses to achieve certain tax breaks.

[4] "Tangentopoli," which literally means "bribesville," was the name given to the scandal and the investigations following the collapse of Andreotti's Christian Democratic government in 1991 (Helicon Publishers, 2000).

[5] By this I am referring to the structures of giving in place within corporate philanthropy in the conventional sense (White, 1995) and other forms of NGO activities.

[6] The table shows a summary of all the reported changes and benefits brought about by the EOC. It is not intended as an account of the changes in one particular business, since the simultaneous application of all of these changes would be unsustainable.

8

Making Space for Communion:
Local — Global Networks

INTRODUCTION

EOC ventures are attempting to renew the network of relationships within and surrounding their businesses. Through living
the Focolare spirituality, business directors are able to re-imagine
the place of business, redefining it as a "social" space, as well as
an economic one, in the utilitarian sense. The dominance of the
economic rationale of profitability, however, does not exist only
within individual firms. It is in the "in-between" space that defines
the relationship between firms that the market logic of competition
is arguably most prevalent. The market economy is perceived above
all as a battle for superiority between corporate bodies. The previous
chapter showed that the EOC has begun to involve the network of
relationship between firms at a local level and on a global scale. This
relationship between companies and with other economic institutions creates space within the economy for the development of a new
business mentality in which alternatives to the dominant values are
practiced and pursued. In this chapter, I will examine the local and
global networks that have grown up through the EOC which enable
this new mentality to grow and flourish. Businesses in Milan and
Brazil will serve as examples of regional groups within the context
of the globalized EOC networks.

EMERGING "EOC SPACES"

One of the main features of the EOC in some ways distinguishes
it from other attempts to reform the economy. Local EOC businesses
are linked to others around the world, all attempting to put into practice the same principles.[1] On the one hand this global consciousness
within the EOC gave the directors a profound sense of contributing
to a project that in some way was universal, one that extends far
beyond their own business: "Our experience is not local, it is global."
At the same time, the global nature of the EOC made them realize
that they were one node in a global network of small but significant

161

businesses, giving them many practical opportunities to expand their own enterprises.

Research in the two case study regions reveals two types of relationship between the directors of the EOC ventures. *Support networks* are specifically linked to the creation of spaces where difficulties and needs can be discussed openly. The second might be called "commercial networks." These networks, which are intertwined with the first, provide business directors and other entrepreneurs with the opportunity to meet and establish ties with their peers.[2]

Although both of the case study regions shared many aspects of these networks, the EOC networks in Milan and Sao Paulo have significant differences. The support that EOC ventures provide for each other is essential to the survival of the EOC as a whole, given the difficulties that the businesses face in attempting to put such high principles into practice within the market economy. Two related networks can be distinguished: the informal and the formal. The informal networks consist of voluntary personal contacts — phone calls, visits, letters, — between two or more business directors on a regular basis. The more formal network of contacts consists of a range of regional, national and international meetings organized by the commissions for the EOC, or by EOC associations that the directors had established themselves. These meetings facilitate the strengthening of personal and commercial contacts and allow various dimensions of the EOC to be examined in greater detail.

Support Networks

In Sao Paulo, the EOC businesses met as a regional group once a year at their annual convention in Araceli, which was arranged to coincide with the *Espri* Annual General Meeting. All of the directors interviewed participated in these annual meetings. The national meeting gave the directors the opportunity to grasp the breadth of EOC developments across the country, giving them a shared vision and sense of participation in the project. The directors stressed how the emphasis of these meetings had altered in recent years. The first few national meetings focused on the technical aspects of business — financial difficulties, technological development, marketing. Given the range of businesses within the scope of the project and the various sectors in which they were operating, this approach became difficult. Meetings of this sort would best be organized according to sector groups. This made the organizers — a group of business people with EOC ventures — reflect on the main purpose of the national meetings and come up with a revised program. The revised meeting focused much more on the spiritual dimension of the EOC and the various ways that businesses were trying to apply this vision. Significant examples of success were highlighted and time was left for quiet reflection as well as for dialogue with more experienced business people. This change in the focus of national meetings appears to have had an important impact on the EOC nationally. One of the directors of *Espri* explained how the change took place:

> We meet once a year. There is a national meeting for the EOC, for the business owners of the EOC and this meeting is very important. What we have seen over the years, through the experience that we have gained, is that in the beginning, the business people wanted these meetings to look at technical things — how to manage a business, productivity, or professional skills. We could see that this is something that all business people can find in their own work. There are organizations set up by the government that do this. They provide a professional analysis of the business. What we felt that was missing was the foundation of the EOC, the exchange of experiences, and witnesses about how to live out these things. It took us a few years to realize this because we thought that we had to be more practical and we could see that this was not the way it was. The people who are involved in the EOC — the owners, managers, administration etc. — need this foundation that is based on lived experience. This is something that you can find in these meetings of the EOC that are made up of people from all sectors, experts etc. There is the need for this basis. This is the only place where you will find this. You can't find this outside.

It is interesting how the business directors themselves recognized the particular "gap" that the EOC could fill. It could not offer expertise in a new form of technology or financial management, but it could offer the "foundation" for the EOC based on the "exchange of experiences and witnesses." In other words, these meetings acted as a focal point for learning from other experiences, reinforcing the underlying ethos among all the businesses in Brazil. Emphasizing the importance of these meetings, other directors echoed this desire to exchange experiences on how the EOC could be applied:

> I would say that first of all there is the joy of knowing that this project is leading the way, that there is global interest in the project

and that all over the world there are people who are fighting for this. Then you can see the evolution of the businesses — all of them are growing and the number of workers involved is growing. There are weaknesses here and there, but the great majority are in evolution and growth. Then there is the experience that this gives us because I have the feeling that here in Brazil, because of the government, because of inflation ... When you hear the experiences from other regions you get the feeling that we are much better off and this comforts us and encourages us to go ahead.

The directors in Brazil, moreover, stressed the importance of keeping the "world vision" alive among themselves through these meetings: "It gives you a world vision of the EOC, and it can even open up new horizons." Although the local vision was important to them, they wanted to meet in order to open up their vision to the global — since without this local sense of the global, there would be little prospect for sharing profits beyond their particular local community. The meetings gave them a profound sense of belonging to a global community, even though their own businesses were firmly situated in a local context. This sense of the "global" was offering them a sense of vast opportunity — "leading the way," "new horizons." It gave them courage and enthusiasm to put the spirit of the EOC into practice in their businesses, despite the inevitable difficulties and possible opposition to the idea at a local level.

Despite the fact that the national meetings took place only on an annual basis among the business directors in Sao Paulo, they felt a strong sense of being a close-knit local community. All the directors knew their counterparts at other businesses personally, were aware of the situations within the other EOC ventures (exact function of other businesses, commercial difficulties, personal problems etc.) and felt supported by the others. Informal exchanges of phone calls, letters and private visits created a strong sense of personal ties among the business directors. This exchange was facilitated by the fact that many of the directors are also on the directorate of *Espri*, the company that manages the industrial park near Araceli. They used the monthly *Espri* meetings to keep up with the other people involved in the EOC near Araceli.

Businesses in the Sao Paulo region were spread over a wide geographical area, with clusters within the various cities in the state of Sao Paulo and in particular, a concentration in the area that surrounds the model town of Araceli. The level of personal contacts between the businesses, however, did not appear to be affected by the variation in distances. All of the directors interviewed had close ties with the other businesses, despite the distances between them, perhaps because of their strong desire that the EOC succeed and their awareness that this is possible only by helping one another overcome the tendency of the market to undermine co-operative relationships.

The personal, however, also extended beyond the local area, as many of the directors had close links with business people in other countries, including other Latin American nations and Europe. "Our experience is not a local one; it is a global experience." Many had contacts with people whom they had known through the Focolare Movement but who had only become aware of their business ties through the EOC. This sense of personal ties throughout the world meant that although the directors had a "world vision," it was not something abstract or detached from their personal experience. Brazilian directors realized that they were participating in a global community with counterparts they knew. Many had participated in at least one of the international conferences on the EOC in Rome, funding their participation personally or through help from people in the Focolare Movement. They regarded these meetings above all as an opportunity to assess the situation of the EOC in the whole world and to gain strength from the knowledge that many other people in different countries were working for the same project.

> This international exchange is important since congresses held for different industrial sectors — chemical, industrial, etc. already exist in the world. Very frequently, however, these only concentrate on the technical aspects and you are not able to give everything ... In our meetings, since we have something in common, there is transparency: in terms of technology, they are looking to see who has it and who needs it; there is transparency on the level of relationships — you transmit everything to the person who needs that information. The experience of the business is shared completely. This is different from other conferences. I think that this is important also because it is a witness to a united world. It bears witness to this united world at a time when here in Brazil everyone is talking about globalization. Globalization, globalization ... there is no way back ... and we can see that as EOC business people we are working for another aspect: the globalization of love. I feel that this aspect — there is already the globalization of technology, finance — but we contribute in this

respect through working for the globalization of love. This means disinterested giving, being prepared to also transfer technology, solidarity. The globalization of love, which is translated into solidarity. This is disinterested giving — sharing.

In this answer, the director in some ways focuses in on the specific aim of the EOC in view of the globalization of the free market — "working for the globalization of love." Although such an idea jars with current theories (and sounds rather quaint), he was specific about what he meant by "love." He was not referring to a sentimental feeling of "one world" but a practical commitment to care for those far away — "love — which is translated into solidarity" — through the EOC.

These informal support networks, however, also translated into practical help for other businesses within the EOC at a local scale. For example, more experienced businesses offered advice to newer businesses on various aspects of technology, expertise and adminis-tration. Wherever possible, they would be happy to offer occasional free services in order to enable other companies to grow and de-velop, seeing this as a service of "sharing" within the EOC. This was particularly the case, but not exclusively, where the businesses were within easy geographical reach of each other:

> There are some businesses nearby, and we work together, sharing the responsibility and our talents. We are in contact with other businesses further away in order to help them through sharing our experience, since our business is a bit bigger and has a little more experience. We offer our administrative experience with the other businesses that need it.

This support network proved to be critical in difficult situations that put at risk the values of the EOC or the future of the business itself. Several directors said that they would have had neither the will nor the strength to continue had it not been for the friendship and support of the other businesses. In particular, one director in Sao Paulo had experienced a tough situation in the past year. One of his partners, who was not of the EOC, had been embezzling from the company. This betrayal of trust created a painful situa-tion that could easily have led the company to close and to lay off all the workers. The director said that without the EOC he would most definitely have had to do this. Many other directors cited this particular situation as if it were happening in their own business.

The personal relationships between the directors in Brazil were facilitated by the existence and development of the industrial park at Araceli. As well as providing a commercial focus for the EOC in Brazil, it also offered the possibility to get to know others participating in the project. Sharing in its development also offered encouragement to those who were experiencing difficulties within their own businesses.

The support networks in Brazil differed in many respects from those in the Milan region, although to some degree the businesses there also participated in informal and formal support networks. As in Brazil, their main function was to provide moral support and encouragement in putting the principles of the EOC into practice, especially in difficult times:

> We hold meetings now and again. There have been a few and they help us an awful lot to go ahead when we share our difficulties. We do not feel that we are on our own. I remember that there was a time last year when we were embarking on a project, and therefore had a lot of apprehension, but when we heard that P was going through a difficult time, we felt that we were in it together — one heart and one soul. This still keeps me going.

They used these meetings to share the practical difficulties of trying to apply the EOC ethos, such as improving the relationship with employees and clarifying the legal status of the business. Likewise, participation in the EOC gave the directors a sense of participating in a common project in which the relationships were founded on "communion." These relationships contained a mutual sense of openness and an ability to speak the truth to one another and even to correct each other:

> The other kind of relationships that have come about and are still emerging, are relationships of communion, you could say, where we talk about common problems we face. What I have noticed is that no one really has the solution to all the problems. There will always be problems, but if you sit round a table and are able to talk about your problem and feel that the other understands you, it is very important. Especially if you understand that the other person understands you not just because he is a business person like you, but because we have a common goal — the desire to share our profits with the poor, the preferential option for the poor. So I can speak to you or another EOC business person and even though we may not actually say it, the aim is the same. So it is important to understand that sometimes there are things that you are doing that are not going well. If you speak to someone

about it, they can analyze your business in truth and in freedom, if you share the same feeling.

The relationships between the businesses in Milan had been formalized in a business association for the EOC formed in 1995. One of the founding members explains the origin of this association:

> It came about because we wanted all the money that arrived to be managed transparently and at the same time not to fall into the hands of just one person. Beforehand, there was one person who did everything, but now we have formed this Association for the EOC … All the money that is given is gathered by the Association.

The main function of the Association, therefore, was to provide an intermediary for the collection of profits that were then passed on to the Focolare Movement. The Association, however, also organizes meetings in conjunction with the commission for the EOC in the region. In 1995, for example, it issued a series of guidelines for businesses that wished to participate in the Association, which are outlined in Figure 8.1 below. Prospective participants signed up to this voluntary agreement on the standards of business practice derived from the various aspects of the Focolare spirituality. Its main aspects are based on guidelines subsequently published by the International Bureau of Economy and Work in 1997. The majority of the directors in Milan also participated in the international EOC conferences in Rome. They too regarded them as important in the development of the EOC.

Several of the guidelines refer directly to the internal geographies of the businesses and the way that these ought to reflect the Focolare spirituality. These involved simple advice, like the creation of spaces designed to make the business "welcoming for collaborators so that they feel at home" and more challenging suggestions, like taking into consideration the "physical needs and difficulties of collaborators." The emphasis placed on creating an internal harmony within the business that is "welcoming and serene" in some ways mirrors the tendency in business to emphasize a spiritual dimension. The underlying rationale, however, is not so much to promote productivity as to express the caring relationships that ought to exist between everyone in the business and with the environment. Thus, the guidelines referring to the internal geographies of the businesses relate mostly to aspects of the physical environment that would improve the relationships between various collaborators.

Figure 8.1 Guidelines for Business Practice within EOC Ventures

Economy and Work
Solidarity. Promote various initiatives in favor of those in need (e.g. loans or direct help to employees in need, donations or contributions for social needs; create new jobs; reconcile the various needs of the business, and make provision to donate part of the profits for the EOC project.

Interpersonal relationships
Starting from the assumption that the "person" is at the center and not work, try, among other things, to check that a) the structure of the business favors the human relationships within it; b) meaningful relationships are established with clients, suppliers, or other people connected with the business; c) the way of running the business, inspired by this new culture, leads to questions over the motivation behind the business.

Ethics and Economy
It would be good to look at the effort made in running the business to maintain a correct relationship with institutions (taxation, inspectors, unions), competitors and with employees (fair and adequate pay, etc.)

Health
The physical well-being of collaborators has to be given particular care and attention, not only because it increases production. It would be good to check: in cases where there is a hazardous activity, whether all the norms of occupational health are being respected; if the physical needs and difficulties of collaborators are being considered (for example: good ventilation, lighting, clean work space, comfortable working position without compromising standards, good seating, etc.); whether shifts are arranged in such a way as to allow adequate periods of rest.

Harmony and Environment
A welcoming and serene atmosphere requires an appropriate environment. Check carefully whether: there is space within the business that responds to the practical needs of welcoming people, meeting, and eating; the environment can be adapted in simple ways to make it more welcoming for collaborators so that they feel at home.

Studies and Professional Training
Ensure that initiatives are undertaken to improve and increase the professional skills within the business as a whole and within the individual sectors (production, administration, commerce etc.); participation in training courses and time set aside for refresher courses and study.

Communications
Employee participation in the decision making of the firm, through seeking and listening to their needs and proposals; analyze the initiatives taken within the business so that the sense of collaboration among everyone can grow and people do not feel isolated in their corner of work.

© Published by *Associazione per una Economia di Comunione*, Milan 1995

As this research was being conducted, however, the businesses in Milan were experiencing greater difficulties than their Brazilian counterparts in establishing support networks with others in the region. Although the businesses in Milan met quarterly to discuss how to progress as EOC ventures and had formalized their firms in an association, several expressed a desire to have more time to get to know other owners:

> Here in Piemonte, in Lombardy … we meet regularly, about three or four times a year, so there is a relationship. I see the relationship as very limited so far — it is difficult for us to get to know each other. We see each other, certainly, but I do not know what the other is going through. In my opinion, we need friendship — not friendship in the sense of wanting the other to be my friend, but knowing the other. Just as I cannot get to know the business of my competitors or acquaintances, I find that I do not know the businesses of the EOC, even though I may know the person who owns it for years. For me this is something that needs to be developed more.

Some of the directors put this lack of contact between the businesses down to the simple geography of the region and the location of the businesses in relation to each other. "There are contacts with other businesses. Not with a lot of them because they are spread out over the territory so it becomes a bit difficult." The region of Milan itself had no common focus for the development of the EOC such as the industrial park in Brazil, which acts as a cluster. This focus on a shared project gave the business directors in Brazil a common focus for their enthusiasm for the EOC outside their own business. In Milan, on the other hand, business directors generally met to discuss their internal problems and not the development of a shared project. In some ways this led them to focus on themselves and their particular regional difficulties, rather than looking outwards to the EOC as a shared space in the wider economy.

Commercial Networks

Other levels of networks that have begun to emerge through the EOC include formal business links between the businesses in the form of contracts and transactions. Although the businesses participating in the EOC cross a wide range of commercial sectors, there is some scope for the businesses to form alliances among themselves. Again, in this respect, Italy and Brazil differ markedly, demonstrating a close link between the levels of personal contacts and commercial contacts. This aspect is much more highly developed in Sao Paulo, despite the fact that the businesses there have the same degree of sectoral variation as in Milan.

The patterns of commercial transactions among the businesses participating in this study showed clearly that in Sao Paulo the level of commercial contacts between them is already fairly highly developed. All of the businesses have some commercial contact with other EOC ventures in the region. In particular, those in the cluster near Araceli have strong commercial links among themselves and with other EOC ventures in Brazil.

The *Aurora* school has arranged special health care arrangements with the health clinic Agape. *Comunione*, the accounting office, services *La Tunica*, Agape and *Ecoar*. *La Tunica* provides the uniforms for *Aurora* and Agape. *Ecoar* provided cleaning products for all of the businesses in the industrial park, as well as *Comunione*, *Aurora* and Agape. The management consultancy ESPACO provides services for all of the above companies. The director of *La Tunica* describes the emerging network:

> We have commercial contacts with various businesses nearby. For example, *Comunione* looks after our accounts; we have a contract with Agape for the health care of our employees, there is a reciprocal relationship; the same applies to *Aurora* — we supplied the uniforms right from the beginning; with ESPACO, I have already mentioned this. We have EOC ventures that are also our clients — the one in Brasilia, Perolini; in Rio Grande, there is a another business, which is also one of our clients; and in Belem there is Feito por nos, which is one of our clients. So there is this working relationship, and then there is also a normal relationship. For example, when I have to buy cleaning products, I will always go to buy them in *Ecoar* for *La Tunica*. Then within the industrial park there is a special relationship between the businesses because we are all trying to build this together.

The geographical proximity of the businesses near Araceli provided an opportunity for development in the local area. Moreover, the fact that the businesses were located in the industrial park gave them a sense of importance within the EOC world-wide. People from different countries interested in the EOC decided to invest in them since they were located in the industrial park. There is an interest in its development both from within the Focolare Movement worldwide and from other authorities outside the Focolare. In January 1998, for example, it was visited by Marco Maciel, the vice-president of Brazil, who then participated in a conference on the subject in Brasilia in May 1998. This continuous interest in the development of the industrial park has provided a strong motivation to succeed and to enable the project to grow.

It was thought that the industrial park could provide a prototype of the EOC for the rest of Brazil and for the world, as part of the model towns of the Focolare. Chiara Lubich envisaged that the towns would have an industrial area, demonstrating that the Focolare spirituality was not primarily a means of retreating from the world but a way of transforming it. As a result the shareholding company *Espri* was established to administer the purchase of the land and the installation of the necessary infrastructure. *Espri* plays a central role in this respect. Eight of the directors who had their own EOC companies were also on the managing committee of *Espri*. In this respect, the business directors in Brazil immediately associated the development of the EOC with creating common projects and not simply the development of their own businesses. They offered voluntary services to *Espri*, with a shared commitment to develop the industrial park.

Through the industrial park it has been possible for the directors to embark on joint projects with other Brazilian businesses and investors from other countries. In 1998 there were five businesses fully installed: *Ecoar, La Tunica, Prodiet, Rotogin* and *Uniben*. *Ecoar, La Tunica* and *Prodiet* are fully owned by Brazilian investors, but the other two have emerged through collaboration among EOC business directors on an international level. *Uniben* is a subsidiary of an Italian investment fund that aims to provide capital for the development of EOC ventures. *Rotogin,* a plastics factory, was established through collaboration with a successful French company, also part of the EOC, which donated its technology to its Brazilian counterpart. Future partnerships between international EOC ventures are being actively sought by the businesses in Sao Paulo. Despite the fact that they were spread out in the city of Sao Paulo, EOC ventures were forming closer contacts across the various sectors in which they operated:

> We have commercial contacts with a few businesses here in our zone. For example, there is a business that is linked to ours here that promotes parties and events. So every time that we need to organize a party or a get together with our employees, a lunch,

we get this business to come in. There is another business that has a vehicle, so every time we have to transport a piece or offer this kind of service, I get in touch with this business. So there is already this kind of relationship.

In the above examples from the Sao Paulo region, the localized clusters of businesses are demonstrating a kind of reciprocal relationship toward their EOC counterparts. There is a kind of unwritten agreement by which businesses will be granted contracts and preferred suppliers based on their participation in the EOC rather than the market price per se. In this case, however, the reciprocity between the different people involved is not restricted to the informal economy, but the directors are using their personal contacts to create a degree of leverage that benefits the EOC as a whole. The directors, moreover, regarded development of these kinds of relationships as critical to the development of the EOC as a whole. Substantial evidence indicates that the directors were committing time and resources to developing common projects as a group.

In the Milan region, on the other hand, the level of commercial contacts among the EOC ventures is low. Most of the contacts were with businesses outside the case study group. In most cases, however, the commercial contacts were sporadic. The directors still focused by and large on the development of their own business, in the hope that through this development it would be possible to contribute to the EOC through sharing profits. Integrating their businesses with others in the EOC was not seen as a priority.

One explanation for the lack of integration in Milan could be that the businesses were in different sectors. It is difficult to imagine what commercial relationship a faucet factory could have with a nursery school. The same thing, however, could be said about many of the businesses in Brazil, which are in different sectors but still find some point of commercial contact. Another explanation could be geographical distance. In Brazil, three clusters of businesses and the industrial park in Araceli acted as a catalyst to the development of the EOC. In Milan, there is not the same degree of clustering, and there is no central focus. Geographical distance alone, however, cannot explain the lack of exchange. In Brescia, for example, there are EOC ventures within several miles of each other in relatively compatible sectors — a textile factory, a retail outlet (selling clothes), a woodworking workshop and a factory that produces breadsticks. Despite their proximity and the fact that the directors of the companies knew each other (at least by name), they shared little business.

Another explanation for this reluctance to integrate with other businesses is perhaps the dominance of a more capitalistic, individualistic culture within the business world in Italy than in Brazil. There is not a lack of will or enthusiasm toward the EOC in Milan — both the business directors in Brazil and Italy were enthusiastic. Instead, there was a difference in the way that the directors believed that they could achieve this goal. In Brazil there was more of a sense of getting on together, helping one another's businesses out.

In Milan the dominant idea was that the individual businesses should compete as best they can in the market without getting too involved in the affairs of other EOC ventures. The underlying mentality of the directors in Milan was that their firms could contribute more by being more competitive rather than reaching agreements with other businesses.

This kind of "corporate individualism" could also be seen in the reluctance to share trade secrets with other EOC ventures (and with myself as a researcher). Many of the directors expressed a desire for more open, transparent relationships with their EOC counterparts but regarded this as an extremely difficult task. Part of this reluctance to get involved can be seen as a reaction to the "tangentopoli" mentality that dominated Italian business in the 1990s. Since many wanted to "come clean" through the EOC, they did not wish to be seen as having "special" relationships with any other businesses or people, no matter how worthy the cause. The directors were aware of the possible implications that such relationships could have in relation to the "anti-trust" laws that were hotly debated in Italy in the 1990s.

Understanding how the support networks and the commercial networks inter-link is critical to the development of the EOC, both at a local, regional and international level. It is the intersection of these sets of personal and business relationships, religious beliefs and business practice, public institutions and private associations that makes the EOC a kind of hybrid network that is both religious, social and economic. The links of friendship that the directors have established (to differing degrees in Brazil and Italy), have enabled networks of trust to consolidate at a local and regional level. The exchange of experience and advice on a personal level almost imperceptibly translated into commercial opportunities:

> We share our difficulties and commercial ideas. Perhaps there is one that has material that could be interesting for another,

so they sent a fax to say "Perhaps this could interest you." Or another may know about a fair that one of the others may be interested in so … there is all this exchange, all this help.

This trust is not simply a belief that the others share in the spiritual vision of the Focolare or that they have good intentions. It is based on a sound knowledge of how the others are working in their enterprises as a professional. It requires a working knowledge of the professional capabilities of the others as well as their commitment to the spiritual vision. Through the development of these links of trust there has been a gradual transition to developing business contacts that can benefit both parties. In some ways, the links that are emerging between the businesses, especially in Brazil, resemble the traditional guilds that emerged primarily to create greater collaboration within certain commercial and industrial sectors of the economy. In the case of the EOC the linkages of solidarity between the businesses, which are spread over a broad range of sectors, are interpreted as "communion."

CULTURAL AND ACADEMIC NETWORKS

In addition to the support and commercial networks outlined above, the EOC has now begun to develop its own local and global networks that seek to promote the development of the project. This is done primarily through academic and cultural discussions, generating new spaces for a different discourse on the economy to emerge.

Since the mid-1990s, an important element of the EOC project has been support for academic studies, predominantly master's theses. Over the past 20 years over 200 theses and dissertations on the EOC have been written and defended at universities worldwide. They cover a variety of academic disciplines, from economics, to business studies, psychology, sociology, and theology. Most are available online through a dedicated archive; as a body they provide a rich source of knowledge on the development of the project.[3] In many instances, these studies have led to further academic research on topics related to the EOC, as well as regular conferences, which provide an important point for networking between academics and business people alike, and an important reference point for the EOC as a whole globally.

Another important development in the EOC has been the creation of a global internet site for sharing news, views and events taking place across the world. The website www.edc-online.org provides an important focal point for the project.

One of most sensitive areas of the EOC is the relationship that exists between the businesses and the Focolare Movement itself. This relationship is interesting, above all, because it defines an area where "spiritual authority," which the Focolare represents, and authority that comes from business expertise can be found. It is also interesting because here the real novelty of the EOC emerges. It is sensitive because it contains the greatest scope for serious misunderstandings involving peoples' "spiritual wellbeing" and "material wealth." Without the spiritual vision of the Focolare Movement and the spiritual community that has come about through the Focolare, the EOC would not exist. The desire to apply this spiritual vision in the economy so as to resolve the problem of inequality led to the EOC being formed in the first place. The application of this vision, however, cannot be static: it is a constant process of verification and renewed commitment based on the individual's free choice to put EOC principles into practice. Maintaining strong links between the businesses and spiritual vision of the Focolare therefore is critical for the project's future growth.

Besides providing the spiritual vision behind the EOC, the Focolare Movement acts as a network of potential contacts for sales and publicity. Since its beginning in 1991, the EOC has had a high profile within the Focolare and members of the Movement have been encouraged to participate actively. Since many within the Focolare cannot contribute to the EOC directly through investment or through starting businesses of their own, the next best thing is to support the businesses by buying from them or assisting them in the promotion of their products. The businesses advertise in the various Focolare publications such as the *Città Nuova* magazine in different languages and the *Economia di Comunione* newsletter. Through these magazines and through presentations of the businesses at meetings organized by New Humanity, EOC ventures become "household names" for the Focolare: "When there is a big meeting, for example ... of 12,000 people, all the directors of our business went to share our experience. Personally speaking, it is great, there are no problems." In their "experience" the directors highlight how they are applying the EOC principles. As a result, their business becomes a natural choice for anyone wishing to support the EOC.

This has certainly been the case for many in Brazil. Strong evidence suggests that several of the new businesses have succeeded primarily due to help from people within the Focolare and from the Focolare as a whole. Nevertheless, reliance on the internal Focolare market for both a sales network through franchises and for a large proportion of direct sales cannot be sustained. Sooner or later the businesses have to compete in open markets.

Despite the close relationship in Brazil between the businesses and the Focolare, the directors interviewed had clear ideas about the nature and limitations of the relationship. They highlighted the distinction between the spiritual relationship with other people in the Focolare on a personal level and the institutional business relationship they have with the Movement through the distribution of profits. In their opinion, maintaining this distinction was important, as it enabled the businesses to grow without interference or pressure from the Movement:

> The life of the business is the life of the business. There is no interference on the part of the Focolare in the life of the business. It has its own management that decides on the goals, but what makes it different isn't whether the Focolare is involved or not, but the fact that in general the people who are directing the business are involved in the Focolare Movement. The business, in a juridical sense, is completely separate from the Focolare Movement. The people who are managing the business are involved in the Focolare Movement.
>
> There is always a good relationship. It works like this — at the end of the month, we work out the profits, and the finance sector automatically separates the proportion of the profits that goes to the Focolare Movement. So the relationship with the Movement as a business is more or less a technical one. We also try to remember to send a report about how things are going each month. On the other hand, there is a personal relationship with the Movement — this report that we send. But there is a good relationship.

None of the Brazilian business directors interviewed suggested any difficulties in their relationship with the Focolare. On the contrary, they stressed that their open relationship was positive for their business. The Focolare helped mainly in the form of moral support, which gave many of the business owners a shared sense of ownership and responsibility with the other people in the Focolare. While retaining the full responsibility for running the business, the directors felt that the continuous interest from other people within the Focolare was a strong incentive to develop in accordance with the EOC. Many of the directors had been invited by the Focolare to present the experience of their business at national and international conferences, which enabled other people within the Focolare to be kept informed in the developments within the EOC.

This close relationship was facilitated by the fact that the industrial park of the EOC was located adjacent to the main Focolare center in Brazil. This meant that decisions relating to the location of businesses in the park were taken in conjunction with the leaders of the Focolare in Araceli. It also meant that the Focolare's conference facilities in Araceli became the "natural" venue for any meetings relating to the EOC, from the local ones to major international conferences. Business people expressed no difficulties with this close relationship. Both the Focolare leaders and the business people interviewed expressed mutual trust and admiration in each other, regarding the relationship as a partnership that was beneficial to both.

Nevertheless, the directors of some of the firms did express the desire to form some kind of independent professional association that would allow them to act as a professional body. They regarded this as a priority for the future growth and development of the project:

> This is a dream that we have … to form an association of businesses that can offer this help and can be a bit more close at hand and a bit more secure. It could offer administrative help, financial help, it could help the business to discover its mission, help with the quality control programs … there are a series of things that could be done together but we are not managing to do them today since we are all spread out. Our dream would be to study this idea more and to transform it into something more.

Through an association, they could see that the businesses would have greater scope to exchange ideas and technology on a regular basis, fostering the development of shared projects. This could take place within the security of a formal association with clear guidelines on the EOC.

In Milan region, on the other hand, the reliance on the Focolare as a potential market for products was less apparent. Most of the businesses advertised in the Focolare press, but did not regard this as the main source of clients. Only one was making use of its particular relationship with the Focolare and its location next to the Focolare Center. The shop sold products from EOC ventures all over Italy and abroad, and the main clients were people who came to Focolare meetings in the nearby center. A quarter of the directors in the Milan region had a clear idea of the relationship that existed between the businesses and the Focolare. For them, as with the Brazilian business directors, the distinction between the role of the business and the Movement was clear-cut and they had no difficulty in explaining the relationship: "With the Focolare, each of us has a personal relationship. There is not a relationship with the business as an entity."

For the rest of the directors in Milan the relationship between the businesses and the Focolare was more complicated. Many of them were puzzled at the question of the relationship between the business and the Movement, as they had never thought about it before: "I think that this is a new question ... With the Focolare there is not a relationship. At least that is what I think ... Perhaps we occasionally offer services for the community. If they ask me to lend them the truck, I do it ..." In some cases the spiritual role that the Focolare plays in sustaining the vision beneath the businesses was becoming confused with the strategic planning of the business itself. In a minority of cases, directors expressed confusion over who was providing them with the decision — giving advice in their business context. For most, decisions on the future of the business were still taken in the boardroom with the advice of the other partners. Others sought advice from others who were living out the spirituality of the Focolare. In some instances, as might have been expected, this had led to bad decisions in terms of the financial success of the business or had led to difficulties in the relationships with other people on the board of managers. Many of the business directors in the Milan region recognized the need for reflection on the nature of the relationship that should exist between the businesses and the Focolare, but were unsure how this should proceed.

Conclusion

This chapter has examined in depth the various networks between the EOC ventures and with the Focolare on a local and global scale. What emerges is the variety of experiences in the two benchmark regions of Milan and Sao Paulo and within the regional groups. In Sao Paulo, the formal and informal support networks between the businesses are strong, and this has had important implications for the rapid development of commercial contacts between the businesses. The development of the industrial park near Araceli as a physical space in which these ideas can be applied plays an important role in building up the networks between the businesses and with the Focolare. It also has a "demonstration effect" in encouraging people that it is possible to apply the EOC in the present. In the Milan region, although there is a formal association for the EOC providing guidelines on the implementation of the project, the support networks between the businesses are weaker. As a result, commercial contacts between the businesses are still limited. In both regions, the relationship with the Focolare plays a central role in the development of the EOC both on a spiritual level, as the source of inspiration and motivation, and on a practical level through adapting "ready-made" networks to serve the EOC. For the business directors in Sao Paulo, the nature of this relationship was clear-cut. In Milan, however, there are queries about how this relationship ought to develop, especially with regards to the sharing of profits and transparency.

The development of EOC networks raises the contentious issue of how such special relationships between businesses can be interpreted. The EOC is based on the altruistic spirituality of the Focolare Movement, and participants interpret the relationships between the businesses as "communion." Collaboration is supposed to improve the prospects of the businesses so as to earn more profits, as it has been with guilds and other business associations. The difference that the EOC ventures cite, however, is that their collaboration is based on the choice to share the eventual gains with the poor. In this way a certain amount of "closure" is acceptable in view of the greater good they are seeking. Such relationships, nevertheless, would be interpreted by skeptics such as Adam Smith as an emerging cartel that can only harm the consumer by increasing prices through tacit agreements among the businesses involved. Within the local areas, moreover, such unwritten agreements based on personal relationships could be regarded as unfair, as they prevent the workings of the "free" market, based on the assumption of anonymous actors working independently and making choices on price rather than personal preference. Such relationships are subject to the "anti-trust" laws of the countries in which they are operating, that in effect enforce the perception of the market as an arena which is (and ought to be) governed by individualistic anonymous economic actors.

In recent years, questions such as those discussed in Chapter 1 have fuelled sustained debate between orthodox economics and socioeconomics. The former argue that businesses ought to operate independently in view of respecting the freedom and openness of the market, whereas the latter argue the opposite, that those freedoms are based on the creation of associations and special relationships (Granovetter, 1985; Amin & Thrift, 1995). They argue that markets that operate in perfect anonymity do not exist in practice; rather, institutions make their choices on a number of criteria that include profitability, but also other more culturally defined criteria.

NOTES

[1]Economic reformers such as the Quakers in Britain in the 19th century also displayed the tendency to collaborate, although this was primarily on a local scale and not internationally. The tendency toward insider dealings within the Quaker networks often led to them being branded as "dishonest," illustrating how inter-firm collaboration in view of a greater good can be interpreted as anti-competitive (see Nevaskar, 1971).

[2]There are similarities here with the networks of businesses formed by other humanitarian associations such as the Rotarians or the Lions Clubs. Such organizations were formed principally to humanize the market economy by applying people-oriented principles both within the business and in the way that profits from the businesses were spent. Over the years, however, they have also formed a natural way for likeminded business people to meet and form contacts (Rotary International, 2000).

[3]http://www.edc-online.org/index.php/publications/theses/online.html?lang=en.

9

Rethinking "Rational Economic Man": Lessons from the EOC

INTRODUCTION

This book has presented the findings of detailed ethnographic research within the EOC. This research has involved examining the cultural roots of the Focolare's economic vision, through reference to archives and participant observation. These findings have been presented using original texts and transcripts (as much as this is possible, given the need for translation). In this way, a detailed picture of the various ideas upon which the EOC is based has been presented — in particular, the Focolare spirituality, the culture of giving, market norms and global economic discourses, and local cultural practices. I have shown the various ways in which these interplay, giving rise to various practices within and between the EOC ventures that aim to create spaces of "communion" within the market economy on a local and global scale. At this point the discussion will return to more theoretical questions introduced in the first chapter. This chapter will consider two related questions. First, what light can the EOC cast on the question of "rational economic man" as an underlying assumption of economics? Second, what does the EOC say about the relationship between religious perspectives and economic vision today? How can these relationships be interpreted in a complex global economy?

"RATIONAL ECONOMIC MAN" — A CULTURAL CONSTRUCT

The starting point for this book was the current global crisis facing the world today. The first chapter explored the economic, social, environmental and political dimensions of this crisis. It proposed that although the crisis is complex and has many proximate causes, at its root, it is actually quite simple. This simplicity lies at the root of modern economics, and the philosophical underpinnings of globalization. It is called *Homo Oeconomicus* or "rational economic man," initially a theoretical construct of 18th century economists to explain the workings of the economy. Over time, however, as outlined in the first chapter, this concept has become a normative principle upon which economic theory and practice have come to rest. It influences public policy, business management, as well as popular culture. I argued, however, that it is a deeply flawed principle in a number of ways. First and foremost, it is an incomplete, and hence inaccurate, reflection of actual economic interactions. It fails to explain even the most basic trends within the economy through ignoring some fundamentally important sources of human capital. These sources of relational and social capital are antithetical to "rational economic man." He has no social dimension. Second, the notion fails to take into account the conundrum of trust in the economy. Finally, through defining what is rational or reasonable in a very narrow way as "self-interest," "rational economic man" ignores the many ways in which human beings construct their sense of "rationality." That rationality is not uniform. Self-interest may seem rational behavior in some instances and for some people, but by no means is it the only rational way of acting — even within the economy. Other deep rooted forms of rationality emerge from different social and cultural norms. Among these, religion is an important factor that needs. to be taken into consideration.

This powerful notion has penetrated many different facets of cultural life. Academics have argued that within Western culture, the "economic" sphere is by and large viewed as the "core" and culture, including religious belief, is seen as a kind of "periphery," a veneer that surrounds it. This broad Marxist perspective, according to Crang (1997), contains at least three different related ideas: economic determinism (Harvey, 1989), economic operation (Bourdieu, 1984) and economic colonialism (Habermas, 1988). These three interpretations of the interrelationship between culture and the economy emphasize the way that post-modern culture can be viewed as the "cultural clothing" of late capitalism, reflecting the market laws of supply and demand. Western society, they argue, has become increasingly dominated by economic forces and the cultural sphere is increasingly seen as an autonomous arena, separate from the meaning of life itself (Featherstone, 1995: 15–33). It has been integrated or entangled within the economy, creating a kind of mass culture that at the same time erodes the memories, customs and myths that constituted traditional cultures (Tanner, 1997). There is increasing talk of a "consumer culture" making it very difficult to separate the cultural and the economic. People are seen as cultural consumers who pick and choose their culture, just as they would vegetables or a new car. Particular cultures, moreover, become marketable products based on their aesthetic value (e.g. Scottish men in kilts, whisky drinkers) or even on their underlying ethical principles (e.g. Germans — hard workers; Irish — welcoming, happy people), reinforcing, by default, certain stereotypes about other cultures incompatible with capitalist working structures. At the extreme, the economic rationale of profit is seen to "colonize the life world" (Habermas, 1987), taking over all other dimensions of human life. All spheres of life, including personal relationships, according to this view, are subject to the instrumental logic of the market that dominates the capitalist economy: it is in the "nature" of capitalism to turn everything and everybody into a commodity, reducing culture to a means-end relationship.

This "economic core — cultural periphery" view has to some extent been counterbalanced within economic geography by renewed interest in the various schools of "social and cultural embeddedness" (Granovetter, 1985; Smelser & Swedberg, 1994) that draw on the work of Polanyi (1957) and Weberian traditions within economic sociology. From this perspective it could be argued that economic action can never be separated from the cultural and social practices in which it is taking place. Economic actors are simultaneously part of a network of social relationships which give meaning to their economic action and shape the way that they act within the market (Grabher, 1993; Wuthnow, 1995). Cultural factors such as regional tastes, religious practices, traditional ways of relating to each other, the status of commerce in a society, or even attitudes toward debt all have profound influences on the nature of the "market." Polanyi (1957), in particular, cited three modes of economic integration — reciprocity, market relations and redistribution — that depend on different kinds of relationship. Harvey (1973) used these modes of integration in his analysis of socialist formulations for social justice. He stressed that all three modes of integration can simultaneously be found within different modes of production and are not mutually exclusive (Harvey, 1973: 205-6). The dependence of the economic sphere on reciprocal relationships has led to increased interest on the relationship between economic success and "social" factors such as the ability to build associations and to network (Platteau, 1994, Amin & Thrift, 1994).

Although stressing the inseparability of the social, cultural and the economic, I argued that none of these conceptualizations of the relationship actually challenged the commonsense distinction between the economic and the non-economic, since the "economic" is still equated with the "market" and the "non-economic"; by

CHAPTER 9

default it is seen as "non-market." Yet it is arguably in examining this commonsense distinction between market/non-market or economic/non-economic that the greatest insight into the relationship between the cultural and the economic can be gained. One way of doing this is by examining those spaces that do not fit easily into being "market" or "non-market," since such spaces may be engaged in some kind of socio-economic life founded on reciprocity, thereby challenging such commonsense distinctions.[1] The examples I gave were co-operative activities of LETS schemes (Bowring, 1998; Lee, 1996) and the emergence of Time Dollars initiatives (Boyle, 1998), which offer no financial reward for what is being done. Such initiatives can be explained with conventional economic discourse, but the explanatory power of such discourses is limited in relation to how those engaging in these activities actually view what they are doing (North, 1999). What is interesting is hence to examine the explanation that they themselves give for their actions. I argued, like Peet (1997), that such explanations could uncover different economic rationalities that go beyond the conventional understanding of rational economic action. They would have to make reference to those cultural factors that helped to frame the wider worldview and sense of purpose, taking into account the way such factors as religious beliefs and localized knowledge shape economic thinking and action.

In his discussion of a humanized conception of economic geography Wallace (1978) proposes that different "alternative perspectives" could cast light onto different economic rationalities. Although some would regard his "project" as fatally flawed due to his assertion that a "Christian perspective" is a "non-ideological paradigm in which to ground an authentically human economic geography," I argued in Chapter 1 that his conception of alternative perspectives is still valid. His difficulty was in not recognizing that there could be a plurality of perspectives within economic geography. More recent work on the relationship between the range of Christian worldviews and geography (Aay & Griffioen, 1998) has demonstrated the potential for different worldviews to co-exist and to be mutually enriching. They also highlight the difficulties that emerge when attempting to rewrite geographies along "confessional" lines, since although these different perspectives may represent a non-ideological view of the world for those who share them, for those who do not share the same beliefs they are entirely ideological.

The Economic and the Cultural within the Focolare

It is from this wider perspective on economic rationality that I sought to examine how the interrelationship between the economic and the cultural is understood within the Focolare, and particularly within the EOC ventures and other institutions involved in the EOC. From the documentation examined in Chapters 2 and 3 on the Focolare Movement, it emerged that within the Focolare spirituality, from the beginnings of the Movement, there has been a very strong relationship between the economic and the cultural. The geographies of the beginning of the Movement in Trent in the 1940s showed that one of the main concerns of the group was to solve the social problems of the city through creating a greater equality among those who were part of the emerging community and with those who had been most affected by the war. They emphasized strongly that the new understanding of God's Love that characterized the start of the Focolare led to changes in the way that they perceived and lived out economic and social relationships. Their aim was not simply a renewal of religion, but a "social revolution."

This relationship has remained strong throughout the history of the Focolare up to the present day and is crystallized in the idea of the Trinitarian perspective (Coda, 1998), through which all human relationships and the cosmos can be regarded as the reflection of the image of God, who is one and three: "The life of the Trinitarian God, in other words, appears to be a perennial 'making space' for the other" (Salvati, 1990: 156). This image of the Trinity as the perfect community in which there is unity and diversity is regarded as the model that can both explain and influence all aspects of human existence (Cambón, 1999). This shared belief in the presence of God in human relationships reflects the communion of the Trinity at the heart of the Focolare's economic vision. The Focolare aims, therefore, not so much to carry out particular initiatives or promote particular causes, but to reawaken the reality of the Trinitarian nature of human relationships:

> In the Trinity everything is in common. Therefore, when Christians live out the communion of goods, they are not carrying out "good works" nor is it an "optional extra" onto their life, but they are simply fulfilling what they were made for: living in harmony with the Trinitarian roots of human existence. (Cambón, 1999: 62)

These relationships give meaning to the expansion of networks of "Focolares" or "hearths" across the globe, giving rise to distinctive "Focolare spaces" where the ethos of the Focolare is applied. The Focolare's spaces also represent the "incarnation" of the Focolare ideal. This can be said about the individual spaces, such as the model towns and Focolare centers, which form tangible landscapes "made over" according to the Focolare spirituality. These spaces can act as privileged places in which the ideas of the Focolare are lived out among communities of differing sizes. In the Focolare perspective, these are places where the Trinitarian relationships are already lived out, and therefore sacred spaces. The Focolare, however, is not limited to these tangible landscapes. The same idea could be applied to the various intangible, more elusive networks of the Focolare, and in particular the EOC, which span space and time, forming inter-linking groups of people who seek to live out Trinitarian relationships within the social, political and economic structures in which they live and work.

The EOC, therefore, can be interpreted in a variety of ways. Ley (1974), in his examination of urban conceptions of good and evil, considered the different interpretations that Marxist and Christian geographers could bring to the same subject. The interpretative key arguably says more about the theoretical suppositions of the author than the subject of the research. In the case of the EOC, the Trinitarian perspective is one possible interpretation among many. It is arguably a privileged perspective as it is the one to which the majority of the subjects of the research adhered. Within this perspective, the value of economic action is the extent to which it can be said to reflect Trinitarian relationships. This clearly begs the complex theological question of how to explain the nature of economic action within the Trinity. The Trinity, God, as a transcendent being has no need for economic action, which is a temporal condition of existence on earth. The Trinitarian perspective, therefore, cannot offer direct answers to questions that relate to economic action, as stressed by Cambón (1999: 196). At most it can offer values, priorities and ideal motivations that can underpin economic action.

Within Focolare spirituality, however, there is a very close link between theory and practice, since the Trinitarian perspective also proposes an epistemological framework that has far-reaching implications regarding the possibility of mystical insight into the nature of God and human existence. The central precept of this epistemology is that human beings not only reflect the life of the Trinity from the exterior, but can participate, in a mystical way, in the Love that is the intimate life of the Trinity.[2] The creation of such Trinitarian relationships is both the end point and the point of departure for the Focolare spirituality. This love, however, also has the capacity to generate new insights since participation in the life of God is the spirit of understanding. Trinitarian relationships, therefore, can result in a new way of thinking: "thinking *in* the Trinity, living in the relationships, living in communion" (Tomatis, in Cambón, 1999: 202).[3] The experiences of those who seek to live this way do not simply replicate a static dogma, but participate in the life of the Trinity and in doing so generate further insights into the way that this perspective can be applied to different fields of human life.

The Focolare spirituality, therefore, engenders a strong sense of moral responsibility to transform relationships in order to make them more Trinitarian, generating greater communion between all. It is this communion that the EOC seeks to generate within the sphere of the economy:

> When ... someone re-finds their faith in the capabilities of the human person for altruism, disinterested giving and sharing, and promotes a "culture of giving" and an "EOC," they know that they are proposing a type of society which is arduous to achieve, but not an utopia ... they are betting on the best part, on the objective capacity to love and on the "trinitarian nostalgia" which exists, also subconsciously, deep within every human being. (Cambón, 1999: 63)

In economic terms, the Trinitarian perspective translated into a *culture of mutual giving,* a constant intertwining of material and non-material donation. The term "giving" in relation to the Focolare spirituality has to be understood as "gift of self" on an existential level. It is not possible to reduce giving to an external act, but has to be seen in view of the relationship that exists between the giver and the receiver. "Giving," therefore, in this respect is intrinsically relational since it is always about establishing a relationship with the other.

When the EOC was launched in 1991, it was viewed by the Focolare Center and the business leaders as an opportunity to live this culture of giving within the sphere of the wider monetary economy so as to redistribute wealth. It was a chance to enculture the monetary economy within the particular vision of the world of the Focolare. Through recognizing that the economic is bound by a cultural vision, and subject to the ethical ideals contained therein, the Focolare was attempting to create a space within the market economy where its

188

ideals would be dominant. It was not trying to create an alternative to the market economy (although there appeared to be some confusion over this within the Focolare), but to transform the relationships within the sphere of the more extensive public economy into ones that could be called Trinitarian. Part of this involved sharing a proportion of the profits of the businesses to fund assistance to the poor and to promote education for a culture of giving.

Although its concept is alien to Western industrialized economic thinking, the experience of the Focolare Movement tacitly supports the Weberian view (Swedberg, 1998) that religions contain their own economic ethic. This vision shapes their understanding of how economic relationships and institutions ought to be regulated in the broadest sense, without seeking to offer precise prescriptions of how such businesses should operate. Within the EOC ventures this sense of God's presence is also reflected in the sense of "calling" the directors felt in responding to the EOC. The businesses themselves, and in particular the industrial parks within the Focolare model towns, became in effect places of pilgrimage for those in search of a "new way." Participation in the EOC affected the choices that they made in how they regulated every aspect of their economic action from the relationship with employees to taxation and environmental concerns. For the majority of the leaders, their actions were part of their religious calling.

For Weber (1958), however, capitalism and Christianity ought to be fundamentally opposed since the former relies on a means-end instrumental rationality and the latter relies on value-oriented rationality. His main concern was in understanding how these seemingly incompatible rationalities actually became compatible. Weber started from the premise that Christianity and capitalism are incompatible, since Christianity is hostile to money-making as a goal in life: "You cannot serve God and wealth" (Lk 16:13). In particular, he highlighted the way that the Catholic laity tended to favor an economically traditional life due to the "weak premium on asceticism due to the possibility of absolution" (Swedberg, 1998: 125). Weber's descriptions of Calvinism and Catholicism have since been disputed (Marshall, 1982) due to his oversimplifications and definitions of religious beliefs, unacceptable even among religious leaders.

The perspective on the relationship between economic action and Catholicism offered by my research into the businesses in Milan and Sao Paulo demonstrates certain aspects of Weber's book, but also differs from it in some important aspects. It is clear that the launch of the EOC marked a decisive point in the lives of those who decided to take part and that they experienced a sense of "calling." This turning point lay, above all, in a transformation in the way that they themselves regarded the relationship between their economic action and the spirituality of the Focolare. In Chapter 6, I considered how directors interpreted the spirituality and applied it within commercial businesses, for which the discourse of the market is usually dominant.

The salient point from which all the responses emerge could be termed the "depth of epistemic commitment" to the Focolare vision possessed by the directors. They explained their actions not so much in terms of financial profitability but in terms of *"giving a soul to the economy."* This epistemic commitment was reflected above all in the substantial risks that they took in order to follow what they believed was a "divine" project. In Brazil, for example, several of the businesses had been set up through the owners selling all that they had in order to invest in the idea. They were prepared to transfer location to Araceli, choosing the location on the basis of a divine plan rather than predetermined financial criteria (such as the cost of facilities). Given the level of financial insecurity at the time within Brazil, this was an extremely high risk, even a gamble. In some ways, their actions reflected a regard for tried and tested "scientific" theories of business practice and management in favor of belief in a spiritual ideal.

Yet, in the mind of those who were taking the risks, this was not blind faith or irrational behavior. Within the context of the EOC, this kind of action was entirely rational and discloses an economic rationality beyond the confines of conventional economic discourse. Their actions were founded on the belief that God's providence would come to the aid of those who followed their consciences: *"Providence helped us to find a marketing outlet that sells all over Italy."* Their profound belief in the Trinitarian relationships meant that God's action was not perceived as a kind of magic formula or good luck, but a reality borne out in their personal experience and that of others. In practical terms, it was a trust that was reflected in the sense of belonging: the trust that God would come to the aid of those who risked everything for the EOC. If their businesses failed, then those who had risked would be sure to be the top of the list of those to be helped.

As discussed in Chapter 8, the experience of those who had lost businesses as a result of the EOC was not examined in a direct way within this research and is rarely discussed among people within the

Focolare. When asked about this, however, the Focolare delegates and directors could cite several examples of EOC ventures that had folded. When asked how the people concerned interpreted this failure, the response was mixed. Some interpreted their failure as business incompetence or the result of circumstances outside their control. These people were generally able to continue their participation in the Focolare and were being helped through these difficult circumstances by other people in the community. Some had gone on to start other EOC ventures.

On the other hand, one person explained how her father had invested his life savings in an EOC venture. The investment was based on good faith that the money would be well spent. The business started to go wrong, however, since its location was determined by proximity to a "model town" rather than economic criteria based on access to suppliers, markets and so forth. Around the model town there was limited access to the specific market it was supposed to be serving. Instead of recognizing the failure and liquidating the project or changing strategy, the project was prolonged and more money was poured into it. In the end it had to close and those who had invested lost everything. In this case, the failure resulted in a profound sense of disillusionment in the EOC and isolation from the Focolare. The sheds that housed the business now lie empty and the machinery is rusting. Although rare, such stories highlight the dangers of an interpretation of the EOC that verges on what could be termed "Trinitarian fundamentalism." They illustrate precisely the kind of situation that Cambón (1999: 196) cites as one of the very real dangers of a "naive" interpretation of the Trinitarian perspective. Those managing the EOC project have been at pains to stress the need for sound business ideas based on technical expertise, also within the sphere of market analysis. Attempts to disregard such expertise in the belief that God will run the business will inevitably result in serious loss of capital and profound disillusionment.

Although it may appear that the EOC tacitly supports Weber's contention of economic ethics based on religious values, the nature of the economic ethic of the Focolare is quite different to that offered by Weber in his analysis of Catholicism. The Trinitarian perspective of the Focolare, in fact, sits uneasily with the interpretation of Catholicism offered by Weber. Within the Focolare spirituality, as discussed above, God is found and served through service to one's neighbor and through mirroring these relationships in those within the Trinity. This emphasis on finding God through others makes it extremely difficult to equate economic action and an instrumental rationality with religion and a value-oriented rationality. Moneymaking in itself is neither good nor bad. What matters is motivation, which will influence how money is made and what is done with it. If making money is the only goal in economic action and everything else is a means to that end, then an action so focused entirely on self could not reflect the Trinitarian relationships. If making money is motivated by an attitude of creating wealth to share with others so as to build up the community, and if those who are involved in that process are treated in such a way as to build up Trinitarian relationships, then it is not only acceptable but could even be regarded as a moral duty. Sharing becomes the principal rationale behind the economic action. The business is regarded not simply as a means to an end, but as an end in itself, as a "social space" (Sorgi, 1991a). Within this social space, the goal of making a profit is paralleled with that of creating an atmosphere of caring among all those who participate and through promoting a more socially and environmentally sustainable world.

The sense of engagement with the free market economy central to this spirituality could be compared in some ways with Novak's (1993) understanding of the "Catholic ethic." Novak highlights the fact that the teaching of Catholicism on "creation" makes it highly compatible with an economic system that emphasizes free enterprise. He argues that, although Weber was right in his understanding that religions can give rise to a particular economic ethic, his understanding of "rationality" and how it gave rise to capitalism is inherently flawed. Weber's understanding of rationality sidelined the value of creativity. Economic thinkers throughout the twentieth century such as Schumpeter, Hayek and Kirzner have repeatedly stressed creativity as central to the continuation of the market. Novak's understanding of the Catholic ethic draws on the rich theological anthropology of "creativity" within the Catholic tradition. He says that the moral strength of capitalism (and democracy) lies not so much in its ability to distribute wealth fairly, but in its ability to promote human creativity. It is also interesting to note that Novak also predicted that such an ethic would be most likely to appear in Latin America since it has traditionally been the source of progressive Catholic thinking.

Through the promotion of EOC ventures, initiative and enterprise have become qualities promoted throughout the Focolare Movement in general, harnessing the creative potential that Novak sees as central to the development of the market economy. Through the EOC, the art of association is promoted, especially at local levels, through encouraging local communities to take stock of their needs and to begin to work to fulfill these needs. The EOC also engenders a sense of public spiritedness and civic responsibility within individuals and in corporate groups that decide to participate in the EOC. This could be seen above all in the attitudes of the business leaders toward the various communities to which they belonged. The EOC provoked a sense of looking outward from the business itself as a source of profit to the place of the business in the wider local community and beyond.

The EOC leaders, moreover, demonstrated the "virtues of civility," that Novak puts at the foundation of the free market. These are "the art of compromise on practicalities," "the habit of showing respect to other persons," and, finally, "the art of speaking kindly" (Novak, 1993: 234). In some ways these virtues are very similar to the "goodwill" that Dore (1983) says is an essential foundation of the economy, since they foster trust among people. The leaders in the case studies emphasized strongly the value of "new relationships" within the economy, with some even going so far as calling them Trinitarian relationships. The foundation of these new relationships was the recognition of the dignity of every person as an equal member of the human family, created in the image of God. In practice, it translated into the desire to promote a "family" relationship with those who worked together and to attend to the needs of those who were part of the business.

Underlying Tensions

The economic ethic of the Focolare upon which the EOC depends offers a powerful transformative vision that goes to the heart of modern economics. As the same time, it is undeniable that the EOC ventures face real difficulties in the interpretation and the practice of this idea in their daily transactions. Given that the leaders' responses and the data relating to the EOC in this study tend to suggest that there are underlying difficulties in putting the Focolare spirituality into practice within the sphere of business, such a critical analysis is essential.

The global overview of the EOC showed that the levels of profits shared in common have not been rising as quickly as expected, and that over the past few years the number of businesses joining has remained steady. Of the firms surveyed, 70 per cent had not shared any profits since they started to participate in the EOC. On the one hand, this high percentage is partly due to the fact that the businesses are young and still have several years of investment before breaking even. On the other hand, it is also a reflection of the fact that many felt that they had to invest within the business itself in order to participate in the EOC. As outlined in Chapter 8, participation in the EOC meant that many of the firms incurred extra costs. It is necessary to examine the possible reasons for these failures, and whether they seriously limit the prospect of the future growth of the EOC.

One tension observed was a general lack of clarity regarding what it means to be an EOC venture. This has resulted from confusion over what it means to live the culture of giving within the business and, consequently, the nature of the relationship between the business and the Focolare. Chapter 8 examined the different ways in which EOC people applied the culture of giving in their business. For some, the ideal of "giving" posed them with moral conundrums since it is impossible to interpret business life *only* as an act of giving. If this were the case then the owners would have to "give" to their employees without expecting them to fulfill their obligations as workers; they would have to "give" to their clients without expecting them to pay for services; they would have to "give" to their suppliers without expecting them to provide a reliable service. Suggestions of such a literal interpretation of the culture of giving could be seen in the examples of directors who did not want to discipline employees who were not pulling their weight, or who failed to reinvest an adequate amount in the firm in order to ensure its long-term survival. This literal interpretation in some ways demonstrated that the business people themselves had not understood how the Focolare spirituality could be related to their enterprises. The interpretation of the Focolare spirituality, on the other hand, had to be balanced against the needs of the business, recognizing that the culture of giving cannot be taken at face value.

The lack of profit donations, however, also resulted from the concerns of some of the business people regarding the lack of information that they received about how the profits would be spent. This too has to be seen in the light of the meaning attached to giving within the Focolare. Normal practice regarding the communion of goods on a personal level reflects the principle in the Gospel regarding almsgiving — "your right hand should not know what the left hand is doing." In other words, one who "gives," does so in trust and has no need to know how or where the gift is used. The responsibility of the giver rests in the act of giving itself.

One of the difficulties with the EOC has been the applicability of this "family" mentality, deeply bound up in the idea of the culture of giving, within the public sphere and on a global scale. It is possible to be accepting and trusting when what is being given is a personal gift, but what happens when the gift is no longer personal, but the result of the work of a group of people, many of whom do not share the same beliefs and trust? Within the world of commerce, it is common practice to receive detailed accounts of donations given to charities and receipts for donations. Within the EOC, since the structures emerged directly from those in place within the Focolare for the communion of goods, the need to communicate how the profits were being spent was not regarded as a high priority. The business people would receive the same notification as everyone else who read the EOC newsletter.[4] Yet the research carried out in the firms showed that this lack of information was beginning to stall the development of the EOC. A desire for information in this respect comes, above all, from a sense of corporate responsibility based on the legal requirement to justify the use of profits to other directors and to employees.

This dilemma dramatizes the critical question of the projection of the private within the Focolare into spheres normally associated with a more public sphere. The sense of intimate "hearth" or family, at the heart of the Focolare spirituality, is one that is normally associated with the private sphere and relies on forms of interaction that could be associated with a high degree of informality and spontaneity. Such informalities have existed since the beginning of the Focolare and are based on the desire to respond to needs with immediacy, and without the need for bureaucratic interference. At a local level, this intimacy is enabled by face-to-face interactions, and transparency is ensured by the limited scale. At a global level, however, there are profound challenges to such a system if it is to retain this specific characteristic of intimacy and to operate within the legal, institutional and political framework of the market economy.

There are striking parallels between this kind of interaction taking place on a global scale within the Focolare and the so-called "moral economies" discussed in Chapter 1. Such moral economies, traditionally linked to pre-industrialized "close-knit" communities, are characterized by high levels of trust (Platteau, 1994) and a high degree of reciprocity. The social structures of such communities would mean that decisions on allocation of resources and wealth distribution are often taken by a leader on behalf of the community. Few questions are asked, since there is certainty that the leader will only act in the best interests of the community. At the same time, transactions between members of the community are often unrecorded and non-monetary. Most transactions are based on mutual help or neighborliness. Yet the main characteristic of these moral economies is their restriction to small geographical areas, and within such communities a limited division of labor. Through the EOC, the Focolare is attempting thus to project a similar vision into the global market economy through the involvement of commercial enterprises. Within the EOC, businesses interact with the rest of the global economy with its highly sophisticated division of labor. Whereas the survival of moral economies relies on the trust generated by knowing the other through living in close proximity, within the EOC this trust is generated through sharing the same Focolare spirituality on a global scale. This trust is stretched out through the intertwining of multiple and overlapping networks of the Focolare binding together and could even be stretched to breaking point.

Justification for sharing profits for the EOC was based above all on the owner's personal participation in the Focolare community, and their understanding that their profits were going to be used to help people whom they regarded as part of the same "global family." In this way, it was irrelevant whether these people were in the business, in the same street, town, or even the same country. They felt the responsibility to help them on the basis that they were part of the same global community in which distance did not matter. In some cases, however, the employees, who were generating the profits, were either unaware of this choice or not in favor of it leading to a tension between the desire to share globally, and to attend to the needs of those closest within the business. In most cases, directors felt it was their responsibility to attend directly to the needs of their closest neighbors while at the same time helping those far away.

The involvement of employees in the sharing of profits, therefore, is an important aspect of the EOC. The data relating to the number of employees who are aware of participating in the EOC demonstrate that this is another source of potential tension, as discussed in Chapter 8. Some firms initially skirted this issue by only employing people who were involved in the Focolare and who therefore were assumed to be in agreement with the aims of the business, to share its profits with the EOC, and were prepared to share the same work ethic. For many businesses, this form of closure could have been an easy road to follow, since it would have overcome the difficulty of explaining the EOC to outsiders and avoided employee opposition to the idea.

On the other hand, for other firms that already had employees who did not belong to the Focolare or even know of its existence, this was not an option. They had no idea that their boss participated in the Focolare, mainly because there had never been any reason to discuss such matters. Business is not a place to discuss participation in religious groups, since these are normally taken as wholly personal matters. The owners thus had to accept the fact that they had to work within the cultural frame of reference of these employees without imposing different sets of standards derived from their own personal visions. At the same time, though, the fact that the profits were being used to serve human needs led business people to question to what extent non-Focolare employees should be aware of the firm's new philosophy and objectives and, if so, how this should be communicated. The EOC created a paradoxical situation in which there were insiders (Focolare people both within and outside the business) and outsiders (non-Focolare employees), although there is no evidence to suggest that there was favoritism on the basis of such distinctions.

The EOC ventures can claim that they reflect the Focolare spirituality when the profits are the result of the consent and full participation of their workers. From the point of view of the Focolare, the EOC is already partially achieved when the owner shares his or her profits, even without the conscious participation of the workers. In this respect, the workers are bound up in a "divine project" due to the fact that they work for the EOC. The EOC, though, can arguably only be fully achieved at the point when the ideal of sharing is not only an end product, based on the decision of one person (or a group of people), but the result of a working process in which these values permeate every level. In other words, businesses are truly EOC ventures only when all of the relationships within the business can be said to be Trinitarian. Clearly there will always be the need for one person to take the decision to share, if the ownership legally rests in that person's hands, but that decision should be the result of consensus rather than personal conviction alone.

NATURE OF PRODUCTS AND SERVICES

The final source of potential conflict between the culture of giving and the EOC relates to the nature of the services and products that EOC ventures provide. As an alternative to the dominant view of global capitalism, the EOC is very different from the other radical "alternatives" put forward in the 1990s. The views of authors such as Latouche (1993) and Sachs (1992) point the way to a "scaling down" of Western high consumption lifestyles in order to make space for those who have not had the opportunity to experience the benefits of economic development: consuming less so that they can consume more. It is a view that regards the globe as a closed ecosystem with finite resources that need to be sensibly, even equitably, divided up among a growing population (Daly, 1996). Enabling the poorest to gain a more equal share of wealth means lessening the "environmental footprint" of Western societies.

The "culture of giving," outlined in Chapter 3 embodies the values cited as critical for the kind of transformations needed in order to reach environmental and social sustainability (Oslon, 1995). Oslon stresses that the revitalization of meaningful community life is critical in the search for a renewed social vision (Oslon, 1995: 30). In this respect, the Focolare demonstrates an extraordinary potential to revitalize the "social imagination." Nevertheless, one has to examine the role that EOC ventures play in changing attitudes toward consumption and whether they are complicit in fostering high consumption lifestyles through the chain of industrial production. Do the businesses, for example, produce goods or services (the name of sharing profits for good causes) that contradict the values of giving underpinning the Focolare spirituality?

In the research into the businesses in Italy and Brazil, those in Sao Paulo demonstrated a greater awareness of the interrelationship between these two levels of economic action and social vision. There was a stronger influence on producing environmentally friendly goods and services that they regarded as compatible with the culture of the businesses in Brazil. In Milan, on the other hand, there was less awareness of how these different levels related to each other. More were engaged in providing goods and services that could be regarded as symbolic of consumer culture. These included luxury items, such as designer sunglasses, and financial services for some of the big fashion houses in Milan. Although it is not possible to equate products with cultural attitudes, clearly the EOC ventures that were providing such goods (so as to share their profits) had an interest in retaining an ethos of consumption that identified with consumerism, or they would inevitably lose business. Their involvement in such relationships with other non-EOC ventures demonstrates the complexity of "claiming the moral high ground" for the EOC. It is something that requires further thought and reflection.

Notes

[1]Sayer and Ray (1999: 6) disagree with this "blurring" of the distinction between the economic and the non-economic, stating that some activities are economic in "nature" (e.g. doing paid employment) while others, though having economic dimensions, are non-economic (e.g. watching television). I would argue, however, that the distinction that they are making is actually between the formal, money economy and other non-monetary forms of economic life. Both have an "economic" dimension, inasmuch as they involve the production, exchange, and distribution of goods (material or otherwise) and services.

[2]To this effect, the work of Coda (1998) points out how living out Trinitarian relationships also leads to a renewal of ontology.

[3]Cambón (1999: 56) says that the Trinitarian unity can add a "supplement of knowledge" onto the competence of those working in different fields of human endeavor, so as to generate new creative solutions which are appropriate to the circumstances. It, therefore, can have an impact at a theoretical level through generating a new way of *pericoretic* thinking. In order for this to come about, it is not sufficient that there be a profound silence which welcomes the words of the other, seeking to understand what they are saying; in the words of Zanghì, a relationship is Trinitarian on the level of thought when "I am myself in you and you are yourself in me" [*Io sono io in te e tu sei tu in me*] (Zanghì, 1998: 83).

[4]As a result of this research the situation has changed. From January 1999, all EOC ventures that give profits for the EOC receive an annual statement from the Focolare center showing how the money has been spent.

10

Challenging Perceptions of Justice:
The Needs of "Distant Strangers"

If my son is in need, it doesn't matter to me whether he is here or on
the other side of the planet — I want to help him. *Gustavo Claría*

INTRODUCTION

The previous chapter considered how the EOC relates to the
various theories regarding the relationship between the principle of
"rational economic man," culture and the economic and how these
are played out from the local to the global. This discussion reveals
that the EOC, both locally and globally, shares an understanding of
the relationship between the economic and the other aspects of life
that influence the understanding of what is "rational." It is assumed
that the cultural embraces the economic, rather than the other way
around. This culture has the potential to transform economic spaces
into social and even "sacred" ones through the Trinitarian relationships. It reveals an economic landscape enriched with new concepts
of rational action, underpinned by "other" rationalities arguably
inseparable from the cultural context in which they were formed.

At this point the discussion turns to the implications that this distinctive understanding of the relationship between the economic and
the cultural could have in relation to one of the fundamental questions
facing the global economy today: how to deal with growing inequalities between rich and poor. The EOC raises important questions with
regards to social justice and the market, both as a theoretical idea and
as a normative vision. Important ideas about social justice emerge from
the research in this book, particularly responsibility for those in need
both near and far — what David Smith (1998) has called the "spatial
scope of beneficence."

HOW FAR SHOULD OUR CARE EXTEND?

The question "How far should our care extend?" raises an
interesting proposition. Is it fair to distinguish between people on
the basis of being near or far from us? In recent years, academics

in the area of human geography have studied this question in depth. In his keynote paper, Philo calls for geographers to open up a new engagement with moral philosophy, so as to "yield fresh insights into geographical issues where the economic 'logic' is already understood but where the moral components are as yet 'invisible'" (Philo, 1991: 18). Although social justice has always been a theme within human geography, since the mid-1990s there has been resurgence in "moral" debates in many geographical texts (e.g. Harvey, 1996; Hay, 1995; Smith, 2000). The emphasis of this new moral turn has highlighted how considerations of space, place and environment are potentially at the heart of moral thinking. Smith (1997) provides an overview of the various re-engagements between the disciplines of human geography and ethical issues.

Given the complexity of the debates surrounding the interface between moral philosophy and geography, Smith cautions against geographers engaging with meta-ethics, but cites two areas where he regards the contribution of geographers as highly relevant: the debate over universalism and relativism and the question of the geographical distribution of goods (with the related question of responsibility to "distant others"). Both of these related debates are highly relevant to the EOC. The question of redistribution is at the heart of the EOC and raises probing questions regarding the nature of distribution. Secondly, the Focolare ethos challenges the prevalent dualistic tendency to describe the morality of the local/particular as "thick" and that of the global/universal as "thin." The Focolare/EOC ethos is arguably an example of a "thick" global morality that is particular, but has universalizing tendencies. The ethos of the Focolare is a global projection of a "morality" rooted in the idea of the local "hearth," the most intimate image of caring and sharing within a family.

Theories of Social Justice

Smith (1994) provides an overview of the various theories of social justice influential on the discourses that still dominate both the market economy and other theories that have emerged in response. He cites the following quote on economic justice that highlights the problem:

> The problem of economic justice can be expressed with remarkable simplicity: On what basis should goods and services be distributed? Answers to this question, however, are as numerous as those to any important philosophical issue. Some (libertarians)

believe that the operation of the free market guarantees justice. Others (utilitarian) hold that the needs or interests of people should be of primary concern. Still others look to how much is deserved, as measured by labor time, or contribution, as the basis for distribution. Equal distribution, since it seems to reflect the common humanity shared by all, is also viewed by many as the core of economic justice. The philosophical problem is to decide which among these and other positions is in fact superior, and to give reasons for one's conclusions that will convince others. (Arthur and Shaw, 1991: 1, cited in Smith, 1994)

Of the different theories discussed in this book, the one that is most deeply implicated in economic affairs in the present day is utilitarianism (Smith, 1997: 59). The overriding concern within utilitarianism is the pursuit of human welfare as the only sound normative basis for making decisions. It places the maximization of well-being (or welfare, utility, happiness, pleasure) as the overriding objective toward which all other objectives should be directed. It reflects the moral principle of equal concern in requiring "impartiality," giving the same weight to each individual's welfare and asking each to give the same concern to all others equally. Classical utilitarianism stressed the pursuit of pleasure or the absence of pain as the universal value that had to be maximized. Such concepts, however, have been criticized strongly, since the pursuit of pleasure is loaded with hedonistic connotations (Nozick, 1974: 42-5). In more recent theoretical elaborations of utilitarianism, the theory has been linked closely to classical economics and welfare theory. In this concept, the idea of happiness is replaced by "utility," meaning that each individual seeks to maximize their own personal preferences within the general structure of the market. It is normally restricted to monetary transactions, but can be extended and applied to whatever gives people a sense of satisfaction. The aggregate pursuit of utility is called "welfare." This principle was reworked by Pareto and became the foundation of economic science: it is in the best interests of everyone if individuals pursue their own self-interest. Egalitarianism can be seen as the inverse of utilitarianism. Goods have to be shared with others somehow and the responsibility for distributing the goods (in some versions of the theory) lies with the state, legitimizing the separation between production and distribution. Social justice is seen as a big cake with slices that have to be distributed out fairly: either people keep their slices and the cake keeps growing, or the slices are shared out differently.

This concept of social justice has been severely criticized on many grounds, but despite this, it has remained the cornerstone of economic thinking and practice. Criticisms range from the impossibility of assuming that human beings perform calculations to maximize their satisfaction to the gross difficulties in measuring utility itself. Etzioni (1989), for example, highlights at least two different and conflicting "utilities" that relate to morality: duty and pleasure. Such utilities cannot be reduced to a single concept of preferences. The concept of preferences itself, moreover, is difficult to accept in view of the numerous special relationships between people and those closest to them. Within this concept of social justice, there is no conception of "relationships," either special ones (family, friends, community) or general ones with unknown strangers. People are viewed as isolated individuals who exist to gain their personal maximization of utility. At best, corporate utility substitutes for personal utility, reflecting a kind of collective utility maximization. Finally, such a universalized concept of social justice is "aspatial," since the position of equality from which it departs does not take into account the actual existing claims to space (territorial, parochial, local) that perpetuate situations of injustice. As a consequence, such concepts are "thin" in terms of vocabulary and in their ability to offer normative answers to the questions of injustice.

Egalitarianism, Impartiality and the EOC

Despite these shortcomings, there are certain aspects of this universalized vision of social justice that can be readily applied to what is happening within the EOC, although they can by no means offer an explanation of the EOC. Within the Focolare, there is a strong sense that equalizing the distribution of wealth is related to social justice Chapter 3, which considered the economic vision of the Focolare, examined how at times the focolarini were mistaken for communists due to their strong emphasis on social revolution and the emancipation of the poor. They regarded themselves as the *principal actors* in creating a fair distribution as a key to achieving a more just society. The underlying principle of social justice, therefore, stressed the inequality of access to resources, particularly money and basic goods such as clothing, housing and food, as a source of injustice. This emphasis on equalization can also be seen very clearly within the EOC: through sharing their profits the directors see themselves as helping to create a more just society. Legitimate self-interest is accepted as a positive force for good — in the sense that free initiative is essential in order to facilitate the pursuit of profit — but it is not regarded as the goal of economic action. It has to be constantly moderated through responsibility toward persons and the environment.

The main difference between the Focolare perspective and the egalitarian/distributionist theories of social justice would appear to reside in who should do the distributing and how. The EOC emerged as the result of the failure of the modern economic system to deliver welfare to the people within the community. This can be seen in particular in Latin America, where the EOC has taken off most vigorously. Traditional theories place the role of redistribution in the hands of the state through taxation. Although the role of the state still has importance for the EOC, which does not set out to replicate state welfare, within the EOC the redistribution of resources is integral part to the production process. The owners are given the responsibility to distribute their profits to the poor through the Focolare, putting into practice the CST principle of "subsidiarity." They do not take on the personal task of sharing out resources, but delegate responsibility for this to those whom they regard as part of their wider community. Through creating a system by which care is administered through community structures both on a local level and global scale, the role of the state in the lives of those helped by the EOC is kept to a minimum. In this way the business is not just the means of "increasing the size of the cake" (in the egalitarian sense), whereas the state is the means of "sharing the cake." Through the EOC, the productive process/business also has the function of redistributing profits in proportion to the increasing size of the cake. This in turn limits the extent to which the corporations can grow since they balance their potential to invest in growth against the need to distribute in the present.

On another level, however, some aspects of these theories of social justice sit uneasily with the vision of the EOC presented in this book. In particular, the ontological vision of Trinitarian relationships raises questions regarding the possibility of impartiality within the market. Within the EOC one has to ask *to what extent is it possible to create Trinitarian relationships while at the same time being impartial?* As discussed above in relation to networks, some of the EOC ventures seem to have difficulties in "respecting" the norms of impartiality within the market, a phenomenon not unique to the EOC. This is occurring on all levels within the EOC — from the creation of EOC associations to the decision to share profits. In a sense, the underlying principle of creating Trinitarian relationships leads owners to view the market not as a series of colliding atoms, but as an inherently relational space. Their aim becomes that of making the economy *more* relational through increasing the number of these special relationships within the market through living out the Focolare spirituality in the workplace.

The creation of these kinds of special relationships within the market could be interpreted by such universalized theories of social justice as "unjust." While improving the well-being of a number of people and increasing their chances of escaping poverty, the processes by which they are helped and the nature of the help received could be deemed as "unfair" by those who favor an openly accountable and democratic system of decision-making that includes a formal application procedure for help. Yet such processes are at odds with the existing process within the EOC, which is inherently relational. Nevertheless, such is the complexity of theoretical considerations of social justice, what is injustice to one theory is perfectly just to another.

The EOC and Feminist Conceptions of Social Justice

The EOC, on the other hand, would seem to be more in tune with a number of contemporary theories of social justice put forward by feminist thinkers as a reaction to these universalized theories. In particular, they stress the relational dimension of ethics. Among such relational ethical theories put forward is the idea of a "politics of difference" by Young (1990b). In Young's view, an adequate concept of social justice must emphasize the relations that lead to domination and oppression rather than focusing solely on the distribution of goods. She rejects universalized theories of social justice that tend to mask the real situations of oppression which are expressed in institutions and groups. In this respect her work parallels that of Simone Weil, cited earlier in this book, in its emphasis on "heeding a call" (Young, 1990b: 5) rather than on "mastering a state of affairs." Although she rejects the kind of communitarianism that Walzer (1983) proposes, on the grounds that such an ideal is unobtainable in contemporary life as it emphasizes face-to-face relations (Young, 1990a: 314), her own work resonates with the need to build meaningful "groups" (rather than communities) that can overcome forms of domination and oppression. Perhaps the main difference with communitarianism, apart from vocabulary, is that Young's vision sees questions of justice/injustice in terms of the relationship between various groups, and therefore is alert to their perceptions of boundaries. Justice is about expanding the network of relationships within particular groups to include others rather than involving the inward-looking promotion of parochial self-interest at the expense of those who are different.

In this respect, there are strong parallels between the work of Young and the Focolare ethos, both in the writings of Chiara Lubich and in the practices of the EOC. The question of social justice in relation to the EOC moves away from one based on the state — with the undertones of impartiality and universality implicit within it. It rests rather on involvement or participation in a community that has a mutual recognition of the duties to and responsibilities of each other. The question is therefore one of belonging rather than one preoccupied by some predetermined rationale of justice. As one Focolare delegate told me in an interview: *"If my son is in need, it doesn't matter to me whether he is here or on the other side of the planet — I want to help him."* What matters is the fraternal relationship that exists no matter how physically near or far the other person might be. This has strong parallels with Young's idea of the increasing importance of groups and movements in which welfare shifts from the state to intermediaries and non-state actors. Within the Focolare this shift in the meaning of community, as imagined by Young, can be seen in action. The Focolare is a global community in which participation is not based on any particular criteria except identification with the ideals and objectives of the group.

The Focolare, though, does not only form a practical example of one of the groups that Young was talking about. It can also cast light, in a more theoretical vein, on the kind of values essential to the "politics of difference" that Young is advocating. One of the remarkable features of this pluralistic ethos is the co-existence of different epistemologies within the one group, without the dilution of one into the other in a form of either religious syncretism or the impoverishment of different traditions in an attempt not to offend others. Although a profoundly Christian spirituality forms the main motivating force behind the actions of the majority of people within the Focolare, great emphasis is placed on the need to foster relationships with each person, especially with those who are "different" in terms of race, gender and religious beliefs. Pluralism, therefore, is not regarded as a necessary evil (as it would be possible to assume) but an essential feature of human society that finds its counterpart in the Trinity.[1] The vocation within the Focolare spirituality to create Trinitarian relationships zeroes in precisely to the place of disunity as locus where Christians are called to be. This preferential choice to "fill the gaps" of disunity between individuals and groups has enabled within the Focolare a fruitful dialogue that takes in people of different Christian traditions, people of different religions, and even people who have no specific religious tradition but who still share a commitment to the promotion of a common culture based on mutual love and respect.

Another theory of social justice particularly in tune with the Focolare ethos is what Gilligan (1982) called an "ethic of care." Recognizing that the theories of social justice have been formulated for the most part from a masculine perspective, studies in behavioral psychology have showed that women related justice to an ethic of care rather than to one of impartiality and fairness. Her view hence stresses the relational dimension of ethics which has as much to do with feeling a sense of responsibility, involvement and duty toward others as it has to do with constructs of impartiality and rational observation. In much the same way, the Focolare ethos is about engaging with others so as to reach a mutual understanding and relationship. In a sense, through its spirituality's perspective of Trinitarian relationships, the Focolare is putting into practice an "ethic of care" often associated with feminist thinking (Smith, 1994: 112) so bringing about Young's (1990b) "politics of difference." The association between these two concepts of social justice is rarely made, but it seems that within the Focolare the two are intimately connected and mutually enriching. The idea that "care" is a distinctively female attribute has been contested (Toronto, 1993) as it could lead to the perpetuation of unwanted stereotypes. Keeping this in mind and without wishing to make "typecast" judgments on the nature of gender differences, the experience of the EOC could cast light on the nature of a "feminized economic geography," if "feminine" is equated with an "ethic of care."

The EOC emerged from a movement that was initially led by women who, during the war, adopted an "ethic of care" as their sole aim and objective in life. In this respect, it evolved from a perspective that presumes a close relationship between the giver and the receiver, emphasizing the relational dimension of care in the construction of a meaningful community. Although the Focolare now involves men and women, the Focolare and the EOC bear the hallmarks of Chiara Lubich's charismatic leadership. The "ethic of care" within the EOC could be translated into an "ethic of caring and sharing" and is seen, above all, in the desire and commitment to care for those both near and far as the main concern of the businesses. This imbues the world of commerce with values traditionally associated with the home or the family — traditionally female "spaces." Such a vision of a "feminization" is far removed from the current literature on the feminization of the economy which emphasizes how capital has become more "flexible" in order to facilitate the entry of more and more part-time predominantly female workers in the paid economy (Walters & Dex, 1992). Unfortunately, feminization is almost always associated with the feminization of the labor force — women in low-paid, low-skilled, insecure, part-time jobs (Agee & Walker, 1990; Allen, 1992). In this regard, feminization has come to mean the predominance of the rational pursuit of profit over every other consideration. In the EOC, on the other hand, "feminization" of the economy means imbuing the structures of the market with values normally associated with the spatially intimate family.

UNIVERSALIZING THE EOC

The EOC demonstrates the possibility of the emergence of new global economic visions based upon alternative perspectives on the dominant discourses of globalization. It offers a radical reworking of the ideal of social justice within the market economy that has the potential for fostering an ethos of "sharing" not only at a local scale but also on a global scale. It offers the possibility of the extension of an "ethic of care" not only at a local scale, but also through its incorporation within the institutions of the market economy, at a global scale. Despite the difficulties encountered by those attempting to apply the Focolare's vision in these first decades, there remains a strong potential for advocating a different, alternative perspective on economic and social life. Such a need is profoundly relevant and is echoed by those seeking solutions to the multiple environmental, social and economic crises the world is facing. The need for "alternative visions" has been advocated on numerous occasions by the United Nations in relation to the implementation of Agenda 21 (Brown & Quiblier, 1994), as well as numerous NGOs and academics seeking ways to envisage a more sustainable world (Cobb, 1995; Daly, 1996; Ekins, 1992; Milbrath, 1995). Within the EOC there is an intertwining of spirituality, economic vision, idealism and realism capable of bringing about a particular blend of social justice, making the economy move in arguably more sustainable directions.

A central question which has to be asked, therefore, is the extent to which such an alternative can be universalized, as well as globalized, given that it has emerged from a religious epistemological framework and its underlying notion of the "hearth" is spatialized at a local level. The Focolare makes powerful truth claims that, although pluralistic to some extent, are rooted in a Christian religious worldview. That particular vision of the world, moreover, forms the rationale behind the EOC. At the same time, as mentioned above, the Trinitarian perspective offers an interpretative key not only for the EOC, but perhaps for all social relationships. The urgent questions being raised through the existence of the EOC hence go to the heart of many debates within contemporary geographical and moral thinking: to what extent is it possible to envisage a "global ethic" external to the market and capable of embracing difference? In view of post-modern skepticism of "grand meta-narratives," is it possible for such an ethic to make reference to epistemological certainties based on religious beliefs? To what extent can modern institutions, such as businesses, reflect these beliefs while remaining pluralistic?

A GLOBAL ETHIC

The question of the construction of a global ethic that transcends the market is, perhaps, one of the most pertinent questions at the turn of the millennium (Küng, 1997a; McNeill, 1999; O'Connor, 1994). Work on this need for a "global ethic" cites the world's religions as a primary potential source for such a global ethos (Küng, 2000; Küng & Schmitt, 1998). Writers stress that within many world religions there already exists the basis of a global ethic capable of reaching a more environmentally and socially sustainable world. The central tenet of this ethic is a renewed emphasis on the "golden rule" to do to others what you would like them to do to you (UNESCO, 1995: 36). They stress that the way forward will be found in the capacity of the different world religions to engage with other religions in the promotion of human rights and responsibilities. In this respect, the Focolare experience can offer some insight into the future prospects for inter-religious dialogue. The emphasis that the Focolare spirituality places on listening, on "making space for the other," has enabled a creative dialogue to evolve within the Movement, between people belonging to different religious traditions, as outlined in Chapter 2.

The Focolare goes some way to rectifying the often narrow-minded interpretation of "salvation" dominant within certain Catholic traditions. The emphasis placed on enabling the other to "be" through engaging in dialogue, without wishing to convert them to a particular belief system, is a long way from the traditional (and often stereotypical) Catholic perspective. The theology from which the Focolare emerges is far removed from the doctrines used to assert racial superiority or imperialism. In practical terms, the expansion of the Focolare network across the world has led to an interest in (even a fascination with) different cultural and religious groups, exploring different ways of seeing the world. This is seen in the many attempts to "dig out" local cultural traditions that may have been abandoned or neglected in order to celebrate the differences within the Focolare community, as was shown in Chapter 3. Such differences are regarded as a mutual enrichment against the background of a shared ethos of caring and sharing.

Despite these universalizing tendencies (or indeed, because of them) post-modern thinking would tend to be deeply suspicious of the Focolare. Its existence touches on the contentious issue of the relationship between the "universal" and the "particular," challenging the relativistic tendencies that have come to dominate some areas of human geography. Within such strands of thinking, as discussed in Chapter 1, the rejection of meta-narratives is often regarded as a "celebration of difference," but seems to forget that difference only exists against a background of profound similarity, illustrated in what Davidson called the "argument from translation" (in Fay, 1996: 90). Davidson argued that to say that others are different is actually an admittance of similarity.[2] Moreover, difference cannot be seen as a value in itself, detached from other values such as freedom:

> The universal right to difference has no moral value unless it is a product of freedom; that is, unless humans are truly free in both the negative and positive sense of freedom, and so they have the resources enabling them to choose what they genuinely wish to choose and to sustain their choices. (Bauman, 1998: 17)

The Focolare approach to this tension between relativism and universalism is rooted in the ideal of the Trinitarian perspective. Such an ideal is itself a culturally bound specific concept, but it has far-reaching implications for the ensuing debates over ethical and cultural relativism. Within the idea of the Trinitarian perspective, there is an implicit rejection of ethical relativism, since there is a shared understanding of the "nature" of the human person, as a being who is in relationship with God and with others. Within such a claim, however, there is also a place for difference, on a cultural level, since there is admittance that such a belief is not universally accepted. Different cultural groups possess distinctive understandings of the nature of the human person. Nevertheless, the Focolare proposes a kind of universalism that it regards as transcending cultural differences: the belief that human beings exist to love, to give. It is only within such love that cultural differences can find space for expression. It is this love, conceptualized in different ways by different cultures — compassion, goodwill, philanthropy, caring, sharing — that the Focolare seeks to universalize rather than contain within a specific belief system. For Christians, the fact that this concept of unity in diversity can be regarded as participation in the life of the Trinity is a powerful motivation to apply it in practice. For those who do not share such a religious faith, the Trinity can also be regarded as an icon of unity in diversity. This distinction between the different levels of "universalizing" is also expressed in the work of Young:

> Universality in the sense of participation and inclusion of every-one in moral and social life does not imply universality in the sense of the adoption of a general point of view which leaves behind particular affiliations, feelings, commitments and desires. (Young, 1990b: 105)

The Focolare ethos neither fits neatly into the "dogmatic rationalism" associated with modernity nor the "ambiguous interregnum" of post-modern perspectives on reality (Friedman, 1989: 217). It embraces some elements of modernity, such as a commitment to justice and freedom, whilst others could be termed more "post-modern," such as attention to difference and relationships. Universality — "building unity" — within the Focolare is seen as an ongoing relational process, a "becoming" and a "striving," therefore, rather than a fixity. Such a process involves the recognition and acceptance of differences within the context of dialogue. Reaching unity for the Focolare is hence not regarded as a question of eliminating differences in favor of uniformity, but about learning to care for and to love the other in both their differences and their similarities and *vice versa*. This approach opens up many new possibilities for building bridges and common perspectives with believers of many different religions and none.

CONCLUSION

This book began with an examination of the various theoretical ideas surrounding the relationship between the economic and the cultural and how these have been applied within human geography. Then, it touched on the elaboration of such ideas within the Focolare

Movement at both local and global scales, giving rise to the EOC. In this way alternative economic geographies operating within the global market have been "uncovered" and "mapped out," both geographically and conceptually. Such economic geographies draw on the spatially intimate image of the "hearth," projecting the underlying values of face-to-face relationships in which *communion* is the dominant form of economic exchange onto a global scale within the institutions of the market economy. This spatially intimate image finds a transcendent counterpart in the ideal of Trinitarian relationships, which is seen as the portent of humanizing values such as solidarity, dialogue, participation and even love, transforming "economic space" into "social spaces" wherein the relational human dimension of economic action is emphasized. In particular, this Trinitarian perspective translates into sharing, as the practical expression of love in action. At this point, one has to ask, by way of conclusion, what are the prospects for the future growth of the EOC in a commercial world which, although relational, is increasingly led by the globalized logic of profitability?

The EOC rests on a spiritual vision which, if considered through the lenses of conventional utilitarian economic discourses, could seem unrealistic and even irrational. This conclusion may seem fatalistic, but it is not intended as such. Indeed, it is only through escaping from the narrow perceptions of rational action afforded by conventional economic discourses that the EOC can be understood fully and the scope for its development grasped. For those immersed in the Trinitiarian perspective that underpins the Focolare spirituality, "otherworldly" ideas such as the mysterious workings of Providence and a radical openness to "the other" make perfect sense. Within the EOC networks the overlaps and conflicts between these apparently opposing visions are played out on a local scale and on a global scale.

Yet precisely in this ability to articulate a radical alternative vision of the role of human agency in personal, local, regional and global economic action lies the strength of the EOC. It emphasizes the space that exists for different ways of thinking and acting, even within a presumably totalitarian global economic system. The Trinitarian perspective has already given rise to a new vocabulary — and new discourses — that sit uneasily with the conventional public economic discourses. One example is the concept of *communion* in the English language. Such concepts arguably represent a rupture with conventional economic thinking, making space for new concepts and also new schools of thought. As with all ruptures, however, it also risks creating confusion, as new terminology (such as "communion") carries connotations, made more difficult through the process of translation. Those advocating the EOC have to play a balancing act between running with the new terminology and attempting to integrate the ideas underpinning the EOC into the current economic discourses.

The persuasive power of the EOC as a working example of a new economic geography, both at a local and a global scale, moreover, will continue to offer inspiration and practical examples of changes that can be applied elsewhere. Certain dimensions of the idea — above all at the level of values and motivations — could be emphasized by other communities and organizations, starting perhaps with other global communities such as religious movements.[3] This would give rise to a variety of diverse "*economies of communion,*" each with their distinctive co-ordination points operating at different scales from the local to the global. Such economies of communion would revitalize the existing structures of giving[4] present within the market economy and maybe encourage the rise of new ones. One could even foresee partnerships and common projects between such movements and groups, leading to new opportunities for the local and global redistribution of wealth within and across the various communities.

Such economies of communion would be based, above all, on establishing the centrality of two principles underpinning the Focolare Movement's EOC within the wider structures of society: the promotion of a culture of giving[5] and the subdivision of profits in favor of the poor. In the first case, promoting a culture of giving would entail fostering, promoting or initiating activities at all levels, promoting the development of cultural attitudes and social behaviors that emphasize the value of giving as a lifestyle choice. Such educational activities would have to focus on the idea of "giving," not simply as the *act* of donating money or things[6] but as *self-giving* in the sense of an underlying value within all relationships with others both near and far. In the words of one of the EOC directors, the culture of giving is "a way of being, a way of acting" and not simply the act of giving itself. Within the Focolare, such activities are carried out chiefly through the development of both the little towns and the Focolare centers. Beyond the scope of the Focolare, such an idea could be adopted by numerous NGOs already working in the fields of development education and sustainability.[7]

It could therefore see the proliferation of economies of communion at a local and global scale, providing new possibilities for economic and social justice. Such economies would not destroy cultural differences, communities and the environment, but thrive on co-operation and solidarity. In the words of the former Secretary General of the UN, Perez de Cuellar: "Trust, loyalty, solidarity, altruism and even love, though readily dismissed by currently fashionable economists, no doubt do play a part in human relationships. Unlike material goods, they grow on what they feed on. No society is capable of surviving without them" (UNESCO, 1995: 50). Through the EOC, new geographies of sharing are being opened up within the market economy, through which the "fashionable" economic theories have given way to a different perspective on economic relationships. One can at least hope that these networks, based on "solidarity, altruism and even love," will continue to "grow on what they feed on" and play a more prominent role in shaping the global economy of the third millennium.

NOTES

[1]This is underpinned by a profound commitment to pluralism, which is expressed succinctly in the words of the theologian Vives: "The revelation of the Trinity shows clearly that the affirmation of being, at its deepest level, is not closure within the self, which excludes plurality, but communication in the plurality" (cited in Cambón, 1999: 91).

[2]The argument from translation is as follows: To claim that the others live in a different conceptual world from us is to claim that they speak and think. To claim that the others speak and think we need to know that they are saying something and therefore to say we know at least some of what they mean. To know what the others mean, we need to be able to translate their utterances into our language. But to be able to translate their utterances we need to ascribe to them various beliefs, desires, attitudes, and ways of connecting these mental elements. But to ascribe such mental elements to them we must assume that they share with us a background of common beliefs, and principles of thought. But to say that we have a shared background of beliefs, desires, and principles of reasoning is to live in the same world as they do (Fay, 1996: 88).

[3]For example, within the Catholic Church, as in other churches, there are hundreds of new movements such as Communion and Liberation, L'Arche, Sant Egidio as well as older ones such as the Catenians.

[4]By "structures of giving" I am referring both to numerous charitable organizations and NGOs, as well as the state structures designed to promote the redistribution of wealth.

[5]The idea of a culture of giving has increasingly come to be understood in terms of financial structures of corporate giving as can be seen from such as White (1995) and Burlingame (1998). Within the Focolare, giving has a much more holistic meaning, as an underlying relationship between individual persons based on a culture that emphasizes self-giving. Within this logic, if the structures of giving, understood in the above sense are to be revitalized, this would mean not simply giving more money but above all rediscovering the subjective relationships between individuals within these structures.

[6]Giving understood in this way does not necessarily lead to a "culture of giving" in the Focolare sense. Such giving could also be motivated by a utilitarian ethos — as in the case of marketing strategies in which freebies are offered or in development strategies where giving resulted in dependence. Within this kind of giving what comes into relief are the power relations through which giving becomes a manipulative force. Such giving often leads to resentment or fear of the giver rather than mutual respect and understanding.

[7]For example, NGOs like Oxfam, Friends of the Earth, Cafod and Christian Aid all increasingly allocate parts of their budgets to the promotion of values on a cultural level. Within the UN, the Commission on Sustainable Development works in partnership with global NGOs for the promotion of a "culture of peace." Such structures could easily be adapted to promote a "culture of giving."

CHAPTER 10

Bibliography

ALLEN, J. and MASSEY, D. (1988) *The Economy in Question* (London: Sage).

AMIN, A. and THRIFT, N. (eds.) (1994) *Globalization, Institutions and Regional Development in Europe* (Oxford: Oxford University Press).

AMIN, A. (1996) *Capitalism in the Age of Globalisation* (London: Zed).

ARAUJO, V. (1994b) "Per una Economia di *Comunione* secondo la dottrina sociale della Chiesa," *La Società*, Anno IV, 3: 501–533, Turin: Cercate a.r.l.

———. (1991) "Una economia per uomini nuovi," *Città Nuova* 19.

———. (1993) *Gesù e l'uso dei beni* (Rome: Città Nuova).

AYRES, R. U. (1998) *Turning Point: The End of the Growth Paradigm* (London: Earthscan).

AYTER, R. and RIBEIRO, F. S. (1994) "Economia de Comunhão: caminho para a unidade dos povos," *Cadernos Escola Social* 5(7) (Sao Paulo: Cidade Nova).

BACK, J. P. (1988) *Il contributo del Movimento dei Focolari alla 'koinonia' ecumenica* (Rome: Città Nuova).

BAER, W. (1995) *The Brazilian Economy: Growth and Development*, 4th Edition (London: Praeger).

BAER, W. and TULCHIN, J. (eds.) (1993) *Brazil and the Challenge of Economic Reform* (Washington: Woodrow Wilson Center Press).

BALDASSARRI, M. and MODIGLIANI, F. (eds.) (1995) *The Italian Economy: What Next?* (Rome: SIPI).

BALLET, J. (1994) "The social enterprise: a theoretical model," *Annales de l'Economie Publique Sociale et Coopirative*, Vol. 65, No. 4: 623–640.

BARNES, T. and SHEPPARD, E (1992) "Is there a place for the rational actor? A geographical critique of the rational choice paradigm," *Economic Geography* 68(1): 1.

BAUMAN, Z. (1998) "On universal morality and the morality of universalism," *The European Journal of Development Research* 10(2): 7–18.

BECKER, B. and ELGER, C. A. (1992) *Brazil: A New Regional Power in the World Economy* (Cambridge: Cambridge University Press).

BELL, R. (1998) *Simone Weil: The Way of Justice as Compassion* (Oxford: Rowman and Littlefield).

BHABA, H. K. (1994) *The Location of Culture* (London: Routledge).

BIAN, Y. (1998) "Getting a job through a web of Guanxi in urban China." In *Networks in the Global Village*, edited by Barry Wellman (Boulder, CO: Westview).

BIELA, A. (1998) "A copernican relvolution in the social sciences." In *Economia di Comunhão* (Sao Paulo: Cidade Nova), pp. 21–30.

BLOCH, M. and PARRY, J. (eds.) (1989) *Money and the Morality of Exchange* (Cambridge: Cambridge University Press).

BLOCK, F. (1990) *Postindustrial Possibilities: A Critique of Economic Discourse* (Berkeley: University of California Press).

BLOCK, F. and SOMERS, M. (1984) "Beyond the economistic fallacy: the holistic social science of K. Polanyi." In *Vision and Method in Historical Sociology*, edited by T. Skocpol (Cambridge: Cambridge University Press), pp. 47–84.

BOFF, L. (1987) *Trinità e società* (Assisi: Citadella).

———. (1990) *Trinità: la migliore comunità* (Assisi: Citadella).

BOOTH, D. (ed.) (1994) *Rethinking Social Development* (New York: Penguin Press).

BOSELLI, G. (1991a) "Una cittàdella pilota," *Città Nuova* 13: 27–34.

———. (1991b) "Una Economia di *Comunione*" *Città Nuova* 14: 27.

BOURDIEU, P. (1984) *Distinction: A Social Critique of the Judgement of Taste* (London: Routledge and Kegan Paul).

215

BOYLE, D. (1998) *Funny Money: In Search of Alternative Cash* (London: Harper Collins).

BRECHER, J. and COSTELLO, T. (2001) *Global Village or Global Pillage: Economic Reconstruction from the Bottom Up* (Cambridge, MA: South End Press).

Brescia Set — Rivista di Provincia (1997) "Fanno il profitto e divono per tre," December 12, pp. 10–11.

BRITTAIN, S. and HAMLIN, A. (1995) *Market Capitalism and Moral Values* (London: Edward Elgar).

BROWN, N. and QUIBLIER, P. (eds.) (1994) *Ethics and Agenda 21* (New York: UNEP).

BRUNI, L. (2007) *La ferita dell'altro — economia e relazioni umane* (Trent: Il Margine).

_____. (2002) *The Economy of Communion: Toward a Multi-Dimensional Economic Culture* (Hyde Park, NY: New City Press).

BRUNI, L. and PELLIGRA, V. (eds.) (2002) *Economia come impegno civile: relazionalità, ben-essere ed Economia di Comunione* (Rome: Città Nuova).

BRUNI, L. and SMERILLI, A. (2008) *Benedetta Economis — Benedetto di Norcia e Francesco d'Assisi nella storia economica europea* (Rome: Città Nuova).

BRUNTLAND, G. H. (1987) *Our Common Future: Report of the World Commission on Environment and Development* (Oxford: Oxford University Press).

BULL, A. and CORNER, P. (1993) *From Peasant to Entrepreneur: The Survival of the Family Economy in Italy* (Oxford: BERG).

BURLINGAME, D. (1998) *Corporate Philanthropy at the Crossroads* (Indiana: Indiana University Press).

BURNS, J. (1981) *Theological Anthropology* (Philadelphia: Fortress).

CALLIARI, G. (1991) *Il vangelo forza dei poveri* (Rome: Città Nuova).

CALVI, M. (1999a) "Così l'utile si sposa con il condividere," *Avvenire*, January 27, p. 15.

_____. (1999b) "E nel mercato arriva la *Comunione*," *Avvenire*, January 30, p. 12.

CÂMARA, H. (1969) *Church and Colonialism* (London: Sheed and Ward).

CAMBÓN, E. (1999) *Trinità modello sociale* (Rome: Città Nuova).

CARDOSO, F. and FALETTO, E. (1979) *Dependency and Development in Latin America* (London: University of California Press).

CATAPAN, D. (1994) "A cultura do dar Cadernos," *Escola Social* 5(6) (Sao Paulo: Cidade Nova).

CERINI, M. (1992) *God Who Is Love in the Experience and Thought of Chiara Lubich* (Hyde Park, NY: New City Press).

CHILDS, P. and WILLIAMS, W. (1997) *An Introduction to Post-colonial Theory* (London and New York: Prentice-Hall).

CLARK, G. L., FELDMAND, M. P., and GERTLER, M. S. (2000) *The Oxford Handbook of Economic Geography* (Oxford: Oxford University Press).

CLARK, M. A. (1995) "Changes in Euro-American values needed for sustainability," *Journal of Social Issues*, 51(4): 63–82.

CLARK, M. and SLEEMAN, M. (1991) "Writing the earth, righting the earth: committed presuppositions and the geographical imagination." In *New Words, New Worlds: Reconceptualising Social and Cultural Geography,* compiled by C. P. Philo (Aberystwyth: Cambrian).

CLIFFORD, J. (1988) *The Predicament of Culture* (Cambridge, Mass: Harvard University Press).

CLIFFORD, J. and FISCHER, M. (1986) *Anthropology as Cultural Critique* (Chicago: Chicago University Press).

COBB, J. B. (1995) "Towards a just and sustainable economic order," *Journal of Social Issues* 51: 83–100.

CODA, P. (1984) *Evento pasquale. Trinità e storia* (Rome: Città Nuova).

_____. (1992) "Nuova evangelizzazione e dottrina sociale," *Nuova Umanità*, 87 (5–6).

CODA, P. and others (1998) *Abitando la Trinità. Per un rinnovamento dell'ontologia* (Rome: Città Nuova).

COLA, S. (1985) *Chiara* (Torino: Leuman).

COLEMAN, J. (1987) *The Church and Christian Democracy* (Edinburgh: Clark).

COLEMAN, J. (1988) "Social capital in the creation of human capital," *American Journal of Sociology* 94: S95–S120.

CORBRIDGE, S. (1993) "Marxisms, modernities, and moralities: development praxis and the claims of distant strangers," *Environment and Planning D: Society and Space* 11: 449–472.

CORBRIDGE, S., THRIFT, N. and MARTIN, R. (eds.) (1994) *Money, Power and Space* (Oxford: Blackwell).

CRANG, P. (1997) "Introduction: cultural turns and the (re)constitution of economic geography." In *Geographies of Economies*, edited by J. Wills and R. Lee (London: Arnold), pp. 3–15.

CRUSH, J. (ed.) (1995) *The Power of Development* (London: Routledge).

DALY, H. E. (1990) "Sustainable growth: an impossibility theorem," *Development: Journal of the Society for International Development* 3–4: 45–47.

DALY, H. E. and COBB, J. B. (1990) *For the Common Good* (London: Green Print).

DAVIES, P. (1997) *Current Issues in Business Ethics* (London: Routledge).

DAVIS, L. (1997) *The NGO-business Hybrid: Is the Private Sector the Answer?* (Baltimore, MD: John Hopkins University).

DE CARLI, M. (1996) *Quando la Chiesa è donna* (Milan: Sperling and Kupfer).

DE MELO, M. G. (1993) "Economia de Comunhão: um fenomeno social," *Cadernos Escola Social* 5(3) (Sao Paulo: Cidade Nova).

DE ROSA, G. and PICCOLI, P. (eds.) (1986) *Giordani e Sturzo: un ponte tra due generazioni carteggio 1824–1958* (Milan: Cariplo).

DESAI, A. B. and RITTENBURG, T. (1997) "Global ethics: an integrative framework for MNEs," *Journal of Business Ethics* 16(8): 791–800.

DI MEANA, P. R. (1992) "All'ascolto di un 'pensiero forte': la dottrina tomista della Trinità," *Salesianum* 54: 30.

DI STEFANO, M. (1991) "Avenues beyond capitalism," *Living City* (New York), August/September, pp. 23–25.

DICKEN, P. (1986) *Global Shift* (London: Harper & Row).

DIRLIK, A. (1997) *The Post-colonial Aura: Third World Criticism in the Age of Global Capitalism* (Boulder, Co: Westview Press).

DOLLAR, D. and KRAAY, A. (2000) "Growth *is* Good for the Poor," World Bank Research Paper http://www.worldbank.org/research/growth/pdfiles/growthgoodforpoor.pdf.

DORE, R. (1983) "Goodwill and the spirit of market capitalism," *British Journal of Sociology* 34 (4), pp. 459–82.

DUCHROW, U. (1995) *Alternatives to Global Capitalism* (Utrecht: International Books and Kairos).

DUNFORD, C. (2000) "The holy grail of micro-finance: 'helping the poor' and 'sustainable'?" *Small Enterprise Development*, Vol.11, No. 1: 40–44.

EARLY, T. (1997a) "Focolare founder takes New York by storm: making ideals a concrete reality," *National Catholic Register* 73(24) June 15–21, p. 1/11.

_____. (1997b) "Love one another: Focolare founder visits black Muslim mosque in Harlem," *Catholic New York*, May 29, p. 33.

EKINS, P. (1992) *A New World Order: Grassroots Movements for Global Change* (London: Routledge).

ELIADE, M. (1959) *The Sacred and the Profane* (New York: Harcourt, Brace and World).

ELLIOTT, L. and ATKINSON, D. (2009), *The Gods that Failed: How the Financial Elite have Gambled Away our Futures* (Vintage, London).

ESCOBAR, A. (1995) *Encountering Development* (Princeton: Princeton University Press).

ESCOBAR, A. and ALVAREZ, S. E. (eds.) (1992) *The Making of Social Movements in Latin America* (Colorado: Westview Press).

ESTEVA, G. (1987) "Regenerating people's space," *Alternatives* 12: 125–52.

ETZIONI, A. (1989) *The Moral Dimension: Towards a New Economics* (New York: Free Press).

FAVALE, A. (1984) *Movimenti ecclesiali contemporanei* (Rome: Las), p. 202.

FAY, B. (1996) *Contemporary Philosophy of Social Science* (Cambridge, USA: Blackwell).

FEATHERSTONE, M. (1995) *Undoing Culture: Globalization, Post-modernism and Identity* (London: Sage).

FELICE, F. (1999) *The Ethical Foundation of the Market Economy: Reflection on Liberal-personalism in the Thought of Luigi Sturzo.* Unpublished transcript of a paper given at an EOC Conference, Hamburg, Germany, September.

FERRUCCI, A. (1992) *Nord-sud che fare* (Rome: Città Nuova).

———. (1993a) "Un impegno per crescere insieme," *Città Nuova* 10: 30–31.

———. (1993b) "Economia de Comunhão: un fenomeno economico," *Cadernos Escola Social* 5(4) (Sao Paulo: Cidade Nova).

———. (1993c) "Economia di *Comunione* nella libertà," *Città Nuova* 6: 32–33.

———. (1994) "Un popolo di uomini-umanità," *Città Nuova* 3: 34–36.

———. (1995) "The EOS: a world-wide family," *Living City,* January, pp. 24–7.

FIELDS, S. (2005) "Continental Divide — Why Africa's Climate Change Burden is Greater," *Environmental Health Perspectives* Vol. 113 (8), pp. A533–37.

FISHER, W. and PONNIAH, T. (2003) *Another World is Possible: Alternatives to Globalization at the World Social Forum* (London: Macmillan).

Focolare Movement (1994) *Relatório anual das atividades socias* internal report, Sao Paulo.

FORESI, P. (1953) *Teologia sociale* (Rome: Città Nuova).

FORTE, B. (1986) "Trinità Cristiana e realtà sociale," *Asprenas* 4: 355–371.

FOUCAULT, M. (1980) *Power-knowledge: Selected Interviews and Other Writings 1972–1977,* translated from the French and edited by C. Gordon (Brighton: Harvester Press).

FOWLER, A. (1998) "Authentic NGO partnerships: dead end or way-ahead?" *Development and Change* 29(1): 137–59.

FRIEDMAN, J. (1989) "The dialectic of reason," *International Journal of Regional Research* 13(2): 217–40.

———. (1994) *Cultural Identity and Global Process* (London: Sage).

FROMM, E. (1957) *The Art of Loving* (London: Allen & Unwin).

FUKUYAMA, F. (1995) *Trust: The Social Virtues and the Creation of Prosperity* (London: Hamish Hamilton).

FURTADO, C. (1963) *The Economic Growth of Brazil: A Survey from Colonial to Modern* (London: California Univ. Press).

GALLAGHER, J. (1997) *Chiara Lubich: A Woman's Work* (Hyde Park, NY: New City Press).

GANDOLFO, G. and MARZANO, F. (eds.) (1999) *Economic Theory and Social Justice* (London: MacMillan).

GIACOMETTI, A. (1995) "Economia di *Comunione,* che cos'è?" *Il Segno,* Milan, May.

GIBSON-GRAHAM, J. K. (1996) *The End of Capitalism as We Knew It* (Oxford: Blackwell).

GIDDENS, A. (1998) *The Third Way: The Renewal of Social Democracy* (Cambridge: Polity Press).

———. (2000) *The Third Way and Its Critics* (Cambridge: Polity Press).

GINSBORG, P. (1990) *A History of Contemporary Italy* (London: Penguin).

Giornale del Popolo (1996) "Bilancio in dare," June 11.

GIOVANNI, G. (1997) "Chiara Lubich, prima cristiana a parlare nella Moschea di Malcom X," *Il Tempo,* Rome, May 18, p. 18.

GIROLAMO, M. (1998) *Da Sturzo a Novak: itinerari etici di capitalismo democratico* (Rome: CISS).

GLOCK, C. and BELLA, R. (1976) *The New Religious Consciousness* (Berkeley: University of California Press).

GOLD, L. (1996) *The EOS in Brazil,* Unpublished M.A. dissertation, University of Glasgow.

———. (2000) "Abrindo espaço para uma nova visão econômica: redes locais-globais de comunhão," *Atti del Convegno* (Sao Paulo: Cidade Nova).

_____. (2001) "L'esperienza dell'Economia di Comunione." In Ferrucci, A. (ed.) *Per una globalizazione solidale* (Rome: Città Nuova).

_____. (2003) "Small enterprises at the service of the poor: the Economy of Sharing Network," *International Journal of Entrepreneurial Research and Behaviour* 9, 5, pp. 166–84.

GOLIN, E. and PAROLIN, G. (2003) *Per un'impresa a piú dimensioni: strategie secondo il metodo Rainbow Score* (Rome: Città Nuova).

GRABHER, G. (1993) *The Embedded Firm: On the Socio-economics of Industrial Networks* (London: Routledge).

GRANOVETTER, M. (1985) "Economic action and social structure: the problem of embeddedness," *American Journal of Sociology* 91 (3): 481–510.

GREEN, D. (1996) "Latin America: neo-liberal failure and the search for alternatives," *Third World Quarterly* 17 (1): 109–22.

GRIFFITH-JONES, S. and SUNKEL, O. (1986) *Debt and Development Crises in Latin America: The End of an Illusion* (Oxford: Oxford University Press).

GUELLA, G. and BASSO, O. (1984) "The communion of goods and work guidelines," Part 1, Internal Focolare document, Focolare Center, Rome.

GUELLA, G. and BASSO, O. (1985) "The communion of goods and work guidelines," Part 2, Internal Focolare document, Focolare Center, Rome.

GUI, B. (1996) "On 'relational goods': strategic implications of investment in relationships," *International Journal of Social Economics* 23 (10/11): 260–78.

GUTIERREZ, G. (1984) *We drink from our own wells: the spiritual journey of a people* (London: SCM press).

HABERMAS, J. (1987) *The Theory of Communicative Action*, translated by Thomas McCarthy (Cambridge: Polity Press).

_____. (1988) *Legitimation Crisis* (Cambridge: Polity Press).

HART, S. (1992) *What Does the Lord Require? How American Christians Think about Economic Justice* (New York: Oxford University Press).

HARVEY, D. (1973) *Social Justice and the City* (London: Arnold).

HARVEY, D. (1989) *The Condition of Post-modernity* (London: Blackwell).

_____. (1996) *Justice, Nature and the Geography of Difference* (Oxford: Blackwell).

HAY, A. M. (1995) "Concepts of equity, fairness and justice in geographical studies," *Transactions, Institute of British Geographers* NS 20: 500–8.

HEMMERLE, K. (1996) *Tesi di ontologia trinitaria* (Roma: Città Nuova).

_____. (1998) *Partire dall'unità. La Trinità come stile di vita e forma di pensiero* (Rome: Città Nuova).

HERR, T. (1991) *Catholic Social Teaching: A Textbook of Christian Insights* (London: New City).

HUTTON, W., MACDOUGALL, A. and ZADEK, S. (2001) "Topics in business ethics — corporate stakeholding, ethical investment, social accounting," *Journal of Business Ethics*, Vol. 32, No. 2: 107–18.

INGHAM, G. (1996) "Some recent changes in the relationship between economics and sociology," *Cambridge Journal of Economics* 20: 243–75.

JAY, E. and JAY, R. (1986) *Critics of Capitalism: Victorian Reactions to Political Economy* (Cambridge: Cambridge University Press).

JOHN PAUL II (1981) *Laborem exercens* (Rome: Vatican Press).

_____. (1991) *Centesimus annus* (Rome: Vatican Press).

JOHNSTON, L. T. (1981) *Sharing Possessions: Mandate and Symbol of Faith* (Philadelphia: Fortress Press).

KHOR, M. (2000) *Globalization and the South: Some Critical Issues* (Penang, Malaysia: Third World Network).

KIRK, J. M. (1995) "Whither the Catholic Church in the 1990s?" In *Capital, Power and Equality in Latin America*, edited by S. Halebsky and R. L. Harris (Boulder: Westview Press).

KLEYMEYER, C. D. (ed.) (1994) *Cultural Expression and Grassroots Development* (London and Boulder, Colo.: Rennier).

KNOX, P. and AGNEW, J. (1989) *The Geography of the World Economy* (London: Routledge), p. 4.

KORTEN, D. (1995) *When Corporations Rule the World* (New York: Kumarian).

KOWARIK, L. (1987) *The Subjugation of Labour: The Constitution of Capitalism in Brazil* (Amsterdam: CEDLA).

KÜNG, H. (1997) *A Global Ethic for Global Politics and Economics* (London: SCM).

———. (2000) "Responsibilities and rights: the quest for a global ethic," *Global dialogue* 2(1): 120–26.

———. (1997) "A global ethic in an age of globalization," *Business Ethics Quarterly* 7(3): 17–32.

KÜNG, H. and SCHMITT, H. (1998) *A Global Ethic and Global Responsibilities* (London: SCM).

LASH, S. and URRY, J. (1994) *Economies of Signs and Space: After Organised Capitalism* (London: Sage).

LATEEF, J. and LATEEF, K. S. (1997) "Italian Focolare Movement leader speaks to Muslim African American audience," *Muslim Journal*, June 13, p. 1/21.

LATOUCHE, S. (1993) *In the Wake of the Affluent Society: An Exploration of Post-development* (London: Zed Books).

LATOUR, B. (1993) *We Have Never Been Modern* (Brighton: Harvester Wheatsheaf).

LAW, J. (1994) *Organizing Modernity* (Oxford: Blackwell).

LEE, R. and WILLIS, J. (eds.) (1997) *Geographies of Economies* (London: Arnold).

LEHMANN, D. (ed.) (1999) "Social movements and religious change," Special issue of the *Bulletin of Latin American Research* 18(2).

LEIBHOLZ, E., LEIBHOLZ, R. and PASSARELLI, V. (1995) "*Femaq*: aumentando a produtividade em época de turbulências," in *Prêmio Mario Henrique Simonsen concurso nacional de case studies*, Chapter 4 (Sao Paulo: Insight Editorial).

LETTS, C., RYAN, W., and GROSSMAN, A. (1997) "Social enterprise. Virtuous capital: what foundations can learn from venture capitalists," *Harvard Business Review*, No. 97: 36–44.

LEYSHON, A. and THRIFT, N. (1997) *Money/space: Geographies of Monetary Transformation* (London: Routledge).

LIPSET, S. M. (1993) "Culture and economic behaviour: a commentary," *Journal of Labour Economics* 11: S330–47.

LUBICH, C. (1981) *Charity* (London: New City).

———. (1984) *May They All Be One* (Hyde Park, NY: New City Press).

———. (1985) *Why Have You Forsaken Me? The Key to Unity* (London: New City).

———. (1987) *Stars and Tears* (London: New City).

———. (1993) "Come la famiglia, così la società," *Città Nuova* 12: 30–31.

———. (1995) "Risurrezione di Roma," *Nuova Umanità* 102.

———. (2001a) *L'Economia di comunione: storia e profezia* (Rome: Città Nuova).

———. (2001B) *La dottrina spirituale* (Milan: Mondadori).

LUND, C. (1998) "Development and rights: tempering universalism and relativism," *The European Journal of Development Research* 10(2): 1–6.

MACDONALD, L. (1995) "A mixed blessing: the NGO boom in Latin America," *NACLA Report on the Americas* 28(5): 30–35.

MACKENZIE, C., LEWIS, A. (1999) "Morals and markets: the case of ethical investing," *Business Ethics Quarterly*, Vol. 9, No. 3: 439–52.

MAHER, L. (1995) *Social Movements and Social Classes* (London: Sage).

MAKEWELL, R. (2001) *Economic Wisdom: Economic References from Scriptural, Philosophical and Classical Sources* (Roseville, Australia: New Frontier Press).

MARCUS, G. E. and FISCHER, M. M. J. (1986) *Anthropology as Cultural Critique* (Chicago: University of Chicago Press).

MARSHALL, G. (1982) *In Search of the Spirit of Capitalism* (London: Hutchinson).

MARWEL, G. (1982) "Altruism and the problem of collective action." In *Co-operation and Helping Behaviour, Theories and Research*, edited by V. Derlega and J. Grzelak (London: Academic Press).

220

MARX K. (1967) *Essential Writings,* selected, and with an introduction and notes, by D. Caute (London: Panther).

McNEILL, D. (1999) "Market ethics as global ethics," *Forum for Development Studies,* 1: 59–76.

MEEKS, D. (1989) *God the Economist: The Doctrine of God and the Political Economy* (London: Fortress Press).

MEYER, W. H. (1995–1996) "Toward a global culture: human rights, group rights and cultural relativism," *International Journal on Group Rights* 3(3).

MILANOVIC, B. (2009) "Decomposing world income distribution. Does the world have a middle class?"http://econ.worldbank.org/view.php?type=18&id=3442.

MILBANK, J. (1990) *Theology and Social Theory: Beyond Secular Reason* (Oxford: Blackwell).

MILBRATH, L. W. (1995) "Psychological, cultural and informational barriers to sustainability," *Journal of Social Issues Special Issue* 51(4): 101–20.

MOFID, K. (2002) *Globalisation for the Common Good* (London: Shepheard-Walwyn).

MORRA, G. (1998) *La dottrina sociale della Chiesa: natura, finalità, e principi essenziali* (Rome: CISS).

MOVIMENTO UMANITÀ NUOVA (1984) *Il lavoro e l'economia oggi nella visione cristiana,* Conference proceedings (Rome: Città Nuova).

_____. (1985) *Verso una nuova umanità,* Conference proceedings (Rome: Città Nuova).

_____. (1988) *Una cultura di pace per l'unità dei popoli,* Conference proceedings (Rome: Città Nuova).

NEF (2000) *Brave New Economy,* CD ROM (London: NEF).

NEF, J (1999) *Human Security and Mutual Vulnerability: The Global Political Economy of Development and Underdevelopment,* 2nd edition (London: IDRC).

NELSON, N. and WRIGHT, S. (1995) *Power and Participation in Development: Theory and Practice* (London: Intermediate Technology Group).

NOVAK, M. (1993) *The Catholic Ethic and the Spirit of Capitalism* (New York: Free Press).

_____. (1998) *Is There a Third Way? Essays on the Changing Direction of Socialist Thought* (London: IEA Health and Welfare Unit).

Nuova Umanità (1992) *Special issue on the EOS* 80/81 (Rome: Città Nuova).

O'CONNOR, J. (1994) "Does a global village warrant a global ethic?" *Religion* 24(2): 155–64.

OSLON, R. L. (1995) "Sustainability as a social vision," *Journal of Social Issues* 51(4): 15–36.

OXFAM (2004) *Guns or Growth http://www.oxfam.org.uk/what_we_do/issues/conflict_ disasters/downloads/guns_or_growth.pdf.*

PALLIOTTI, O. (1993) "Avevano tutto in comune," *Città Nuova* 10: 27–30.

PASSUELLO, F. (1997) *Una nuova frontiera: il terzo settore* (Rome: Lavoro).

PEARCE, J. (1996) *At the Heart of the Economy* (London: Calouste Gulbenkian Foundation).

PEET, R. (1997) "The cultural production of economic forms." In *Geographies of Economies,* edited by R. Lee and J. Wills (London: Arnold), pp. 37–46.

PEIXOTO, M. (1994) *Empresa e economia de comunhão* (Sao Paulo: Cidade Nova).

PELLIGRA, V. (2007) "Intentions, Trust and Frames: A Note on Sociality and the Theory of Games," Working Paper CRENoS 200702, Center for North South Economic Research, University of Cagliari and Sassari, Sardinia.

PHILO, C. P. (ed.) (1991) *New Words, New Worlds: Reconceptualising Social and Cultural Geography,* Conference proceedings (Aberystwyth: Cambrian).

PICÃO, D. (1993) *Economia de comunhão: premessas biblicas* (Sao Paulo: Cidade Nova).

PLATTEAU, J. P. (1994) "Behind the market stage, where real societies exist," *Journal of Development Studies,* 30(3): 537–77.

POLANYI, K. (1957) *The Great Transformation* (Boston: Beacon Press).

Pontifical Council for Justice and Peace (2007) *Compendium of the Social Doctrine of the Catholic Church,* Vatican Press.

POPE BENEDICT XVI (2009) *Caritas in Veritate — Charity in Truth* (Dublin: Veritas Publications).

POVILUS, J. (1992) *United in His Name: Jesus in Our Midst in the Experience and Thought of Chiara Lubich* (New York: New City Press).

POZZI, N. (1994) "Dove nasce la cultura del dare," *Città Nuova* 6: 30–32.

PRESTON, D. (ed.) (1987) *Latin American Development: Geographical Perspectives* (London: Longman).

PRESTON, R. H. (1991) *Religion and the Ambiguities of Capitalism* (London: SCM Press).

PROCTOR, W. (1983) *An Interview with Chiara Lubich* (New York: New City Press).

QUARTANA, M. (1992) "*Femaq*: l'azienda dell'uomo e la città," *Città Nuova* 7: 34–39.

QUARTANA, P. (1992) "L'Economia di *Comunione*: un passo più in là," *Città Nuova* 2: 34–35.

RAHNEMA, M. and BAWTREE, V. (eds.) (1997) *The Post-development Reader* (London: Zed Press).

RAWLS, J. (1971) *A Theory of Justice* (Cambridge, Mass: Harvard University Press).

RAY, L. and SAYER, A. (eds.) (1999) *Culture and Economy after the Cultural Turn* (London: Sage).

RESSL, M. (1999) *The EOS: Prospects and Developments.* Unpublished Dissertation, University of Vienna.

RIBEIRO, S. F. (1993) *Economia de comunhão: aspectos antropològicos* (Sao Paulo: Cidade Nova).

ROBERTSON, E. (1978) *Chiara* (Dublin: Christian Journal Press).

_____. (1989) *The Fire of Love: A Life of Igino Giordani — Foco* (London: New City).

_____. (1993) *Catching Fire* (Guilford: IPS).

SACHS, J. R. (1991) *The Christian Vision of Humanity. Basic Christian Anthropology* (Collegeville, MN: Liturgical Press).

SACHS, W. (ed.) (1992) *The Development Dictionary: A Guide to Knowledge as Power* (Johannesburg: Witwatersrand University Press).

SAMUELSON, J. (1998a) "Global capitalism R.I.P?" *Newsweek,* September 14, pp. 20–22.

SAMUELSON, P. A. (1998B) *Economics: An Introductory Analysis,* 18th edition (New York: McGraw-Hill).

SAYER, A. and STORPER, M. (1997) "Ethics unbound: for a normative turn in social theory," *Environment and Planning D: Society and Space* 15: 1–17.

SAYER, A. and WALKER, R. (1992) *The New Social Economy: Reworking the Division of Labour* (Oxford: Blackwell).

SCHUMACHER, C. (1998) *God in Work* (Oxford: Lion).

SCHUMACHER, E. F. (1973) *Small is Beautiful* (London: Abacus).

SCOTT, A. (1990) *Ideology and the New Social Movements* (London and New York: Routledge).

SECONDIN, B. (1991) *I nuovi protagonisti* (Rome: Pauline).

SEN, A. (1987) *On Ethics and Economics* (London: Blackwell).

_____. (1993) *Moral Codes and Economic Success* (London: DERP), no. 49.

_____. (1994) *Beyond Liberalisation: Social Opportunity and Human Capability* (London: DERP), no. 58.

_____. (1999) *Development as Freedom* (Oxford: Oxford University Press).

SHATTUCK, A. (2008) *Financial Crisis and the Food Crisis – Two Sides of the One Coin* http://www.stwr.org/food-security-agriculture/the-financial-crisis-and-the-food-crisis-two-sides-of-the-same-coin.html.

SILVANI, A. et al. (1993) "La localisation régionale des grappes d'innovation en Italie — du troisième Italie ou Lombardie?" *Revue d'Économie Régionale et Urbaine* 2: 289–307.

SILVERMAN, D. (ed.) (1997) *Qualitative Research: Theory, Method and Practice* (London: SAGE).

SINGER, H. W. and SAKAR, P. (1992) *Debt Crisis, Commodity Prices, Transfer Burden and Debt Relief* (Sussex: Institute of Development Studies).

SLATER, D. (1985) *New Social Movements and the State in Latin America* (Amsterdam: Centro de Estudios y Documentacion).

_____. (1992) "Trajectories of development theory: capitalism, socialism and beyond." In *Geographies of Global Change,* edited by R. J. Johnston, P. J. Taylor and M. J. Watts (Oxford: Blackwell).

_____. (1994) "Power and social movements in the other occident," *Latin American Perspectives* 13–14.

SMELSER, J. and SWEDBERG, R. (eds.) (1994) *Handbook of Economic Sociology* (Princeton, NJ: Princeton University Press).

SMITH, A. (1981) *An Inquiry into the Nature and Causes of the Wealth of Nations* (Indianapolis: Liberty Classics).

SMITH, A. D. (1990") Towards a global culture?" *Theory, Culture and Society* 7(2–3): 171–92.

SMITH, D. M. (1994) *Geography and Social Justice* (Oxford: Blackwell).

_____. (1997) "Back to the good life: towards an enlarged conception of social justice," *Environment and Planning D: Society and Space* 15: 19–35.

_____. (1998) "How far should we care: on the spatial scope of beneficence," *Progress in Human Geography* 22: 15–38.

_____. (2000a) "Moral progress in human geography: transcending the place of good fortune," *Progress in Human Geography* 24(1): 1–18.

_____. (2000b) "Social justice revisited," *Environment and Planning A* 32: 1149–62.

_____. (2000c) *Moral Geographies* (Edinburgh: Edinburgh University Press).

SORGI, T. (1991a) *Costruire il sociale* (Rome: Città Nuova).

_____. (1991b) "Un modello diverso," *Città Nuova,* 15/16: 36–39.

SPAMPINATO, A. (1993) *L'economia senza etica è diseconomia* (Rome: Centro Internazionale Studi Luigi Sturzo).

SPARKES, R. (2001) "Ethical investment: whose ethics, which investment?" *Business Ethics: A European Review*, Vol. 10, No. 3: 194–205.

SPILLER, R. (2000) "Ethical business and investment: a model for business and society," *Journal of Business Ethics*, Vol. 27, No. 1–2: 149–60.

STERBA, J. P. (1981) "The welfare rights of distant peoples and future generations: moral side-constraints on social policy," *Social Theory and Practice* 7: 99–119.

STOHR, W. B. and FRASER TAYLOR. D. R. (eds.) (1981) *Development from Above or Below* (Chichester: Wiley).

STUDDARD, K. (2004) *War Economies in a Regional Context: Overcoming the Challenges of Transformation,* International Peace Academy Publication http://www.ipacademy.org/PDF_Reports/WARECONOMIES.pdf.

STURZO, L. (1960) *La vera vita. Sociologia del soprannaturale* (Bologna: Zanichelli).

SWEDBERG, R. (1998) *Max Weber and the Idea of Economic Sociology* (Princeton: Princeton University Press).

SWEDBERG, R. and GRANOVETTER, M. (1992) *The Sociology of Economic Life* (Boulder, Colo.: Westview Press).

TANNER, K. (1997) *Theories of Culture: A New Agenda for Theology* (Minneapolis: Augsburg Fortress).

TAYLOR, C. (1995) *Philosophical Arguments* (Cambridge, Mass.: Harvard University Press).

TAYLOR, R. (2000) "How new is socially responsible investment?" *Business Ethics: A European Review*, July 2000, Vol. 9, No. 3: 174–79.

The Economist (1996) "Cultural explanations," November 9, p. 26.

The Economist (1999) "Philanthropy in America — the gospel of wealth," May 30, pp. 23–25.

The Jerusalem Bible (1968) (London: Eyre and Spottiswoode).

THOMPSON, G. (1990a) *The Political Economy of the New Right* (London: Pinter).

THOMPSON, J. (1990b) *Ideology and Modern Culture* (Stanford: Stanford University Press).

THRIFT, N. and OLDS, K. (1996) "Refiguring the economic in economic geography," *Progress in Human Geography* 20 (3): 311–37.

TRIGG, R. (1998) *Rationality and Religion: Does Faith Need Reason?* (Oxford: Blackwell).

TRONTO, J. (1993) *Moral Boundaries: A Political Argument for an Ethic of Care* (London: Routledge).

TRUSTED, J. (1992) "The problem of absolute poverty — what are our moral obligations to the destitute?" In *The Environment in Question — Ethics and Global Issues,* edited by D. E. Cooper and J. A. Palmer (London: Routledge), pp. 13–27.

UN (2001) *"We the Peoples": The Role of the United Nations in the Twenty-first Century* (New York: UN Publications).

UNDP (2001) *The Human Development Report 2001* (Oxford: Oxford University Press).

UNDP (2005) *The Human Development Report 2005.* New York, UN Publications http://hdr.undp.org/statistics/data/indicators.cfm?x=3&y=3&z=2.

UNESCO (1995) *Our Creative Diversity, Report of the Commission on Culture and Development* (New York: UN Publications).

UNICEF (1998) *The State of the World's Children* (New York: UN Publications).

WALLACE, I. (1978) "Towards a Humanised Conception of Economic Geography," in *Humanistic Geography: Problems and Prospects,* edited by D. Leys and M. Sameuls (London : Croom Helm), pp. 91–108.

WALLACE, I. (1998) "A Christian reading of the global economy." In *Geography and Worldview: A Christian Reconnaissance,* edited by H. Aay and S. Griffioen (Lanham, MD: University Press of America).

WALZER, M. (1983) *Spheres of Justice: A Defence of Pluralism and Equality* (Oxford: Blackwell).

_____. (1994) *Thick and Thin: Moral Argument at Home and Abroad* (Notre Dame and London: University of Notre Dame Press).

WATTS, M. (1993) "Development 1: power, knowledge and discursive practice," *Progress in Human Geography* 17(2): 257–72.

WEBER, M. (1958) [1904–5] *The Protestant Ethic and the Spirit of Capitalism,* translated by Talcott Parsons (New York: Scribners).

_____. (1978) [1922] *Economy and Society,* 2 vols., translated by Hans H. Gerth and Claus Wittich (Berkeley: University of California Press).

WEIL, S. (1951) *Waiting for God* (New York: Harper Colphorn).

_____. (1968) *Science, Necessity and the Love of God* (London: Oxford University Press).

WUTHNOW, R. (1994) "Religion and economic life." Chapter 25 in *The Handbook of Economic Sociology,* edited by N. Smelser and R. Swedberg (Princeton: Princeton University Press).

YOUNG, I. M. (1990a) "The ideal of community and the politics of difference." In *Feminism/postmodernism,* edited by L. J. Nicholson (London: Routledge) pp. 300–23.

_____. (1990b) *Justice and the Politics of Difference* (Princeton, NJ: Princeton University Press).

ZADEK, S. (1997) *Building Corporate Responsibility* (London: Earthscan).

ZADEK, S. and MAYO, E. (1997) "Ten reasons why society does matter," *New Economics Magazine* 41: 4–7.

ZAMAGNI, S. (1999) "Sul fondamento e sul significato dell'Economia di Comunione." In Bruni, L. (ed.) *Economia di Comunione: per una cultura economica a più dimensioni* (Rome: Città Nuova).

ZAMBONINI, F. (1991) *Chiara Lubich: l'avventura dell'unità* (Cuneo: Paoline).

ZANGHÌ, G. (1998) "Una riflessione sul postmodernismo," *Gen's* 3–4: 83.